Genetic
and
Acquired
Disorders

To the children and families who persevere and thrive despite battling
the medical conditions described in this volume.
And to our families.
P.C.M. & S.R.S.

Genetic *and* Acquired Disorders

Paul C. McCabe
Steven R. Shaw

Current Topics *and* Interventions *for* Educators

A JOINT PUBLICATION

For information:

 Corwin
A SAGE Company
2455 Teller Road
Thousand Oaks, California 91320
(800) 233-9936
Fax: (800) 417-2466
www.corwinpress.com

SAGE Ltd.
1 Oliver's Yard
55 City Road
London EC1Y 1SP
United Kingdom

SAGE Pvt. Ltd.
B 1/I 1 Mohan Cooperative
    Industrial Area
Mathura Road, New Delhi 110 044
India

SAGE Asia-Pacific Pte. Ltd.
33 Pekin Street #02-01
Far East Square
Singapore 048763

Printed in the United States of America.

Library of Congress Cataloging-in-Publication Data

Genetic and acquired disorders: current topics and interventions for educators/editors, Paul C. McCabe, Steven R. Shaw.
    p. cm.
"A joint publication with the National Association of School Psychologists."
Includes bibliographical references and index.
ISBN 978-1-4129-6871-3 (cloth)
ISBN 978-1-4129-6872-0 (pbk.)

  1. Educational psychology. 2. Children—Mental health services. 3. School health services. 4. Genetic disorders. 5. Communicative disorders in children. 6. Children—Diseases—Treatment. 7. Pediatrics. I. McCabe, Paul C. II. Shaw, Steven R. III. National Association of School Psychologists.

LB1051.G3845 2010
371.7'13—dc22

2009047382

This book is printed on acid-free paper.

10 11 12 13 14 10 9 8 7 6 5 4 3 2 1

Acquisitions Editor:	Jessica Allan
Associate Editor:	Joanna Coelho
Production Editor:	Libby Larson
Copy Editor:	Paula L. Fleming
Typesetter:	C&M Digitals (P) Ltd.
Proofreader:	Theresa Kay
Indexer:	Jean Casalegno
Cover Designer:	Rose Storey

Contents

Preface

This book exists for two primary reasons: (1) the incredible pressures on educators to address children's medical issues in school settings and (2) the rapid pace of news and information delivery, which often occurs despite safeguards to ensure credibility and verifiability. Educators are charged with making policies, differentiating instruction, providing educational accommodations, managing the physical plant, providing special education services, collaborating with families, and working with the community in response to children's medical, physical, and psychological issues. However, educators often have little training, support, or information to address these important issues. When faced with a medical question, many people (including us) turn to the Internet. Although much information from the Internet is high quality, much is not. Peer-reviewed scientific papers are often given the same weight in search engine results as advertisements for the latest snake oil. Information about medical issues is (1) presented in esoteric medical science journals with little relevance to schooling, (2) included as part of an encyclopedic but cursory overview of many topics, or (3) summarized and simplified on Web sites with questionable accuracy and oversight. We developed this book to give support and information to educators based on a critical review of scientific research that is credible, in depth, and practical.

Genetic and Acquired Disorders is the second book in a three-volume series entitled Current Topics and Interventions for Educators. This series presents detailed reviews of recent scientific research on a variety of topics in pediatrics that are most relevant to schools today. Current Topics and Interventions for Educators is intended to provide not only detailed scientific information on pediatric issues but also glossaries of key medical terms, educational strategies, case studies, handouts for teachers and parents, and discussion questions. Readers are presented with critical reviews of scientific medical research, including discussion of controversial issues. The authors of each chapter have completed scholarly reviews of the extant research and carefully considered the quality of research design, methodology, and sampling in determining what can be considered empirically valid conclusions versus conclusions based on hyperbole, conjecture, or myth. We believe that this information will help educators address the pediatric issues that affect schoolchildren and be better equipped to discuss these issues with parents, staff, and medical teams.

This book originated from a regular feature in the National Association of School Psychologists (NASP) publication *Communiqué* called "Pediatric

School Psychology." We edited and published many detailed articles that provided in-depth, critical evaluation of research to keep school psychologists current on medical knowledge that could impact their practice in the schools. We found that school psychologists shared this information with policy makers, administrators, social workers, teachers, therapists, and families. This feedback told us that there is a wider audience for these topics.

Educators, students, school nurses, administrators, policy makers, and school psychologists can use this book in a variety of ways. This book can serve as a reference tool, textbook for a course, or a basis for continuing education activities in schools. The literature reviews are critical, challenge popular understanding, and often present controversial information. We would also like the information in this book to serve as grist for discussion and debate. More than ever, educators are charged by law, regulation, or circumstance to address medical issues, despite lacking medical training. Therefore, consultation, reasoned discussion, debate, and consensus building can lead to improved educational services for children with medical and psychiatric issues.

Genetic and Acquired Disorders: Current Topics and Interventions for Educators is a 14-chapter volume divided into three sections: (1) advances in health care and coping with loss in schools; (2) chromosomal, genetic, and metabolic disorders; and (3) acquired disorders. The volume opens with a discussion of advances in medical science and how these advances have led to new challenges for families and schools. Contrastingly, despite advances in medical science, coping with the death of a member of the school community is commonplace and requires a comprehensive intervention approach. The section on chromosomal, genetic, and metabolic disorders includes the controversy concerning rare chromosomal disorders, phenylketonuria, the genetics of autism, the biological basis of shyness, and families of children with genetic disorders. The section on acquired disorders includes chapters on prenatal alcohol exposure, prenatal exposure to antidepressants, celiac disease, maternal postpartum depression and behavior problems, asthma and quality of life, food allergies, and diabetes. Although not inclusive, this volume covers topics that are among the most urgent and current in pediatrics in the schools.

—*Paul C. McCabe and Steven R. Shaw, Editors*

Acknowledgments

A large-scale project like this cannot take place without the assistance of many people. Jennifer Bruce and Sarita Gober provided many hours of editorial assistance in this project. Their support, skill, and good humor made this project possible. In addition, external reviewers read chapters and provided valuable comments. All chapters were improved because of the efforts of these students, educators, and scholars. The reviewers are Tiffany Chiu, Ray Christner, Jason Collins, Janine Fisher, Sarah Glaser, Sarita Gober, Terry Goldman, Michelle Harvie, Tom Huberty, Susan Jones, Robin Martin, Tawnya Meadows, Tia Ouimet, Mark Posey, Sara Quirke, Amira Rahman, Shohreh Rezazadeh, Jennifer Saracino, Christopher Scharf, Khing Sulin, and Jessica Carfolite Williams. Of course, the authors deserve the lion's share of appreciation, because their expertise, hard work, talent, and timeliness made this work possible. Many thanks for their knowledge and generosity in sharing it.

We would also like to thank the National Association of School Psychologists (NASP) publishing board and the editorial staff of NASP and Corwin for their encouragement and expertise in improving the content of this book and believing in the project.

Paul McCabe would like to thank his colleagues at Brooklyn College of the City University of New York for their logistical support and encouragement of this project. He would also like to thank the many talented, hardworking graduate students who have worked with him over the years to contribute to the "Pediatric School Psychology" column and this project. Finally, he would like to offer grateful thanks to friends and family for their love and encouragement, and especially to Dan.

Steven Shaw would like to thank the physicians from the Greenville Hospital System, South Carolina, who shaped his views of how education and pediatrics interact. Most notable of these physicians are Desmond Kelly, Nancy Powers, Mark Clayton, Lynn Hornsby, Curtis Rogers, and William Schmidt. And, of course, thanks to Isabel, Zoe, and Joyce for their love, support, and patience.

About the Editors

Paul C. McCabe, PhD, NCSP, is an Associate Professor of School Psychology in the School Psychologist Graduate Program at Brooklyn College of the City University of New York. Dr. McCabe received his PhD in Clinical and School Psychology from Hofstra University. He holds undergraduate degrees from University of Rochester and Cazenovia College. Dr. McCabe is a New York State–certified school psychologist, New York State–licensed psychologist, and a Nationally Certified School Psychologist (NCSP). Dr. McCabe serves on the editorial boards of several publications in school psychology and developmental psychology and has consulted at state and national levels on issues of early childhood assessment and best practices, pediatric issues in schools, and training in school psychology. Dr. McCabe conducts and publishes research in (1) early childhood social, behavioral, and language development and concomitant problems; (2) pediatric school psychology and health issues addressed by schools; and (3) social justice issues in training, especially training educators to advocate for gay, lesbian, bisexual, and transgendered youth.

Steven R. Shaw, PhD, NCSP, is an Assistant Professor in the Department of Educational and Counselling Psychology at McGill University in Montreal, Quebec. Dr. Shaw received a PhD in School Psychology from the University of Florida. He has been a school psychologist since 1988 with clinical and administrative experience in schools, hospitals, and independent practice. He has conducted workshops and consulted with educational policy makers to address the needs of children with borderline intellectual functioning in the United States, Canada, Pakistan, Moldova, Poland, India, and Egypt. Dr. Shaw conducts and publishes research in (1) the behavior and language development of children with rare genetic disorders; (2) resilience factors for children with risk factors for school failure, especially borderline intellectual functioning; and (3) pediatric school psychology and health issues addressed by schools.

About the Contributors

Sarah A. Bassin, PhD, is a Pediatric School Psychologist with the University of South Carolina Medical School. Her clinical and research interests involve autism, developmental disabilities, and adjustment of children with medical issues.

Jennifer E. Bruce, BSc, is a graduate student in School/Applied Child Psychology in the Department of Educational and Counselling Psychology at McGill University in Montreal, Quebec. She received her undergraduate degree from McMaster University in 2007. Her research experience as well as her clinical experience involves improving quality of life for families of children with genetic disorders and developmental disabilities.

Tiffany Chiu is a student in the Neurosciences program at McGill University in Montreal, Quebec. Her interests include genetic causes of developmental disabilities in children and international delivery of medical services.

Brian Dalpiaz, BA, is a graduate student in the School Psychologist Graduate Program at Brooklyn College of the City University of New York. Brian received his undergraduate degree in Psychology from Georgetown University. He works as a Mental Health Associate on the child psychiatric unit of the Mount Sinai Medical Center in Manhattan, New York. Brian's primary areas of academic and professional interest include academic classroom intervention, as well as childhood mood and anxiety disorders.

Erica J. Deming, MS, CAS, NCSP, is a School Psychologist in the Rochester City School District in Rochester, New York. Erica received her master's degree and Certificate of Advanced Study in School Psychology from Rochester Institute of Technology in 2004. She holds an undergraduate degree from Nazareth College in Rochester, New York. Erica is a New York State–certified school psychologist and a nationally certified school psychologist. Professional interests include identification of learning disabilities, especially in young children, and effective learning and behavioral interventions for children in the primary grades.

Caryn R. DePinna, MSEd, received her graduate degree from the School Psychologist Graduate Program of Brooklyn College of the City of New York. She holds an undergraduate degree in Psychology from the State University of New York College at Geneseo. Caryn has published research on alternative treatments for autism and has several years of work experience with the autistic population. Caryn's other interests lie in treatments for childhood mental illness and classroom strategies to address children with ADHD.

Jessica B. Edwards George, PhD, NCSP, is an Assistant Professor of Psychiatry and Pediatrics at the University of Massachusetts Medical School in Worcester. Dr. Edwards George received her PhD in Counseling and School Psychology from Northeastern University in Boston. She holds her undergraduate degree from Binghamton University—State University of New York (SUNY) in Binghamton, New York. Dr. Edwards George is a Massachusetts- and Rhode Island–licensed psychologist, Massachusetts-licensed school psychologist, and a Nationally Certified School Psychologist (NCSP). She conducts and publishes research in the area of psychosocial and behavioral factors of adherence to medically necessary dietary regimens, specifically celiac disease and other pediatric gastrointestinal disorders. Clinically, Dr. Edwards George serves as a pediatric consultation-liaison psychologist at UMass Memorial Children's Medical Center in Worcester, Massachusetts, where she also has a pediatric psychology outpatient practice working with youth with chronic illnesses and comorbid psychological difficulties and their families.

Debra L. Franko, PhD, is a Licensed Psychologist and Professor in the Combined School and Counseling Psychology program in the Department of Counseling and Applied Educational Psychology at Northeastern University in Boston. She is also a Visiting Scholar in Psychology at Wesleyan University and the Associate Director at the Harris Center for Eating Disorders at Massachusetts General Hospital. She received her BA in Psychology at the University of Michigan and her PhD from McGill University in Montreal, Quebec. Dr. Franko's research interests are in the areas of eating disorders and obesity. Her clinical specialty area is health psychology with an emphasis on eating disorders of adolescents and adults. Her most recent efforts have focused on the prevention of eating disorders in adolescents and college women, as well as online programs to increase healthy eating in children and adolescents. She is on the editorial boards of the *International Journal of Eating Disorders* and *Body Image: An International Journal of Research.* She serves on the Board of Directors of the Academy for Eating Disorders, where she is also a Fellow. She has authored over 95 peer-reviewed journal articles and book chapters in the area of eating disorders, body image, and obesity. Her recently published book, *Unlocking the Mysteries of Eating Disorders: A Practical, Life-Saving Guide to Your Child's Treatment and Recovery,* was published by McGraw-Hill.

Adrienne Garro, PhD, is an Assistant Professor in the Department of Psychology at Kean University in Union, New Jersey. Dr. Garro holds an undergraduate degree from Johns Hopkins University and received an

MEd and PhD in school psychology from Temple University in 2000. She has been a certified school psychologist in New Jersey and Pennsylvania since 1994 with clinical and consulting experiences in schools, outpatient clinics, and health care settings. Dr. Garro has conducted and published research related to child and family adjustment to pediatric chronic illness. Her additional areas of research include the role of cultural factors in child and family intervention and assessment and intervention with infants and preschoolers who are at risk for developmental disabilities and school problems.

Sarah Glaser, BA, is a graduate student within the School/Applied Child Psychology Program at McGill University in Montreal, Quebec. She holds an undergraduate degree from Boston University. Ms. Glaser conducts research on the interaction between intellectual disabilities and mental health issues.

Lindsay Glasser, BA, is a graduate student in the School Psychologist Graduate Program at Brooklyn College of the City University of New York. Lindsay received her undergraduate degree in Psychology with a minor in Sociology from the State University of New York at Buffalo. She previously worked as a Behavioral Health Specialist for People Inc. of Western New York (WNY), serving individuals with mental and developmental disabilities. Currently, Lindsay's interests and research are focused on gender identity disorders in children, as well as advocacy for individuals with disabilities.

Sarah E. Groark, MA, is a graduate student in the School Psychologist Graduate Program at Brooklyn College of the City University of New York. Ms. Groark received her MA in Humanities and Social Thought from New York University. She holds an undergraduate degree from The Evergreen State College. Ms. Groark has worked as an educator with special needs populations in both public and private schools in New York City. Her research interests include early intervention and school-based interventions for behavioral disorders.

Jessica A. Hoffman, PhD, NCSP, is an Associate Professor in the Department of Counseling and Applied Educational Psychology at Northeastern University. Dr. Hoffman received her PhD in School Psychology at Lehigh University and completed her predoctoral internship and postdoctoral fellowship in Pediatric Psychology at the Children's Hospital of Philadelphia. Dr. Hoffman is a Massachusetts-licensed psychologist and school psychologist and holds the national certification in school psychology. She is the recipient of an early career (K) award from the National Institute of Child Health and Human Development to promote healthy eating in schools. Dr. Hoffman is on the editorial board of *School Psychology Review.* Her research focuses on the development of healthy eating behaviors among preschool and school-aged children.

Khing Su Lin is a student in the Neurosciences at McGill University. Her areas of interest are infectious diseases that affect cognitive development and multicultural issues of delivery of medical services.

Tia Ouimet is a graduate student in School/Applied Child Psychology in the Department of Educational and Counselling Psychology at McGill University in Montreal, Quebec. She received a BSc from McGill University in 2007 and was a Research Assistant in the McGill Child Development Laboratory for Research and Education in Developmental Disorders and the Resilience, Pediatric Psychology, and Neurogenetics Connections Laboratory before beginning her master's work with Dr. Steven Shaw in the Resilience, Pediatric Psychology, and Neurogenetics Connections Lab. Her research experience, as well as her clinical experience of working closely with children with autism, has led her to pursue research that has the goal of improving theory, assessment, and intervention implementation for children with developmental disorders.

Doris Páez, PhD, NCSP, is Adjunct Professor of Psychology at North Carolina State University and school psychologist with the Winston-Salem Forsyth County Schools. She has held several leadership positions with the National Association of School Psychologists. Her clinical and research interests concern bilingual school psychology and school adjustment after major medical issues.

Danielle Parente, BS, is a graduate student in the School Psychologist Graduate program at Brooklyn College of the City University of New York. Danielle received her undergraduate degree from Brooklyn College with a major in Psychology. She has worked as a recreational therapist on an inpatient psychiatric unit. Danielle received advanced training in suicide awareness and then worked as a trainer in suicide awareness for school psychology students and other educators at Brooklyn College. Danielle plans to specialize in early childhood school psychology practice.

W. Mark Posey, PhD, NCSP, is a School Psychologist and Codirector of the Department of Developmental Pediatrics at the University of South Carolina School of Medicine. He completed his doctoral degree at the University of South Carolina in School Psychology. Dr. Posey is licensed as a school psychologist in the state of South Carolina. His clinical and research interests include management of children with ADHD, the psychological adjustment of children with medical issues, and the assessment of children with autism.

Sara Quirke, BSc, is a master's student in the School and Applied Child Psychology Program at McGill University in Montreal, Quebec. She has been working as a Research Assistant in the Autism Spectrum Disorders Clinic at the Montreal Children's Hospital since 2007. Through the clinic, she has gained experience working with young children and adolescents with autism and their families. Sara has also taken courses as part of a graduate degree in Education, which has allowed her to develop a unique perspective into inclusive schooling and teachers' needs in this environment. She is interested in pursuing research pertaining to stress in families with a child with autism and the factors that predict positive developmental outcomes in children with disabilities.

Shohreh M. Rezazadeh, MA, is a graduate student in School/Applied Child Psychology in the Department of Educational and Counselling Psychology at McGill University in Montreal, Quebec. She received a BSc from the University of Ottawa and an MA from McGill University. Her research experience as well as her clinical experience involve acquisition of language skills for children with genetic disorders, autism, and developmental disabilities.

Elizabeth M. Schneider is a graduate student at the University of South Carolina. Her research interests include ADHD treatment and teaching children with developmental disabilities.

Gillian W. Thomas, FCP-C, is a Nurse Practitioner with Total Family Care of Winston-Salem (Cornerstone Health Care). Her clinical interests involve the family coordination of services for children with medical problems and developmental disabilities.

SECTION

I

Advances in Health Care and Coping With Loss in Schools

1

Advances in Health Care and Medical Science

Presenting New Challenges for Schools

Paul C. McCabe and Steven R. Shaw

The last several decades have seen tremendous progress in the medical science, research, and technologies that can be used to prevent and fight childhood disease. As a result, children born with or who acquire a medical disorder or disease are much more likely to survive the condition and live longer, healthier lives. However, a greater chance for survival does not come without complications. Although children with serious medical conditions may survive, they often experience physiological, psychological, and emotional effects secondary to the medical condition and/or the treatment. Many of these effects continue into adulthood. In addition, changes in the way medical treatments are administered have increasingly emphasized outpatient care and de-emphasized inpatient stays, in part due to advanced technologies and medications that make this possible. Therefore, most, if not all, treatment may be administered on an outpatient basis. This paradigm shift places an increased burden on families to oversee the child's treatment and follow-up, as well as on educators, who must coordinate home instruction or make necessary preparations for the child's re-entry to the classroom. It is important to examine how advances in medical science and medical treatment strategies have affected schools and the role of educators in ensuring every child in the class has a chance to succeed.

ADVANCES IN MEDICAL SCIENCE

Increased Survival Rates

The survival rates for most childhood medical conditions have improved dramatically over the past several decades, even in light of increased prevalence rates for some diseases. For example, while the incidence of all forms of invasive cancers has increased over the past 30 years from 11.5 cases to 14.5 cases per 100,000 children, the 5-year survival rates also increased, from 58 percent in 1975 to almost 80 percent in 2005 (Ries et al., 2008). The number of live births of low birth weight (LBW) and very low birth weight (VLBW) infants increased 11.8% and 24.3%, respectively, from 1980 to 2000, while infant mortality declined 45.2% during the same period (Iyasu & Tomashek, 2002). Incidence rates of new cases of pediatric AIDS in the United States decreased 4% from 2003 to 2005, and in 2005, only seven children under the age of 13 died from AIDS-related causes (Abdelmalek & Elston, 2008). Prevalence rates for both type 1 and type 2 diabetes are rising worldwide, yet rates of death from diabetes-related complications have dropped three- to sixfold over the past 50 years (Portuese & Orchard, 1995).

Although survival rates for childhood illness are improving, the long-term consequences of surviving a major medical condition and treatment remain significant. For instance, while rates of death attributed to type 1 diabetes in childhood have dropped due to better insulin maintenance and prevention of acute metabolic complications, the chronic effects of insulin therapy over time cause significantly greater chances of death from cardiovascular disease by adulthood (Portuese & Orchard, 1995). Advances in care of LBW and VLBW infants has significantly reduced infant mortality, but their survival has introduced new challenges in terms of rehabilitation and long-term outcomes arising from complications due to prematurity. Treatments for childhood cancer, including chemotherapy and stem cell transplants, have significantly increased survival rates, but they carry with them significant short- and long-term side effects. Thirty years ago, many children with chronic illnesses died from complications before reaching the age of 5, whereas nowadays most children are surviving their illnesses and participating in general education. However, the side effects and long-term consequences of treatment can be significant.

Greater Specificity of Medical Diagnosis and Treatment

Research advances have been employed to design more refined and narrowly targeted technology, methods, and pharmacological interventions to combat disease. Forty years ago, brain scans consisted of fixed image scans of moderate detail, useful for identifying gross abnormalities. Modern scanning technology offers substantially greater image clarity, including three-dimensional rendering as well as the ability to monitor brain processes at work, both of which are helpful in identifying more subtle abnormalities of function. Treatments for childhood cancer consisting of powerful, broadly acting radiation, chemotherapy, and radical surgery (removing large amounts of cancerous and interconnected healthy tissue) have paved the way for increasingly refined treatments and surgery, which use computer-generated modeling and lasers that target the cancer cells directly with less collateral damage to surrounding healthy cells. Research on bone marrow and stem cell transplants is promising and predicts even more targeted interventions, as new, healthy cells will target and replace malignant ones.

Medications have also advanced significantly in past decades and now have much greater specificity of action and reduced side effects. Historically, psychopharmacological treatment for psychotic symptoms involved broad-acting dopamine antagonists such as chlorpromazine (Thorazine), which also induced marked side effects, including drowsiness, cardiovascular changes, neuromuscular reactions, dyskinesias, autonomic reactions, and so on. More recent antipsychotic medications, such as aripiprazole (Abilify), are highly targeted to specific dopamine receptors and offer partial antagonist (blocking) action while facilitating other necessary dopamine transmissions. This differential action is believed to moderate dopamine receptors involved in psychotic symptoms more effectively while decreasing the range and intensity of potential side effects.

Medications for controlling asthma have improved from bronchodilators, which minimized acute symptoms, to anti-inflammatory and antileukotriene medications and immunotherapy, which seek to control long-term effects and prevent the occurrence of acute asthma attacks. Medications to abate allergy symptoms have improved to include sustained-release mechanisms with targeted antihistamine action, which minimizes side effects such as drowsiness, enabling children to remain in school and alert (McCabe, 2008). Children with diabetes can successfully participate in general education using insulin pumps, oral or injected medications, or both in addition to dietary management. HIV medications, such as integrase inhibitors, entry inhibitors, nucleosides reverse transcriptase inhibitors, nucleotide analogs, and protease inhibitors, have demonstrated efficacy in reducing the reproduction of the HIV strain. Many of these HIV medications are combined into one pill, making it easier for children to adhere to the regimen. Better medicines allow for shorter hospital stays and greater ability to reintegrate with normal daily activities while still effectively fighting disease.

Increased Emphasis on Outpatient Care

Outpatient services increased 29% from 1992 to 2000, while the rate of inpatient hospitalization and length of stay plateaued or decreased during the same time (Bernstein et al., 2003). This is largely due to financial pressures of cost containment, as well as the scientific and technological advances described above that have allowed a shift from primary care in hospitals to outpatient settings, ambulatory settings, or home. The treatment of certain childhood medical conditions, such as cancer, will likely continue to require a period of hospitalization due to the complexity of the treatment and need for continual monitoring. However, even these treatments increasingly are conducted on an outpatient basis. Whereas a cancer treatment may have previously required a 2- to 4-week hospital stay, current methods may use a hybrid approach with a 1- to 2-day admission followed by 6 to 10 outpatient visits (Blank & Burau, 2004; Shaw & McCabe, 2008). It is increasingly likely that many pediatric conditions will be treated on an outpatient basis, which means that families and schools will be expected to step into the caregiving role previously fulfilled by the hospital treatment team. This trend reflects a decentralized approach to health care, where parents, schools, and outpatient clinics must share the burden of care and new roles may be assigned to ensure continuity of treatment (Shaw & McCabe).

CHANGING ROLE OF SCHOOLS

Schools are responsible for ensuring a free and appropriate education is provided to all children, including those who are experiencing a medical condition. Schools are challenged to develop flexible education plans that meet the needs of the child's medical regimen. For example, a child may not immediately and fully transition back to school from an inpatient setting but instead be reintegrated in a staggered fashion that reflects a medical protocol requiring brief inpatient stays, ongoing outpatient visits, and recuperation time at home. The use of medications to continue treatment beyond the hospital is common practice, which means that schools are increasingly educating children who are medicated for a variety of reasons.

Increase in Pharmacological Interventions

Recent evidence suggests an increasing trend for medication therapy as a primary treatment strategy. For example, use of psychotropic medications with children has tripled over the last decade, with prevalence rates as high as 6.3%, comparable to adult utilization rates (Zito et al., 2003). Between 6 and 9 million children are diagnosed with a serious mental illness (NAMI, 2004), and most are receiving psychiatric medications, many of which have not been extensively studied for efficacy and long-term effects in children. In some cases, the medications are not prescribed for their original intended purpose. For example, prescriptions of antipsychotic medications to children increased fivefold from 1995 to 2002, and over half of those prescriptions were written not for psychotic symptoms but for behavioral or affective disorders, conditions for which antipsychotics have not been extensively studied (Cooper et al., 2006).

In addition to the millions of children receiving psychopharmacological interventions, over 7 million children suffer from seasonal allergies (Bloom & Cohen, 2009), 9 million children suffer from asthma (Akinbami, 2006), almost 200,000 are diagnosed with type 1 or type 2 diabetes (NIDDK, 2008), and almost 250,000 children suffer from cancer (Ries et al., 2008). Between 2002 and 2005, pediatric prescription medications to treat type 2 diabetes increased 135% to 166%, asthma medications increased 47%, ADHD medications increased 40%, and antihyperlipidemics (cholesterol-lowering) drugs increased 15% (Cox, Halloran, Homan, Welliver, & Mager, 2008). This means that at any given time, educators are likely to encounter one or more children receiving medications that may significantly alter physical states, arousal, attention, cognition, behavior, and emotional functioning.

Multidisciplinary Approach

An Individualized Education Plan (IEP) must account for the physical, psychological, and academic consequences associated with the medical condition and treatment. Best practices call for school multidisciplinary teams to collaborate with medical and community agencies and the family to identify an education strategy that accommodates the medical regimen while optimizing the child's opportunity for as normal a schooling experience as possible. Education teams need to be knowledgeable of the medical condition, the nature of the treatments administered, and typical side effects. The child may have academic, physical, socioemotional, and adjustment needs resulting from the condition, treatment, multiple absences from school, or a combination of these factors. For example, many pharmacological interventions, which are designed to attack dangerous infectious or malignant agents or remedy neurological conditions, cause side effects that significantly impact learning and behavior. These side effects include sedation, restlessness, irritability, lethargy, fatigue, difficulty focusing, pain, nausea, emotional lability, tremor, dyskinesias, and so on. When the education team is able to anticipate and mitigate these effects through careful planning of an IEP and/or an individualized health plan, in cooperation with the family and medical team, the child's adjustment and responsiveness to instruction is maximized.

2

Grief and Bereavement

Roles for Educators

Steven R. Shaw, Tiffany Chiu, and Khing Su Lin

Cindy Johansson, media specialist at Piney Woods elementary school for the last 14 years, drove to school just as she did every day. Her daughter, Sara, a second grader at Piney Woods, rode with her. At 7:15 Wednesday morning, Cindy lost control of her car and slid into an oncoming truck. Both Cindy and Sara were killed in the accident.

At 8:20 that morning, most of the students had already arrived at school ahead of the 8:30 first bell. At this time, news of the accident reached Charlotte Hall, the principal of Piney Woods. Ms. Hall was personally devastated by the news of her friend and colleague of the last 14 years. As media specialist, Cindy Johansson knew all of the students and teachers. She had won awards and grants to fund computer upgrades for the old library. She was certainly one of the best regarded and central figures at Piney Woods. Moreover, 26 classmates in Sara's second-grade classroom had lost a peer and friend.

Ms. Hall informed the school district's central office of the loss of a colleague and a student. Social workers, school psychologists, and school counselors from other schools in the district converged on Piney Woods to assist. Ms. Hall and the school district leadership decided to take the following actions:

- Assign each of the social workers, school psychologists, and counselors to a classroom.
- Summon teachers from each classroom to the principal's office individually and tell them of the news.

- Tell the students at the end of the school day.
- Allow any parents who heard about the accident to pick up their children at school if they desired.
- Send home children with a note informing all of the parents of the situation.
- Make follow-up counseling available for several weeks.

As the plan developed, many issues emerged. About one third of the teachers did not feel emotionally prepared to return to class after being told the news. They were allowed to go home. Some of the teachers decided to tell their students early in the day. The professionals in the classrooms were not always well prepared to manage classes. Many classes watched videos, had extended outdoor recess, completed basic worksheets, or had story-reading time. Throughout the school day, the building was unusually quiet, and the sound of crying was heard in the hallways.

When the children were told about the accident, they responded in a variety of ways. The mental health professionals were watching for students with unusual reactions. Students with extreme reactions were removed from the classroom quietly for individual counseling sessions and to prevent contagion of their emotional responses to classmates. There were developmental differences in the way children received the news. The older children were more upset about the news, as their understanding of death was more mature. A student in kindergarten asked, "Without Ms. Johansson, where will we get our books?" Students were allowed to speak openly about their feelings. Some students talked about how much they would miss Ms. Johansson and Sara. Others told stories about losing relatives or the death of pets.

Significant emotional healing of faculty and students would be required. Long-term counseling was required for 16 students at the school, 8 of them students in Sara's class. Counseling for teachers and for professionals responding to this situation was made available. This challenging and emotional situation is common in schools. Although no one wants to think about the pain that death or crisis brings to a school, preparation and planning for such events is required.

INTRODUCTION

Death is a taboo topic of discussion in the Western world. This taboo is more pronounced when the topic involves school-aged children. Approximately 1 out of every 2,000 students dies each year, with the incidence of deaths being highest for the high school population (Nader, 1997). The most frequent causes of student deaths are accidents, homicides, and suicides. Among children and adolescents younger than 20 years old, 7,031 motor vehicle deaths, 3,418 homicides or legal interventions, and 1,774 suicides occurred in 2006 (Centers for Disease Control and Prevention [CDC], 2009). These sudden and traumatic events are not uncommon. Moreover, a significant number of children will succumb to severe illness such as cancer, HIV, infection, and a variety of congenital issues. Issues related to student death will likely affect all educators at some point in their careers (Jimerson & Huff, 2002).

Although traumatic events affect entire schools and communities, other deaths affect individuals. Approximately 900,000 children younger than 18 years old have lost their parents due to death (Dowdney, 2000).

These students are often going through grief and bereavement individually, and navigating the grief and bereavement process alone is daunting for many students. Without support, the grief and bereavement process can lead to adjustment disorders, mental health problems, and academic and social problems (Boelen, van den Bout, & de Keijser, 2003; Kato & Mann, 1999). Often, extended families and other support groups do not talk about death and loss with children. Educators may provide support to children so that they do not grieve alone.

At some time, all educators address the culturally taboo topic of death in a school setting (Holland, 1993). Addressing such issues is beyond the scope of training of many educational professionals (Mauk & Sharpnack, 1997). Moreover, an emotional component often affects the educational professional almost as much as it does the schoolchildren. For interventions to be most effective, school personnel must be prepared so that they can respond in a timely and supportive manner that leads to constructive navigation of the grief and bereavement process for all students and staff (Ayyash-Abdo, 2001).

BACKGROUND

Grief and bereavement intervention encompasses a variety of formal programs, techniques, and approaches to help students, families, and faculty adjust to major loss, such as death, crises, and catastrophes (Poland & Poland, 2004). Educators are not usually well trained or experienced in addressing issues surrounding death, crises, and catastrophes. Moreover, discussing such issues with children and adolescents is extremely uncomfortable for most adults (Webb, 2002). However, these events affect the short- and long-term learning environment. Schools, as important members of the community, have important roles to play in helping students, families, and faculty members adjust to traumatic and emotional events. Because grief and bereavement practices have great religious, cultural, family, and individual variation, sensitivity to different practices must be exercised. Moreover, children show significant developmental differences in how they understand death and how they grieve.

Some deaths affect entire communities, such as when a teacher or student dies. These deaths affect entire schools or even school districts. Because children grieve differently from adults and from each other, the challenge is to have appropriate mental health services available but appreciate that not all children wish to participate in a communal grieving process. The most common mistake that grief and bereavement programs make is to insist that all children grieve in the same manner. Research evidence shows that such a forced approach can create alienation between some children and school professionals.

Other deaths may affect entire communities to a degree but affect a single child most of all. This occurs when a parent, sibling, family member, or best friend dies. Other types of loss, such as the death of a pet or even the loss of a special toy, can result in significant grief responses. Although the loss of a special toy may seem trivial compared to the loss of a parent, understanding the nature of the relationship that has been lost and understanding loss from the child's perspective are critically important aspects of assisting children through the grief and bereavement process.

For schools to respond effectively to community and individual grief and bereavement situations, planning for such events is required. Although a large base of research support is absent, some studies support the idea that advanced planning leads to more rapid and complete recovery of functioning among the school community. Also, advanced planning and education of teachers leads to faster and more appropriate assessment and treatment of children having adjustment issues and symptoms of posttraumatic stress disorder.

Preparation includes the development of a grief and bereavement response team to coordinate and mobilize resources; effective communication; training for faculty members; the involvement of parents and community members; and coordination with area resources, such as firefighters, medical professionals, and law enforcement. Although planning and training are critical, each situation is different. Flexibility and compassion are required to guide the team to provide effective interventions.

IMPLICATIONS FOR EDUCATORS

In cases of loss, educators must address multiple issues and implications. Below are listed the best practices in managing especially difficult situations concerning grief and bereavement.

How to Tell Students About a Death

- Ask students if they know what happened. Ask them how they found out about the death.
- Share the information that you have about the death directly and honestly.
- Allow students to ask questions. Answer honestly. In many cases, the answer to questions on a topic as complex as death is "I don't know."
- Have students share memories of the deceased person.
- Talk about a memorial and ways to remember the person, such as a display of pictures, cards, and notes; a candle-lighting ceremony; a book of letters and pictures for the family; a donation to a favorite charity in the person's name; or a donation of books to the library in the child's or teacher's name.
- Discuss common grief reactions (and be sure to define *grief*) that a student might experience, such as difficulty concentrating, sudden surges of emotion, or strong feelings of anger or sadness.
- Talk about productive approaches to cope with emotional reactions, such as talking to a parent or trusted adult, being physically active, taking time to be alone, listening to music, writing in a journal, or reading books related to death.
- Have an art activity or something physical to do after the sharing. Many children prefer to draw their reaction to death rather than verbalize it.
- Have in place a "safe room" where students can go if they need some time alone, want to talk to someone, or just want to be away from the class for a period of time.

Notification and Announcement Procedures

Having all of the facts surrounding the situation verified is critical when announcing a death (Wass, Miller, & Thornton, 1990). Administrators must contact the family of the deceased and appropriate authorities to get the facts before providing intervention. Giving students and faculty members the necessary facts assists in dispelling counterproductive rumors. However, the privacy of families needs to be respected. Any final announcement of death requires verification from the family or law enforcement agencies.

Contacting school district administrators is important for several reasons. Plans for communicating with law enforcement, fire, hospital, and community resources are usually addressed at the district level rather than at the school level. In addition, mobilizing school district professionals as needed is usually managed at the school district level. Central school districts also have the advantage of being less emotionally involved in a grief and bereavement situation. Major decisions concerning coordination of notifications and announcements can be made at the school district level. If the death was a suicide, it is essential that central administrators have input into intervention planning.

In addition, key school district administrators need to be contacted as quickly as possible for purposes of media relations. Many school districts have media relations specialists who manage media contacts, and all information to the public must be funneled through the school district media specialist. No other school professional should address the media without coordination with the school district administration and media relations expert (Holland, 1993).

Establish a calling tree: A calling tree can be used to notify district-level personnel, as well as building staff. The calling tree can be used to notify all school personnel that a faculty meeting will be held before school to outline intervention plans. If the death occurred during nonschool hours or during vacation, then this process allows staff members to work through their own issues before they assist their students.

If a death occurs when school is in session, then notification and intervention have an increased immediacy (Murphy, Chung, & Johnson, 2002). First, a memorandum should be hand delivered to every teacher. The most frequent recommendation is to give all teachers the facts about the tragedy and instructions to share the information with their students, as well as suggestions for assisting students. This memo can also invite all staff to a faculty meeting after school. The majority of students should stay in their classrooms. Only those closest to the victim or those with personal issues of their own should be sent to the school's support personnel. Second, use the public announcement system. Principals are urged to plan carefully and rehearse what they will say. Choice of words, voice tone, and inflection are important and set the tone for management of the tragedy (Stroebe, Schut, & Stroebe, 2005).

Parent Notification

Families of students require information concerning a death that affects the school. Information should be delivered to parents as soon as possible. A balance must be maintained between providing enough information to dispel rumors and protecting the privacy of the deceased. The most efficient approach is to develop a fact sheet or letter to be sent to parents via students. The letter contains basic information about the event and about possible indicators that the child may have an emotional reaction that requires attention. This letter, in most cases, would not contain the name of the deceased, especially when the death involves a student. However, the name would be used in communications within the school to the faculty and, in most cases, with the students. The letter sent home would contain a brief description of the cause of death when the facts are known but would avoid unnecessary details.

Determine the Degree of Trauma

Different levels of resources are required for each situation. Assessing the degree of trauma is important for managing the short- and long-term intervention needs. A higher degree of emotional trauma often requires more resources over a longer period of time than grief and bereavement resulting in less trauma (Tonkins & Lambert, 1996).

- Who died? Was the person a longtime or popular member of the school?
- What happened? Unexpected and violent deaths, such as homicides or suicides, tend to result in more challenging coping problems than deaths from long-term illness.
- Where did the death occur? A death that occurs on school grounds results in more severe trauma than a death that occurs in a hospital. Identify who witnessed the death to target appropriate interventions. In addition, deaths occurring at schools result in students questioning their personal safety.
- What other tragedies have affected this particular school or community? Resulting trauma is much worse in situations where past crises, catastrophes, and deaths have been experienced by the community.
- In cases of auto accident or homicide, it is important to know who the perpetrator was, if known. In cases where the person believed to be responsible for the death has not been caught or is also a member of your school community, the level of trauma increases.

Concerns About Death Due to Suicide

If suicide is suspected in the death of a student or faculty member, then community members often experience additional emotional trauma. There are feelings of guilt, loss, and fear. The fear in schools is that suicide can be contagious and "copycat" suicides may take place. The American Association of Suicidology (AAS; 2009) recommends many of the same procedures as for all deaths with additional "postvention" (that is, intervention with those who knew the person who committed suicide) to address issues surrounding suicide. The purpose of postvention is twofold: (1) to reduce the chances of anyone else committing suicide by avoiding glamorization of the events causing death and (2) to assist staff and students with the grieving process. Postvention activities provide an opportunity to teach students the warning signs of suicide so that intervention to prevent further suicides can be implemented. No matter the situation, educators require training to recognize symptoms of depression and warnings of suicide ideation among students. The main recommendations of the AAS include the following:

- Do not dismiss school or encourage funeral attendance during school hours.
- Do not dedicate a memorial to the deceased. (Although the AAS recommends not making a memorial in cases of suicide, other scholars support the use of memorials.)
- Do not have a large school assembly.
- Give the facts to students.
- Emphasize prevention and everyone's role.
- Provide individual and group counseling.
- Emphasize that no one is to blame for the suicide.
- Emphasize that help is available and that there are alternatives to suicide.
- Contact the family of the deceased.

EDUCATIONAL STRATEGIES

Educators perform multiple, specific roles. To maximize efficiency and clarify what to do when grief and bereavement issues arise, these roles should be discussed and even rehearsed. It is also important to recognize that each person has his or her unique history concerning crisis and loss. It is not unusual for the personal history and issues of professionals to resurface (Brown & Goodman, 2005). Each student and each professional should be given permission to feel a range of emotions. There is no right or wrong way to feel. Typically, individuals go through a predictable sequence of emotional reactions following a crisis:

1. High anxiety
2. Denial
3. Anger
4. Remorse
5. Grief
6. Reconciliation

Below are suggested roles and functions for educators.

The Roles of Principals
- Coordinate direct intervention efforts.
- Be visible, available, and supportive and empower staff.
- Provide direction to teachers about how much to set aside the curriculum.
- Give permission for tests to be postponed in many classes.
- Communicate with central administration and other affected schools.
- Contact the family of the deceased.

- Inform staff and students about funeral arrangements.
- Ensure that memorials are appropriate.

The Roles of Teachers

- Provide accurate information to students.
- Lead classroom discussions that focus on helping students to cope with the loss.
- Dispel rumors.
- Answer questions without providing unnecessary details.
- Recognize the varying religious beliefs held by students.
- Model an appropriate response.
- Give permission for a range of emotions.
- Identify students who need counseling and refer to building support personnel.
- Provide activities to reduce trauma, such as artwork, music, and writing.
- Set aside the curriculum as needed.
- Discuss funeral procedures.

The Roles of Counselors, School Psychologists, and Social Workers

- Be available.
- Cancel other activities.
- Locate counseling assistance (check community resources).
- Provide individual and group counseling.
- Contact parents of affected students with suggestions for support or further referral.
- Follow the schedule of the deceased and visit classrooms of close friends.
- Support the faculty (provide counseling as needed).
- Keep records of affected students and provide follow-up services.

DISCUSSION QUESTIONS

1. What should an educational professional do if he or she is too personally anguished and upset to be a productive member of the grief and bereavement support team?

2. When a teacher sees a student's school performance deteriorate after the death of a peer, what is the appropriate action for the teacher to take?

3. Some parents may become emotional or upset when they find out that issues surrounding death and dying were discussed in school. How should schools respond to such concerns?

4. How would educators discuss death differently with a class of ninth graders versus a class of first graders?

5. When a student dies at a school, should faculty members go to the funeral? Should fellow students and their families be invited to funeral services? What if the services are held during regular school hours?

6. In situations concerning death and dying, religion often arises. What considerations should be given to religion in grief and bereavement interventions?

RESEARCH SUMMARY

- Much scholarly thought and writing, but little empirical research, exists on the issue of grief and bereavement interventions in schools.
- The research is limited largely because it is difficult to determine the outcomes of effective grief and bereavement interventions.
- Two components of effective responses are clear: planning and flexibility. Well-organized and trained school staff respond and communicate in a cohesive manner.
- It is important that school staff respond with one voice to reduce the confusion and panic often inherent in a situation involving the death of a member of the school community.
- Flexibility is also important, as children of different developmental levels, cultures, personalities, and family backgrounds grieve differently.
- Using a cookbook approach to grief and bereavement interventions is likely to lead to problems for some students.
- It is important to consider the developmental level of students when informing them about death. Death concepts are immature prior to age 7, especially concepts concerning the permanency and irreversibility of death. Older children may have a better understanding of death but lack coping skills.

RESOURCES

Cassini, K. K., & Rogers, J. L. (1989). *Death and the classroom: Teachers guide to assist grieving students.* Cincinnati, OH: Griefwork of Cincinnati.

Doka, K. (Ed.). (2008). *Living with grief: Children and adolescents.* New York: Hospice Foundation of America.

Klicker, R. L. (1999). *A student dies, a school mourns: Dealing with death and loss in the school community.* London: Taylor & Francis.

Lowenstein, L. (2006). *Creative interventions for bereaved children.* Toronto, Canada: Champion Press.

Wakenshaw, M. (2002). *Caring for your grieving child.* Oakland, CA: New Harbinger.

HANDOUT

GRIEF AND BEREAVEMENT IN THE SCHOOLS

Death of a student, a faculty member, or a parent triggers a difficult and emotional time in schools. The grief and bereavement process may affect an individual student or an entire school community. Most educators do not have much experience or training with grief and bereavement issues in school-age children, yet schools can play an important role in helping individuals or groups of students navigate the bereavement process.

Basic Skills

- Simple and heartfelt statements are most effective. A simple statement such as "I'm sorry your mom died" is much more effective than a long attempt to comfort.
- Listen and respect the child's feelings and fears. Give students a private place to talk and share feelings with a teacher or counselor.
- Do not be afraid to say the word *dead* or *death*. These words help create an atmosphere of acceptance.
- Let students know that it is okay to cry, be angry, be sad, and even to laugh. Recognize that laughter and play do not mean that a child is not grieving. Educators should not be afraid to show their own sadness.
- The student may need a place to be alone, even in school.
- Trust your own judgment. If something the child is telling you does not seem right, then call home and discuss it with the parent and consult with the school counselor or psychologist.
- Attend the funeral, if possible.
- Send a note to the family, expressing your sadness at their loss.

Teachers can expect to observe a variety of reactions in the classroom. These reactions may come and go for as much as 6 months after the event. Although students may require frequent support, these behaviors are not usually indicative of a long-term problem. Students with problems that last longer than 6 months, who appear to be getting worse, who show evidence of self-harm, or who have severe emotional reactions require referral to mental health professionals.

Common Reactions to Grief and Bereavement

- Shortened attention span
- Problems with concentrating
- Not completing school assignments
- Headache, stomachache, or other physical concern
- Fatigue
- Sadness and isolation from others
- Overly sensitive
- Increasingly disruptive in the classroom
- Hyperactive, impulsive, and disorganized behaviors
- Difficulty following directions

There are major developmental differences in how children navigate the grief and bereavement process. Although individuals differ widely in how they express feelings of grief and bereavement, the following are typical behaviors observed at different ages.

Between the Ages of 3 and 5 Years

- Bedwetting and/or needing to sleep with an adult are common.
- Asking questions about the meaning of death
- Playing "death"
- Regression of developmental skills, such as toileting, feeding, and language
- Preschoolers do not understand the word *forever*. As such, they do not often understand the permanence of death.
- Preschoolers also do not understand the irreversibility of death. They may expect the deceased to walk back into their lives at a later time.

Between the Ages of 6 and 10 Years

- Playing "funeral"
- Increasing shyness
- Increasing acting out
- Poor schoolwork
- Young school-age children begin to realize that death is permanent, but they think that only old people and pets die.
- Older school-age children know that death can happen to young and old and has many causes. Many children begin to fear the death of their own parent, siblings, or themselves.

Between the Ages of 11 and Adolescence

- Anger is normal.
- Feelings of everything being unfair
- Self-medication with alcohol or drugs
- Search for spirituality or religion
- Increase of risky behaviors
- Teenagers often intellectualize death and may even fantasize about their own death, but they do not think it will ever happen to them.

SECTION II

Chromosomal, Genetic, and Metabolic Disorders

3

Rare Chromosomal Disorders*

Shohreh M. Rezazadeh and Steven R. Shaw

Austin is a 5-year-old boy who is entering kindergarten. He is a happy child, but he has a number of unusual behaviors. When he plays with his favorite toys, he shakes and turns them. He frequently giggles, but for no obvious reason. Austin seldom interacts with other children except to provoke a response. He enjoys positive (laughter) and negative (crying) reactions from his peers. For example, sometimes he grabs a toy out of his sister's hands, not because he wants to play with it but because his sister becomes agitated and screams at him. Austin usually just drops the toy on the floor as he runs away giggling. He becomes preoccupied with various toys and repeats the same activity many times each day. His repetitive behaviors, such as playing with spinning objects and moving his fingers across his line of vision, can absorb his attention completely. He has received a diagnosis of autism and fragile X syndrome.

Because of Austin's behavior and social and cognitive issues, an Individualized Education Plan (IEP) has been developed by his teachers, therapists, and parents. His IEP has extensive treatment plans for attention problems, mood swings, tantrums, and hyperactivity. At this point, he has not experienced many mood swings or tantrums (although he has thrown some tantrums). Yet mood swings and tantrums are very common in children who have autism and fragile X syndrome.

Angela is a 9-year-old girl diagnosed with Williams syndrome. In addition to a number of health issues, such as cardiac issues and early puberty, she shows a distinctive facial appearance, an "elfin face." Angela also has moderate intellectual disabilities. She is overly and, sometimes, inappropriately friendly with both

*Adapted from Shaw, S. R. (2003). Rare chromosomal disorders. *Communiqué, 32*(4), 37–39. Copyright by the National Association of School Psychologists, Bethesda, MD. Use is by permission of the publisher. www.nasponline.org

strangers and people she knows. Angela talks too much. Her teacher says that Angela engages in a running conversation all day with anyone within earshot. Angela has reading decoding skills at a second-grade level. Yet she does not recall most of her conversations and has minimal reading comprehension.

Because of Angela's behavior and social and cognitive issues, an IEP has been developed by her teachers and parents. There are concerns about her safety because of Angela's friendly nature. Therefore, she receives extensive social skills training, including differential reinforcements of lower rates of talking and social behavior.

INTRODUCTION

Developmental disabilities, constellations of complications of the nervous system of the developing brain, are present from birth. These complications consist of deficits in children's cognition, language, behavioral functioning, sensory functions, motor development, and overall learning ability (Burack, Hodapp, & Zigler, 1998).

In the past, the causes of many developmental disabilities were unknown, but advances in genetics research have led to an understanding of the causes of many developmental disabilities. These advances have furthered the understanding of how genetic anomalies affect the brain mechanisms of cognition, language, and behavior. These discoveries have fundamentally changed the way educators and researchers understand developmental disabilities. The findings from genetic research are of particular value in predicting cognitive and behavioral outcomes in children with developmental disabilities, making it possible for clinicians to arrive at a primary cause for symptoms associated with different disabilities. This information can guide educators in distinguishing among developmental disabilities and designing specific, targeted treatment interventions.

BACKGROUND

Fragile X syndrome and Down syndrome are relatively common chromosomal disorders. Most educators have received training or have experience working with children with these disorders. However, hundreds of rare genetic disorders also affect the lives and education of children. Under IDEA, children with genetic disorders are labeled under categories such as Other Health Impairment; Orthopedic Impairment; and Moderate, Trainable, Severe, or Profound Intellectual Disabilities. Educators provide effective functional analysis of behavior and operant-conditioning models of education to children with severe to profound mental retardation. However, many parents are dissatisfied with this approach, because they want to know *why* the problems are happening and *what* the likely future will be. Despite revolutionary advances in understanding the human genome, the majority of families of children with severe developmental disabilities do not know why their child has impairments. Accurate diagnosis of children with rare chromosomal disorders is a prerequisite for prognosis, treatment planning, and genetic counseling of families (Singer & Berg, 1997). Educators and the children and families with whom they work would benefit from an improved understanding of rare chromosomal disorders.

Down syndrome and fragile X syndrome represent the most common developmental disabilities for which the genetic causes are known. In Down syndrome, an extra copy of the 21st chromosome contributes to intellectual disabilities. In fragile X syndrome, a break or fragmentation in the arm of the X chromosome contributes to a disruption in production of the FMR1 protein. In turn, the FMR1 protein affects the functioning of regions of the brain responsible for reasoning and memory (Hessl et al., 2005). In both fragile X syndrome and Down syndrome, mild to severe intellectual impairment is present. However, research findings have already begun to show characteristics unique to each of these disorders.

Genetics Evaluation

A medical evaluation by a geneticist is similar to most other medical evaluations. However, family history is emphasized. Geneticists will frequently ask detailed questions about the medical and developmental history of first-, second-, and third-degree relatives. Information concerning ethnic group status, religion, or national origin may be asked. Many families become part-time genealogists to answer the geneticist's questions completely. In addition, the geneticist will ask detailed questions about behavior, developmental milestones attainment, and overall cognitive development. The geneticist will conduct a physical examination of heart, lung, blood pressure, reflexes, and physical measurements. There will also be a careful examination of the skin, hair, toes, fingers, and facial structure to look for specific characteristics of identified syndromes (Jones, 1997). Depending on the issues of interest, a sample may be taken for genetic analysis. Usually, the sample is blood. However, amniotic fluid, bone marrow, or other tissue samples may be collected.

Samples are then sent to a cytogenetics laboratory for analysis. Usually, chromosomes cannot be seen with traditional light microscopes. However, during cell division, chromosomes become condensed to the point where they can be viewed with a light microscope at 1,000x (Engels et al., 2007). During this cell division phase, laboratories treat chromosomes with an inhibitor to arrest them in their most visible state. Chromosomes are then stained with a variety of treatments. This allows the bands of each chromosome to become visible. Thus, each chromosome shows its unique pattern of bands, looking much like a bar code. Chromosomes in pairs are usually arranged according to size and banding into a karyotype. A karyotype is an organized profile of an individual's unique chromosomal patterns. The karyotype is examined by geneticists for abnormalities in structure or number of each chromosome pair.

Chromosome Abnormalities

A familial predisposition for chromosomal breakage or problems with early cell division may exist. Also, environmental causes, such as exposure to radiation, lead, carcinogens, or other substances known to be mutagenic, can contribute to chromosome abnormalities. For most children, however, the cause of chromosome abnormalities is unknown. Chromosomal abnormalities can be roughly divided into numeric and structural types.

Numeric Abnormalities. There are relatively few numeric abnormalities. Numeric abnormalities involve the loss or addition of an entire chromosome. The addition of a chromosome is called *trisomy*, whereas the loss of a chromosome is called *monosomy*. The vast majority of monosomies and trisomies result in death soon after conception. Examples of trisomies that often survive to full term are trisomies of the 13, 18, and 21 chromosomes. Children with trisomy 13 and trisomy 18 (Edwards syndrome) usually die within the first year after birth; multiple dysmorphic features and severe dysfunction of organ systems are present. Down syndrome (trisomy 21) is, by far, the most common trisomy; children with this condition are most likely to thrive.

Monosomies and trisomies of the sex chromosomes usually have less severe effects than do numeric abnormalities of the autosome. For example, Turner syndrome is a monosomy of the X sex chromosome (45, XO), and Klinefelter syndrome is an addition of an X chromosome in males (47, XXY). Although there is a great degree of variation, many persons with these numeric abnormalities of sex chromosomes have little functional impairment.

Structural Abnormalities. Structural abnormalities are far more common and far more complex than numeric abnormalities. Structural abnormalities involve some type of damage to the chromosome. The expression of the structural abnormality is dependent on the type, size, and location of the defect (Baker et al., 2002).

The most common type of structural abnormality is called a *deletion*. In deletions, part of the chromosomal material is missing. Advances in chromosomal analysis have resulted in improved understanding of gene deletions. There are many well-defined deletion syndromes, such as Prader-Willi (15q; Holland, Whittington, & Hinton, 2003), Angelman's (15q), Williams (7q, although other locations have been linked; Meyer-Lindenberg, Mervis, & Faith Berman, 2006), DiGeorge (22q), and Cri-du-Chat (5q).

A second type of structural abnormality is *translocation*. In a translocation, material from one chromosome is traded with material from another chromosome. There is some evidence that many cancers are caused by translocations. For example, chronic myeloid leukemia is caused by a translocation of sections of chromosome 9 and chromosome 22.

A third type of structural abnormality is *inversion*. In an inversion, a part of the chromosome is broken in two places, rotates 180 degrees, and reattaches to form a chromosome where the structure is out of order. In many cases, inversions are familial, and no major problems present (Anderlid et al., 2002).

Potential for Intervention

Specific genes and specific behavioral phenotypes are now being identified at a rapid rate, and one can better differentiate among developmental disabilities based on their unique identified sets of symptoms. Each developmental disability has a genetic cause that is responsible for its distinct patterns of cognitive, behavioral, and physical characteristics. These clusters of features occur with high probability in relation to a genetic developmental disability relative to other disorders (Dykens & Rosner, 1999). Phenotype research has accurately identified specific areas of cognitive, behavioral, and physical characteristics for a range of genetic developmental disabilities (Dykens, Hodapp, & Evans, 2006).

The value of having knowledge about the genetic etiology of developmental disabilities and their associated behavioral phenotypes is vast. Such knowledge is hypothesized to provide the means for early diagnosis, preventive measures, and effective interventions (Hodapp, DesJardin, & Ricci, 2003; Hodapp & Dykens, 2005). Currently, treatment interventions for genetic developmental disabilities and other childhood disorders are nonspecific; that is, treatment interventions are not tailored to genetic developmental disorders and are, instead, one-size-fits-all. Current treatment practices do not encompass the phenotypic information, and disorders are treated with the functional deficits and delays in mind rather than with an intervention or treatment designed specifically for the disorder.

By fine-tuning the research on behavioral expression of genetic developmental disabilities, information about the early signs, symptoms, and potential risk factors for emergent problems can be addressed (e.g., Udwin & Yule, 1991). Most importantly, genetic and behavioral research will need to describe the predictable behaviors arising from the genetic factors associated with a developmental disability that increase the probability of making the child vulnerable or at increased risk for further developmental adversities (Fidler, Hodapp, & Dykens, 2002). Such information can prompt the development of preventative and early intervention support. In addition, behavioral phenotype research can focus on determining the age of onset for specific developmental deficits and weaknesses to ensure timely interventions are in place—early interventions will reduce later negative developmental impacts. Furthermore, the developmental course of behavioral expressions will need to be described to provide accurate information about the changes that might occur because of development. This information will help prompt changes in treatment to target areas of weakness and strength. Lastly, information about strengths and protective factors are also important to establish to promote the sustenance of treatment programs.

In sum, advances in genetic research have the potential to inform educators about the unique causes and characteristics of developmental disabilities that were once viewed as homogenous. Previous research on behavioral phenotypes of genetic developmental disabilities has had little impact on guiding targeted and tailored interventions, because such findings have not been transferred from the field of genetic research to educational applications. Future phenotype research will need to focus on addressing specific questions to help devise preventative interventions and tailor those interventions so they reflect the probable long-term developmental outlook of the child with the disorder.

Future Work

The scientific knowledge being developed and applied toward children with rare chromosomal disorders is growing at an exponential rate. Much of the groundbreaking work is coming from the microbiologists, geneticists, and cytologists involved directly or indirectly with the Human Genome Project. However, for this work to have a major effect on the lives of children and their families, there must be an interdisciplinary effort. The importance of understanding developmental, cognitive, academic, and behavioral phenotypic expression of rare chromosomal disorders has been long known but little acted upon (Carey, 2003). Geneticists traditionally focused on physical morphology to assist in clinical diagnoses. Yet due to the work of speech and language therapists, parents, educators, and psychologists, now speech, behaviors, cognitive abilities, and loss of specific skills are major diagnostic criteria for a variety of disorders. These projects would not have reached their current level of success were it not for the coordinated efforts of microbiologists, laboratory geneticists, clinical geneticists, social workers, speech and language therapists, genetics counselors, neurologists, developmental pediatricians, parents and other family members, and educators—and, of course, the children. Complex problems require complex efforts. As challenging and frustrating as working with children with rare chromosomal disorders can be, improved understanding leads to positive interventions that improve the lives of these children and their families.

IMPLICATIONS FOR EDUCATORS

Chromosomal disorders manifest in different ways, and their effects on cognition and learning can vary according to the type, extent, and characteristics of the genetic anomaly. Thus, it is important that teachers have a thorough knowledge of how these disorders impact on learning and educational outcomes for affected children. This knowledge will inform decisions about the most appropriate teaching strategies for each individual child. Below are some questions teachers may ask to help them create an optimal learning environment for students with special needs.

- *What kind of training should teachers acquire to work with students with special needs?* Teachers should obtain in-depth knowledge about the characteristics of children with rare chromosomal disorders through conferences and workshops. Teachers should obtain information about the learning characteristics of these children, such as about their strengths and adaptive functioning. These can serve as guides for teachers in adapting the curriculum to meet the needs of special learners. Further, teachers must maintain close contact with parents/caregivers to ensure children's medical needs are adequately monitored in school.
- *What modifications should teachers make to the curriculum to assist students with special needs?* Teachers should work as part of a team with the school psychologist, special educators, speech and language therapist, and occupational therapist in identifying optimal curriculum and classroom environments for special learners. With input from these professionals, teachers should consider what skills the leaner has and how to best use those skills.

EDUCATIONAL STRATEGIES

- Remember that children are individuals, not simply "a disorder." Children with the same genetic disorder often behave differently and have markedly different sets of skills.

- As such, a behavioral approach that reduces problem behaviors and builds positive behaviors is the first line of educational strategy.
- Some disorder-specific behaviors (e.g., food hoarding for Prader-Willi syndrome or overfriendliness to strangers for Williams syndrome) require disorder-specific strategies.
- Always include parents and other therapists in any behavior-change system. Generalization of skills across settings demands a team effort.
- Behaviors are influenced by multiple domains. Collaboration with medical professionals, speech and language pathologists, occupational therapists, physical therapists, and school nurses is often required for successful educational programming.

DISCUSSION QUESTIONS

1. How will advances in genetic sciences change the way that educators work with children with developmental disabilities?

2. What are some ways that parents of children with rare chromosomal disorders can receive support?

3. What might the role for physicians, neurologists, or geneticists be in developing an educational program for children with rare genetic disorders?

4. How might schools benefit from having a genetics counselor/educator as a member of the student support team or special education staff?

5. What are some of the primary challenges for developing a parent support group to address the needs of children with rare chromosomal disorders and their families?

RESEARCH SUMMARY

- There may be a familial predisposition for chromosomal breakage or problems with early cell division. Some chromosome abnormalities have environmental causes, such as exposure to radiation, lead, carcinogens, or other substances known to be mutagenic.
- Chromosomal abnormalities can be roughly divided into numeric and structural types.
- There are relatively few numeric abnormalities. Numeric abnormalities involve the loss or addition of an entire chromosome. The addition of a chromosome is called trisomy, whereas the loss of a chromosome is called monosomy. Down syndrome (trisomy 21) is by far the most common trisomy, and children with this disorder are the most likely to thrive.
- Structural abnormalities are far more common and far more complex than numeric abnormalities. They involve some type of damage to the chromosome. The most common type of structural abnormality is

called a deletion. There are many well-defined deletion syndromes, including Prader-Willi, Williams, and Cri-du-Chat (5q).

- Educators often think of chromosomal disorders as removed from their day-to-day activities. However, educational professionals and primary care pediatricians are on the front lines of developmental issues for children. The first major criterion that may indicate a chromosomal disorder is severe developmental delay. Low muscle tone and dysmorphic features are other major criteria. The primary care pediatrician typically makes a referral to the geneticist. Some examples of educator involvement include the following:
  - o Developing parent and sibling support groups
  - o Educating teachers and parents
  - o Communicating with physicians
  - o Translating medical information for parents
  - o Noting unusual patterns of development (e.g., loss of skills, sudden onset of atypical behaviors, complete resistance to academic and behavior interventions)
- When an unusual developmental trend is detected, educators may be in the best position to investigate causes, such as home or school stressors, major environmental change, or other nongenetic triggers of atypical behaviors.

RESOURCES

Burack, J. A., Hodapp, R. A., & Zigler, E. (Eds.). (1998). *Handbook of mental retardation and development.* Cambridge, England: Cambridge University Press.

Wilson, G. N., & Cooley, W. C. (2006). *Preventive management of children with congenital anomalies and syndromes.* Cambridge, England: Cambridge University Press.

The following Web sites offer reliable information on chromosomal disorders:

American Academy of Pediatrics, "Genetics and Birth Defects": http://www.aap.org/healthtopics/genetics.cfm. Provides in-depth information regarding the assessment and treatment of children with genetic developmental disorders.

March of Dimes: www.marchofdimes.com

National Dissemination Center for Children with Disabilities: www.nichcy.org

National Organization for Rare Disorders (NORD): www.rarediseases.org

Online Mendelian Inheritance in Man® (OMIM): www.ncbi.nlm.nih.gov/omim/

HANDOUT

CHILDREN WITH RARE CHROMOSOMAL DISORDERS

Children with rare chromosomal disorders have multifaceted needs. Keeping track of all of the professionals helping the child is challenging. Below are descriptions of important consulting professionals and suggestions of questions that parents can have for each professional.

List of Consulting Professionals

Geneticist or Pediatric Geneticist: A scientist who is involved in studying the genes contributing to brain development and behavior. A pediatric geneticist is able to identify the genes responsible for various chromosomal conditions affecting children.

Genetics Counselor: A scientist who provides assessment of the genetic risk to the family for a disorder.

Neurologist: A medical doctor who is able to evaluate and diagnose conditions and problems related to the nervous system (the brain, spinal cord, muscles, nerves) and recommend ways to manage or treat those conditions.

Occupational Therapist: A health professional who is trained to assess a child's gross motor (e.g., walking) and fine motor skills (e.g., hand grip) and organization of sensory information (e.g., vision, touch, hearing). An occupational therapist is involved in designing interventions to help a child carry out his or her day-to-day functional activities.

Speech and Language Therapist: A health professional who evaluates and diagnoses problems related to a child's communication and language development. He or she will design treatments that will help a child's speech production, articulation. They may also use augmentative and alternative communication systems (e.g., Picture Exchange Communication System [PECS]).

Psychologist: A psychologist provides psychological and academic assessment for children in order to evaluate their areas of developmental strengths and weaknesses. In addition to psycho-educational assessment, psychologist is involved in the design and implementation of interventions to help children overcome their academic difficulties. They further provide consultation to school personnel and families in this area.

Questions to Ask Consulting Professionals

- *Ask Geneticist:* How does a gene contribute to my child's disability?
- *Ask Genetics Counselor:* What are the likelihoods of my other children inheriting these genes and having this disorder? Is prenatal genetic testing possible to assess the risk to the fetus?
- *Ask Neurologist:* Which area of the brain is implicated in my child's disability? What treatments are available to help my child?
- *Ask Occupational Therapist:* What activities are off limits for my child due to his or her disability? How can the school make things easier to accommodate a student's physical disability?
- *Ask Speech and Language Pathologist:* Can a child with language delay ever catch up?
- *Ask Psychologist:* What special educational services are available to accommodate his or her learning needs? What can be done to improve my child's behavior?

4

Phenylketonuria (PKU)*

Implications for Educators and Schools

Paul C. McCabe and Lindsay Glasser

Within the first week of her life, Paige was diagnosed with phenylketonuria (PKU) during a routine screening for newborns. Having no previous knowledge of this rare genetic disorder, her parents worked with doctors and dieticians to learn about the treatment for Paige, which includes adhering to a strict diet, and her prognosis. With ongoing support of and collaboration between her school and home, Paige has maintained control of her phenylalanine (Phe) blood levels through adherence to a phenylalanine-restricted diet. Paige has shown no deficits in intellectual functioning, indicating that the diet has proven effective. She is now a 13-year-old adolescent who does, however, exhibit minor behavioral concerns, specifically with impulse control and maintaining attention.

Like most 13-year-olds, Paige is becoming increasingly independent, and her difficulties with impulse control have contributed to some dietary noncompliance. Since her Phe levels must be carefully monitored and adjusted in the event of any noncompliance, her parents have brought their concerns to her teacher and the school psychologist. Several plans were implemented to help Paige regain control of her diet and understand the potential side effects of going "off-diet." Paige was given the opportunity to plan meals at home and suggest acceptable items for the school's vending machines and was assigned to be a mentor to another student with PKU in a younger grade to gain a sense of responsibility. Additionally, the school psychologist provided training as well as ongoing support to the school's faculty regarding the treatment of PKU.

*Adapted from Coluccio, F., & McCabe, P. C. (2004). The effects of phenylketonuria (PKU) on executive function and behavior. *Communiqué, 32*(7), 35–37. Copyright by the National Association of School Psychologists, Bethesda, MD. Use is by permission of the publisher. www.nasponline.org

INTRODUCTION

Phenylketonuria (PKU) is a rare congenital disease that can be detected at birth through routine screening. An individual with PKU has an impaired ability to process the amino acid phenylalanine (Phe), which is found in most protein-containing foods, including most meats and fish, milk products, eggs, nuts, and chocolate, as well as low-calorie foods containing aspartame (i.e., NutraSweet). If left undetected within the first year, the child may develop severe cognitive and developmental delays. Although there is no cure, proper treatment of PKU, involving a Phe-restricted diet, can minimize or prevent intellectual disabilities.

BACKGROUND

Phenylketonuria is caused by the pairing of recessive genes carrying the PKU markers. Universal screening procedures at birth for all newborns have helped to identify the presence of the disease at its earliest possible point. In individuals with PKU, the enzyme that metabolizes the amino acid phenylalanine, named phenylalanine hydroxylase (PAH), is impaired, absent, or inactive.

Prevalence, Symptoms, and Treatment

PKU affects approximately 1 in 10,000 to 20,000 live births and is between 3 to 10 times more prevalent among Whites and Native Americans than among Blacks, Latinos, or Asians (Hardelid et al., 2006; Koch, 1999). Although it has no cure, PKU is the most common treatable genetic disease (Antshel & Waisbren, 2003). Effective treatment includes avoiding foods high in phenylalanine (a phenylalanine-restricted diet). However, since a child with PKU still needs to consume sufficient quantities of proteins and essential amino acids for normal growth and development, care must be taken to design and follow a balanced diet.

At one time, discontinuing the phenylalanine-restricted diet was considered safe between the ages of 6 and 10 years. However, Koch (1999) recommended that the dietary therapy be continued into adulthood to prevent long-term effects caused by elevations of Phe. This becomes especially true for adult women with PKU, who should continue the diet during pregnancy to prevent fetal damage (Cerone, Schiaffino, Di Stefano, & Veneselli, 1999; Koch). Other research supports Koch's recommendation that the diet continue through adolescence and into adulthood to prevent decline in intellectual performance or motor performance (Cerone et al.; Seashore, Friedman, Novelly, & Bapat, 1985; Surtees & Blau, 2000). Early discontinuation of the diet can result in "long-term deficits in verbal fluency, spatial cognition, and eye-hand co-ordination" (Griffiths, 2000, p. 83). Furthermore, in 2000, a National Institutes of Health (NIH) panel of experts concluded that treatment of PKU required a "diet for life" (NIH, 2000). Additionally, a phenylalanine-restricted diet can be beneficial in improving intelligence and minimizing social deficits even in individuals who have had a late diagnosis, meaning they were not screened at birth or were diagnosed after infancy (Koch).

Another option in treatment includes the use of the drug sapropterin dihydrochloride. This drug, the first pharmaceutical treatment developed to manage PKU, was approved by the FDA in 2007 (Rollins, 2008). This pharmaceutical treatment, known on the market as Kuvan, can reduce the blood phenylalanine concentration, providing a higher tolerance for phenylalanine in diets or possibly allowing a less restricted or nonrestricted diet (Levy, Burton, Cederbaum, & Scriver, 2007).

When PKU is left untreated, the most common result is severe intellectual disabilities. When identified and treated in the first weeks of life, intellectual disabilities are preventable (Antshel & Waisbren, 2003). However, children with PKU may still experience some academic difficulties (Arnold et al., 1998; White, Nortz, Mandernach, Huntington, & Steiner, 2001). Because the symptoms of PKU may not be seen until intellectual disabilities occur, newborn screening is vital for the prevention of effects of this disorder.

Cognitive and Neurological Effects

Seashore and colleagues (1985) examined the intellectual functioning of 14 children with PKU who were no longer on the Phe-restricted diet. Of these children, 10 experienced significant declines in intellectual functioning, measured by a difference of up to 31 standard score points on intelligence tests. The researchers also found that the group of children performed poorly on neuropsychological functioning tasks that require cognitive and integrative skills. Similar findings were shown in a study of adolescents who discontinued dietary treatment at an average age of 11 years and were tested 6 years later (Cerone et al., 1999).

Huttenlocher (2000) reported that the average brain size of an individual with untreated PKU is about 80% that of a normal brain. Other researchers have also reported that individuals with PKU demonstrate microcephaly, or smallness of the head (Surtees & Blau, 2000). Seizure disorders are also common in untreated cases of PKU (Huttenlocher; Surtees & Blau). Arnold et al. (1998) found motor function deficits in children with PKU related to a shortage of dopamine in the central nervous system. Fine-motor and visual-motor integration deficits have also been seen in children with PKU (Huijbregts et al., 2003). Welsh, Pennington, Ozonoff, Rouse, and McCabe (1990) identified hyperactivity, attention, perceptual-motor difficulties, and aggressiveness as other conditions often seen in untreated PKU. These conditions can be avoided or reduced through strict adherence to a phenylalanine-restricted diet and/or administration of sapropterin dihydrochloride.

Executive Dysfunction. Executive function has been defined as "the ability to maintain a problem-solving set that is appropriate for goal acquisition, including formulation, planning, self-monitoring, mental flexibility, and the ability to change strategies in response to new information" (Luciana, Sullivan, & Nelson, 2001, p. 1638). Welsh and colleagues (1990) also included organization and impulse control, and Antshel and Waisbren (2003) defined *executive function* as the "processes required for sustaining attention, inhibiting impulsivity, and maintaining information 'on-line'" (p. 458).

Even with dietary compliance or medication treatment, PKU can have a detrimental effect on neuropsychological functioning. The skills that seem to be most affected are those mediated by the prefrontal region of the brain (Arnold et al., 1998; Griffiths, 2000). This area is associated with planning and execution of cognitive processes during goal-oriented problem solving. In children with PKU, deficits in problem solving using abstract reasoning, mental processing, sustained attention, interhemispheric transfer, and visual-motor skills have been identified (Huijbregts et al., 2003).

The dysfunctions in this area may be caused, in part, by dopamine deficiencies in the central nervous system (Luciana et al., 2001; White et al., 2001). The increased concentrations of Phe in the blood result in decreased uptake of other amino acids, because Phe crosses the blood-brain barrier more easily. Tyrosine, required for dopamine synthesis in the brain, is one such amino acid that is decreased in the presence of elevated Phe levels. In individuals without PKU, PAH converts phenylalanine into tyrosine, which is a precursor for the biosynthesis of dopamine. However, increased concentrations of Phe due to the inactivity of the PAH enzyme leads to a deficiency of dopamine and is, thus, a contributing factor to executive dysfunction.

In a study by Welsh and colleagues (1990), children showed specific executive function deficits, including poor planning and mental flexibility, which correlated with current and mean lifetime Phe blood concentrations. Because most children on dietary therapy for PKU have normal intelligence as measured by standardized intelligence tests, intelligence tests may not be sensitive enough to identify the subtle cognitive deficits in these children. The findings of this study suggest that tests of executive functioning may be more suitable and sensitive measures of cognitive development in children with PKU than standardized intelligence tests.

Maternal Phenylketonuria

Children who are born to mothers with PKU, referred to as maternal phenylketonuria (MPKU), are at risk for the same conditions that occur in children with the disorder themselves. Like children with PKU, children with MPKU are at a greater risk for executive function deficits and ADHD (Waisbren & Azen, 2003).

The prenatal development of the child is influenced by the mother's adherence to the Phe-restricted diet. Children with MPKU present with intellectual disabilities more often when the mothers are not on a Phe-restricted diet (Waisbren & Azen, 2003). Children whose mothers are in control of their Phe blood levels before conception did not differ from children without MPKU. Mothers who did not control their diet until after 10 weeks into the gestational period rated their children as hyperactive, aggressive, and impulsive. Antshel and Waisbren (2003) also found microcephaly (73%), low birth weight (40%), and congenital heart disease (12%) in their sample of children of mothers with untreated PKU.

Timing and Degree of Exposure

Antshel and Waisbren (2003) also examined the extent of deficits as a function of whether a child was exposed to phenylalanine postnatally (i.e., PKU) or exposed prenatally (i.e., MPKU). They found that executive function deficits were correlated with levels of phenylalanine, indicating that the toxicity is dose dependent. The findings suggested that although both PKU and MPKU offspring have executive function deficits, the specifics of those deficits are different.

Children with PKU show executive function deficits in the ability to initiate, sustain, shift, and direct attention, all dependent on a well-functioning executive control system. These deficits are consistent with ADHD inattentive type (Antshel & Waisbren, 2003). Children with MPKU have more difficulties with the behavioral components of executive function, such as impulse control. Their executive function deficits are more consistent with ADHD combined type. The results of this study also suggest that children with PKU have right-hemispheric dysfunction, because they have more difficulty "seeing the big picture." MPKU offspring have more left-hemispheric difficulties related to processing specific details, which is mediated by the left hemisphere. These results suggest that the timing and severity of exposure to phenylalanine, either prenatally or postnatally, has differential effects on the developing central nervous system that may be seen later in the form of behavioral anomalies and executive function deficits.

PKU provides a unique opportunity for researchers to examine the direct effects of a toxic substance on neural development both before and after birth. By studying children and adolescents with PKU and carefully monitoring their phenylalanine and tyrosine levels, researchers may develop an enhanced understanding of the intricacies of the dopaminergic system, particularly in the frontal region. This has additional ramifications for the classification and treatment of related dopaminergic disorders, such as ADHD and schizophrenia.

In addition, researchers are discovering new proteins that are safe for individuals with PKU and could be used as dietary substitutes. For example, a protein extracted from whey during cheese production, glyco-macropeptide (GMP), is the first known natural protein that is safe for individuals with PKU (van Calcar et al., 2009). Researchers are identifying ways that these safe proteins can be substituted for the naturally occurring proteins that are harmful for those with PKU.

IMPLICATIONS FOR EDUCATORS

An important task for educators working with a child with PKU is the assessment and determination of specific cognitive deficits. School psychologists can help assess secondary symptoms from PKU effects, and teachers can assess academic and behavioral progress. If deficits are occurring, it is important to develop instructional plans that seek to improve executive function skills. Additionally, executive function deficits found in children with PKU are consistent with ADHD inattentive type (Antshel & Waisbren, 2003). Careful differential diagnosis by the school psychologist is necessary to determine appropriate treatment and individualized intervention.

Most children with PKU will require ongoing monitoring and specialized programming involving contingency management, counseling, self-monitoring, and contracting. Deficits in executive function areas such as problem solving, consequential thinking, and insight and judgment might increase the likelihood of the child testing his or her diet or going "off-diet."

Dietary Compliance

The amount of appropriate phenylalanine intake, called "tolerance," is individually determined by a medical professional and varies depending on PAH residual activity, metabolism, and rate of growth of the child (Ogier de Baulny, Abadie, Feillet, & de Parscau, 2007). Thus, each child may have individualized dietary requirements. Open communication with the parents is critical to ensure adherence to treatment, and any variations of the diet or the child's behaviors should be discussed and managed.

The Phe-restricted diet contains the same list of prohibited and permitted foods for all children with PKU; only the quantity varies. The only foods that contain no phenylalanine are sugar, oil, pure starch, and water (and products made of these ingredients, such as hard candy and soda). Foods containing low amounts include fruits, vegetables, cereals, and bread. Foods with the highest concentrations of Phe include meat, poultry, fish, nuts, and dairy products (NIH, 2002).

Educators and other school personnel can become actively involved in encouraging students with PKU to comply with their diets and avoid temptations. Schools often provide tempting treats, including birthday and pizza parties. Vending machines are prevalent, as well as alternatives to the traditional school meal, including catered foods, buffet-style lunches, and fast food. School personnel can take a three-pronged approach to encourage dietary compliance.

Meet With the Parents. First, a teacher, counselor, school nurse, or school psychologist can meet with the child's parents to assess their knowledge about PKU. This conversation may also include the school's practices in terms of classroom snacks or treats, as well as lunches. It is important to assess the parents' understanding of their child's possible food opportunities and what can be done realistically to keep phenylalanine-laden foods away from their child. Although most parents are well informed of their child's dietary restrictions by the time he or she is school aged, they may not be aware of the occasions where inappropriate foods are offered or when appropriate foods are not provided at all (Carey & Lesen, 1998).

Meet With the Student. Next, a meeting should be planned with the student to assess the student's knowledge of his or her diet, as well as the likelihood of compliance. As the student reaches adolescence, compliance becomes more difficult, as peer pressure mounts and adolescents struggle for independence in behavior (including eating and drinking). Many adolescents will test their diets to see if there is any truth to warnings given by parents and other adults (Carey & Lesen, 1998). Efforts to encourage autonomy in dietary compliance are recommended and likely to be more effective than trying to control the adolescent's diet.

Educate the School Community. Finally, an individual who is familiar with both the child and PKU (e.g., teacher, school psychologist) should work to educate the entire school community on the disorder and related dietary needs. School personnel can assist the teacher and nurse in ensuring compliance and increasing awareness. Staff trainings, workshops, and distribution of handouts providing a list of current resources and research are some suggestions for promoting awareness. Staff can also help to make certain that alternative foods are available for both intra- and extracurricular activities.

EDUCATIONAL STRATEGIES

- Educate all school personnel who may work with or supervise a child with PKU, including educators, nurses, psychologists, administrators, and kitchen and lunchroom staff, about the disorder and dietary requirements and/or medication regimens.
- Maintain open communication with family regarding any updates to the child's treatment, learning, or behavior. Encourage the family to notify the school with any new developments, especially new dietary changes or medications.
- Follow a three-pronged approach to encourage dietary compliance within the school.

  1. Meet with the child's parents to assess their knowledge about PKU. Ensure they are fully aware of their child's possible food opportunities and what can be done realistically to keep phenylalanine-laden foods away from their child.

  2. Meet with the student regarding his or her diet. Encourage autonomy in dietary compliance and provide opportunities for the student to plan or recommend foods provided by the school (cafeteria, vending machines, etc.).

  3. Educate the entire school community on the disorder and related dietary needs, as well as the consequences of the child going "off-diet."

- In addition to assisting the student and his or her caregivers, educators can help to make certain that alternative foods are available for both intra- and extracurricular activities.
- Be familiar with the behavioral and cognitive deficits a child with PKU may display and notify the school psychologist, nurse, and parent if any changes or concerns are noted.

DISCUSSION QUESTIONS

1. How can schools support phenylalanine-restricted diets and minimize the temptation for children with PKU to go "off-diet"?

2. What can parents of children with PKU do to ensure the teacher and other school personnel are aware of the restricted diet and risks associated with noncompliance?

3. What strategies should be used to encourage the child to stay on-diet? How can the child become involved?

4. Since certain dysfunction in cognitive abilities, such as executive functioning, cannot be easily identified through a standardized test, how can these problems be identified?

5. How might a child with executive dysfunction behave in a classroom? How can this student be supported?

6. Given the negative effects of going off-diet for a child with PKU, does the school have an ethical or legal obligation to ensure the child remains on the restricted diet, even if the child's parents refuse to comply or are negligent in ensuring compliance?

RESEARCH SUMMARY

- An individual with PKU does not have the ability to process the amino acid phenylalanine (Phe), which is found in most protein-containing foods, including most meats and fishes, milk products, eggs, nuts, and chocolate, as well as low-calorie foods containing aspartame (i.e., NutraSweet).
- The disease can manifest in two ways:

  1. Prenatally, resulting from a mother with PKU, called maternal phenylketonuria (MPKU)

  2. Postnatally, caused by pairing of recessive genes carrying the PKU markers (PKU)

- If the disease is undetected within the first year after birth, the child may develop severe cognitive and developmental delays. Other consequences of the disorder include dysfunction in executive function, including the ability to initiate, sustain, shift, and direct attention and diminished impulse control. Since these symptoms are characteristic of ADHD, careful differential diagnosis by the school psychologist is necessary to determine appropriate treatment and individualized intervention.
- Although PKU has no cure, proper treatment, involving a Phe-restricted diet, can minimize or prevent intellectual disabilities.
- Because most children on dietary therapy for PKU have normal intelligence as measured by standardized intelligence tests, such tests may not be sensitive enough to identify the subtle cognitive deficits in children with PKU. Rather, tests of executive functioning may be more appropriate measures of cognitive development in children with PKU.
- Although there have been varied recommendations for the duration of the restricted diet, an NIH panel of experts concluded that treatment of PKU requires a "diet for life."
- Recent research is identifying naturally occurring proteins (such as GMP, which is created during cheese production) that may be tolerable for individuals with PKU and could be used as protein substitutes.

RESOURCES

Mayo Clinic: www.mayoclinic.com/health/phenylketonuria/DS00514. This is a user-friendly resource dedicated to PKU.

National Center for Learning Disabilities: www.ncld.org/ld-basics/ld-aamp-executive-functioning/16-executive-functioning. This Web site includes a fact sheet on executive functioning, problems associated with it, and strategies to help.

PKU.com: www.pku.com. Web site dedicated to PKU includes information, personal stories, discussions, local clinics, literature, cookbooks, and additional resources.

PKU Perspectives: www.pkuperspectives.com. Provides recipes and supplies low-protein foods.

HANDOUT

PROMOTING THE WELL-BEING OF CHILDREN WITH PKU

Phenylketonuria (PKU) is the most common treatable genetic disease. Currently, the most effective and available treatment is lifelong adherence to a phenylalanine-restricted diet.

- Discuss your child's individualized daily tolerance of foods containing phenylalanine with his or her primary care physician.
- Consult with a nutritionist to determine a safe and appropriate diet that works with your family's lifestyle.
- Inform the school, especially your child's teacher, that your child has PKU. Provide a list of prohibited and permitted foods and also provide a few extra snacks the teacher can keep in the classroom.
- Maintain open communication with the child regarding his or her diet. Address questions or concerns honestly and utilize available resources when needed.
- Encourage your child to participate in directing his or her diet as early as possible. The more involved your child feels, the greater likelihood of compliance.
- Minimize the focus on food and keep a positive attitude about the diet.
- Ensure your child's school is well informed and educated on the PKU diet.
- Notify any individual who may supervise the child outside of the home or school setting. Examples include sports coaches, parents of friends, neighbors, etc.

When PKU is identified and treated in the first weeks of life, intellectual disabilities can usually be prevented by maintaining a restricted diet. However, children with PKU may still experience some academic difficulties.

- Notify the child's parents, doctor, and school if you observe any decline in executive functioning, such as the ability to initiate, sustain, shift, and direct attention, or other academic skills or behaviors.
- Connect with support groups and utilize available resources to keep up-to-date with news and new treatment options.

5

Genetics of Autism*

Theories, Findings, and Implications

Sarah Glaser and Tia Ouimet

Trevor and Ethan are 6-year-old identical twins. Although their motor skills developed typically, their infrequency of eye contact and delay of language by the age of 2 prompted their mother to seek help. The pediatrician assured her that because boys tend to develop later than girls, and because her sons were 5 weeks premature, there was no need for concern.

At 30 months, Trevor developed a limited vocabulary and improved in his communication abilities, such as pointing at objects and gesturing. Ethan didn't exhibit progress in these areas, prompting their mother to see a specialist. The mother recalled similar developmental difficulties in her niece when she was a toddler. Six months later, the twins were diagnosed with autistic disorder and began 30 hours a week of applied behavior analysis (ABA). Trevor's symptoms improved dramatically within 10 months of therapy. He was able to formulate short sentences, engage in social behaviors such as laughing and smiling, and play with others. Ethan showed only a slight improvement in language and no progress in social skills.

Both boys began preschool while continuing an ABA program of 10 hours a week. Trevor experienced a smooth transition, whereas Ethan found it challenging to get along with others and frequently hit his classmates. His mother decided to remove him from daycare and resume 30 hours of ABA per week. Trevor was re-evaluated and was diagnosed with Asperger syndrome. Their mother is now thinking of elementary schools and is worried about Ethan's ability to integrate into a regular classroom. She is considering the option of sending one or both of

---

the twins to a specialized school. She does not want to separate the twins, as they are close, but she feels that Trevor will excel if placed in the regular school environment. She is also exploring the option of medication to control Ethan's aggressive behavior.

INTRODUCTION

Autism is a heritable, complex neurodevelopmental disorder characterized by distinct impairments in the areas of social interaction, speech development, and range of interests and activities. Autism is the most severe manifestation of a broad spectrum of disorders known as autism spectrum disorders (ASD) that share these essential features but vary in their degree of severity and/or age of onset. Within this spectrum, there are currently five official diagnoses:

1. *Autistic disorder:* Characterized by deficits before the age of 3 years in social interaction and communication (e.g., spoken language), accompanied by repetitive patterns of behavior, interests, and activities.

2. *Asperger's disorder:* Presents with similar but milder symptoms as seen in autistic disorder but without a language delay or cognitive impairment.

3. *Pervasive developmental disorder—not otherwise specified* (PDD-NOS): Symptoms do not meet the criteria for autistic disorder because of late age at onset or atypical symptoms. Symptoms include impairment in the development of social interaction with either a deficit in communication skills or repetitive patterns of behavior, interests, and activities.

4. *Rett disorder:* Normal development occurs for the first 5 months after birth, followed by deceleration of head growth, loss of learned hand skills, loss of social engagement, poorly coordinated body movements, and severely impaired language development. This genetic disorder only presents in females.

5. *Childhood disintegrative disorder:* Characterized by normal development for at least the first 2 years after birth, followed by a loss of learned skills (before age 10 years) in language, social skills or adaptive behavior, bowel or bladder control, play, and/or motor skills.

Autism is recognized as the most common neurodevelopmental disorder, with estimates ranging from 1 in 100 to 1 in 300 children diagnosed with an autism spectrum disorder (CDC, 2009; Fombonne, 2003). Researchers believe that autism may have many genetic and nongenetic causes. In some instances, autism is a feature of an identifiable genetic condition; however, often no specific cause can be determined. During the past few decades, scientists have made significant breakthroughs in understanding the genetics of autism. Through newly developed technologies, researchers are now focusing on specific chromosomal regions that may contain autism-related genes. Recognizing autism spectrum disorders as a genetic condition is essential, because it can affect treatment and therapy options and can allow health care providers to estimate the likelihood of recurrence in other family members.

BACKGROUND

The vast majority of cases of autism have no identifiable cause. Family and twin studies indicate a significant genetic influence, although many different genes are involved, and the modes of genetic transmission are complex and not completely understood (Volker & Lopata, 2008). It is important to understand these genetic contributions, as this understanding can enable future diagnoses and appropriate intervention strategies for individuals and their families. Lack of knowledge in this area can prevent the ability to identify families at risk.

Knowing Which Families Are at Risk

The only group known to have an elevated risk of ASD is siblings of affected individuals. Twin studies are often used to determine how the disorder is passed on in families. These studies verify the concordance or presence of a specific trait in identical or fraternal twins. Since the first autism twin study was conducted in 1977, ample research has shown that autism is highly heritable, with 60% to 90% concordance in identical twins and 5% to 10% concordance in fraternal twins (Bailey et al., 1995). The concordance rate for nontwin siblings of affected children ranges from 2% to 10% (Smalley, Asarnow, & Spence, 1988). This rate is much higher than the prevalence rate in the general population, a factor that highlights the importance of genetic factors in autism. Studies have consistently shown that males are at least 4 times more likely to develop autism than females, with an average male-to-female ratio of 4.2:1 (Fombonne, 2002; Skuse, 2000).

Techniques to Identify Genetic Contributions

Since the development of genetic technology in the 1990s, much genetic research has attempted to explain the heritability and cause of autism. There are three main approaches to identifying chromosomal regions (loci) that are likely to contain relevant genes: whole-genome scans, cytogenetic studies, and candidate-gene approaches. Whole-genome scans search for the linkage of autism to shared genetic markers in populations of families with more than one affected member. Cytogenetic studies point to relevant chromosomal abnormalities in affected individuals and their families. Candidate-gene approaches evaluate genes known to affect brain development in these significantly linked regions (Muhle, Trentecoste, & Rapin, 2004). Genome-wide linkage scans have identified at least 10 genes in the causation of autism in regions 2q, 7q, and17q, with 7q yielding the most consistently positive results (Muhle et al.; Autism Genome Project Consortium, 2007).

Since the discovery of newer high-resolution genetic technologies, large-scale collaborative research projects have been founded. For example, the Paris Autism Research International Sibpair Study (PARIS) contributed greatly to the understanding of autism. This international collaborative project recruited 51 families from seven countries (Austria, Belgium, France, Italy, Norway, Sweden, and the United States). They found four chromosomal regions that overlapped with regions on chromosomes 2q, 7q, 16p, and 19p and discovered other susceptibility regions that overlapped with the 15q11-q13 region identified in previous candidate gene studies (Paris Autism Research International Sibpair Study, 1999). Six additional regions on chromosomes 4q, 5p, 6q, 10q, 18q, and Xp were also located. In addition, the Autism Genetic Resource Exchange (AGRE) is the first collaborative gene bank for the study of autism spectrum disorders and one of the largest shared resources for the study of these disorders, with a collection of over 900 families made available to the greater scientific community.

Known Genetic Causes

During the last 20 years, researchers have been searching for the genes contributing to the cause of autism. Even though significant discoveries have been made and promising hypotheses formed, the specific genes that may be responsible for the majority of cases are still unknown. Researchers estimate that 10% to 15% of ASD cases can be accounted for by rare genetic mutations. It is believed that anywhere from 2 to 15 mutations in specific genetic loci contribute to autism (Schanen, 2006). Despite the abundance of research findings in the past several decades, the following review is not meant to be an exhaustive list of genetic causes.

X-linked Genes. Single-gene disorders, caused by structural defects on one specific gene, are passed on to children from a carrier parent. Rett disorder, one of the disorders included within the autism spectrum, and fragile X syndrome (FXS) are two of the most common single-gene causes of autism spectrum disorders. Individuals with these syndromes contain mutations on two X-linked genes, MECP2 and FMR1, respectively. Within the last decade, researchers have discovered that mutations on MECP2 are identified in more than 80% of females with Rett disorder, revealing its strong genetic component (Freitag, 2007).

Fragile X syndrome is one of the most frequently known causes of intellectual disabilities in males, and recent studies have indicated that approximately 20% to 40% of individuals with the disorder possess autistic features (Persico & Bourgeron, 2006). Individuals with FXS are predominantly male. They possess mutations on the FRX1 gene and are characterized as having abnormally large testes, oversized ears, a prominent jaw, and high-pitched speech. About 2% to 5% of children with ASD possess FRX1 mutations, making it one of the most frequent genetic causes of autism (Freitag, 2007).

Chromosomal Duplications. Chromosomal duplications result when a particular region or even the entirety of a chromosome is duplicated. For example, an abnormality on chromosome 15 resulting in 15q11.13 duplication has been implicated in approximately 1% to 5% of autism cases (Freitag, 2007). Individuals possessing this chromosomal anomaly are characterized as having epileptic seizures during childhood, hypotonia (low muscle tone), severe motor and speech difficulties, and intellectual disabilities (Freitag; Schanen, 2006). Two known syndromes associated with 15q11.13 duplication include Angelman syndrome and Prader-Willi syndrome (PWS). Children with Angelman syndrome, in addition to the aforementioned symptoms, often exhibit a happy appearance, stereotyped hand-flapping movements, mouthing of objects, hyperactivity, and excessive laughter (Freitag). The estimated prevalence of Angelman syndrome in ASD is estimated to be 1% or less of the general population (Cohen et al., 2005). In contrast, children with PWS are characterized as having poor sucking reflex as infants, growth retardation, and a delay in sexual development (Freitag). Both of these syndromes yield a high rate of susceptibility to ASD, with up to 85% of children with Angelman syndrome and PWS meeting criteria for autism (Schanen).

Chromosomal Deletions. In contrast to chromosomal duplication disorders, chromosomal deletion disorders result when a part or parts of a chromosome are deleted. There is evidence that two syndromes resulting in chromosomal deletions, Smith-Magenis syndrome and Phelan-McDermid syndrome, contribute to autism. Smith-Magenis syndrome, which results from a deletion of chromosome 17p11.2, is characterized by intellectual disabilities, absence of speech, marked sleep disturbances, small stature, facial abnormalities, and stereotyped behaviors such as self-hugging, hand clasping, and body tensing (Cohen et al., 2005). Phelan-McDermid syndrome, also referred to as 22q13 deletion syndrome, results from microdeletion of the SHANK3 gene on chromosome 22q13.3. Symptoms of individuals with this syndrome include hypotonia, global developmental delays resulting in moderate to severe intellectual disabilities, excessive chewing of objects, severely impaired speech, accelerated physical growth, and increased tolerance to pain (Cohen et al.; Wilson et al., 2003). It should be noted that the exact representation of these two syndromes within the ASD population has not yet been discovered, and their genetic relationship to autism has been disputed (Cohen et al.).

Candidate Genes. Currently, numerous candidate gene studies are underway in which researchers are assessing mutations on multiple genes that may contribute to the etiology of autism. Candidate genes that are thought to be involved in ASD play an important role in brain development, and it has been hypothesized that abnormal levels of serotonin, dopamine, and acetylcholine neurotransmitters in the brain may be involved in autism (Muhle et al., 2004). It was reported recently that an astounding total of 89 candidate genes have been implicated as possible genetic contributors to ASD (Yang & Gill, 2007). Chromosomes 2, 3, 6, 15, 17, and X have been the subject of increasing investigation, with some promising evidence that mutations on these genes cause an increased risk for autism. The best-replicated locus from linkage studies is chromosome 7, and variations in its FOXP2 and RELN genes have been found in some children with ASD (Freitag, 2007).

Multiple Gene Complications and Unknowns

Despite the fact that several rare genetic syndromes are known to cause autism, the vast majority of cases are believed to have a complex cause, with multiple genes interacting to create the symptoms of the disorder. The large number of genetic abnormalities found in families with at least one individual with autism indicates that many genes are likely to contribute. Some researchers believe that autism results when children inherit three or four mutated genes from their parents. The inheritance of autism among families, coupled with the fact that relatives of affected individuals often show subtle related symptoms, suggests that most forms of autism result from mutations on multiple genes, each of them contributing "small increments of risk" (Gupta & State, 2007). Therefore, it is hypothesized that individuals who inherit many abnormal genes from their parents may exhibit a more serious form of autism.

Although many genetic syndromes and chromosomal abnormalities have been implicated in autism, various factors have made it difficult for researchers to pinpoint the exact causes. One problem involves the relatively low rate of known medical disorders accounting for the expression of ASD, which does not allow for meaningful epidemiological studies (Cohen et al., 2005). In addition, a high percentage of the genetic syndromes associated with autism include intellectual disabilities as a secondary condition. Intellectual disabilities are associated with autism in general, and it is extremely difficult to pinpoint whether the association of the genetic syndrome with autism is due to specific association between the two disorders, mediation via intellectual disabilities, or a combination of both causes (Cohen et al.). Despite these issues, it is clear that genes play an important role in the etiology and expression of autism, and future researchers likely will be able to gain more insight into the biological basis of autism.

Possible Environmental Causes

Although it is widely accepted that complex genetic mechanisms are implicated in ASD, the environment can also play a role. While epidemiological studies have not supported the identification of any one causal environmental factor, there is evidence of an environmental influence (Herbert et al., 2006).

Early childhood exposures to antibiotic treatments and the measles, mumps, and rubella (MMR) vaccination have been hypothesized as contributing to risk of autism. The MMR vaccine is administered when children are 15 to 18 months old, around the time when symptoms of autism typically emerge. This fact, combined with media publicity regarding the possible link of autism to the MMR vaccine, has raised a great deal of concern for parents and practitioners. However, epidemiological investigations of this hypothesis have consistently failed to establish an association between the MMR vaccination and autism (Fombonne, Zakarian, Bennett, Meng, & McLean-Heywood, 2006). Clinical studies have failed to identify a phenotype that could characterize a small group of autistic children presumably at risk of MMR vaccine-induced autism. Another hypothesis related to vaccinations concerns the cumulative exposure of young children up until the age of 2 to thimerosal, a vaccine stabilizer that contains 50% ethylmercury. Epidemiological research on the thimerosal-autism association has also been consistently negative, with studies failing to show any association (Fombonne et al.). Biological studies of ethylmercury exposure have also failed to support the thimerosal hypothesis. There has been no sound evidence to suggest a causal link between vaccinations and incidence of autism.

Isolated case reports have suggested that a range of possible prenatal infections and exposure to toxins could be a factor in the development of

ASD (Rutter, 2005). These include various maternal circumstances that could affect the fetus, including hypothyroidism, thalidomide use, use of mood-stabilizing medication, cocaine or alcohol abuse, and a congenital *Herpesviridae* family virus known as *Cytomegalovirus*. None of these have been prominent in any epidemiological studies of autism, and it is unlikely that they constitute risk factors for ASD (Rutter). Prenatal exposure to the *rubella* virus has been linked to autism but is also not likely to account for many cases (Newschaffer et al., 2007). Furthermore, it is of little relevance in many countries due to the rarity of congenital rubella following population-wide vaccination programs (Rutter).

The associations between autism risk and maternal obstetric characteristics, labor and delivery complications, and neonatal factors have also been investigated. Recently, large studies have evaluated individual perinatal events. Uterine bleeding, caesarean section, low birth weight, preterm delivery, and low Apgar score (i.e., the Activity, Pulse, Grimace, Appearance, and Respiration test given to a newborn baby) are among the few factors that have been more consistently associated with autism, whereas results for most other factors have been unclear (Newschaffer et al., 2007).

Although a link between environmental exposures and ASD is plausible, little evidence supports an association between specific environmental exposures and autism.

The Role of Genetic Counseling and Testing

With increasing public awareness of autism spectrum disorders, particularly their genetic influences, families are increasingly demanding information regarding their risk of having another affected child. Genetic counselors, who typically work in clinical, pediatric, and psychiatric settings, are now able to use research to provide advice to families about recurrence risks (Simonoff, 1998). It is recommended that families seek the service of a genetic counselor, as counseling for ASD can be particularly challenging due to its wide range of symptoms (Freitag, 2007; Simonoff). Genetic counseling can be educational for both parents and children, providing them with detailed information about the disorder and its transmission. It can facilitate an earlier diagnosis for families, in turn leading to many advantages, such as early intervention strategies in schools, specialized treatment plans, and appropriate and immediate medical care for the child. Through genetic testing, underlying medical conditions, such as Down syndrome, can also be ruled out. Genetic counseling is recommended for families if there is a family history of intellectual disabilities or autism (Filipek et al., 1999).

Despite these benefits, genetic testing can also have possible negative implications for families. The first issue regards the current lack of research regarding the effectiveness of genetic counseling for ASD, as well as questions surrounding its validity (Freitag, 2007). Because researchers do not yet have a clear understanding of the specific genes involved in autism, prenatal diagnosis is presently limited to rare chromosomal defects and single-gene syndromes. In addition, genetic testing for rare conditions with autistic features is often expensive and stressful, and screening for these types of disorders may not be available in many settings outside of a research study (Muhle et al., 2004). The concept of genetic testing can be intimidating and confusing for many families, and it is important that the counselor meets with parents to clarify the meaning of the information given by the test (Simonoff, 1998). It is also crucial for families to realize that genetic testing or counseling alone does not provide treatment or behavioral management of affected children.

IMPLICATIONS FOR EDUCATORS

The prevalence rate of autism spectrum disorders in the general population has been steadily rising for the past 30 years, although the reasons behind this recent phenomenon remain unknown. Early intervention strategies are becoming increasingly important for children at risk for developing autism, yet no conclusive evidence exists regarding what type of treatment to use and when it should be implemented (Canadian Paediatric Society, 2004). Despite this fact, most published research studies agree that earlier and more intensive intervention—ideally before the age of 2 or 3—typically leads to better outcomes for children (Canadian Paediatric Society).

Home- and School-Based Treatment and Interventions

There is no single treatment protocol for all children with autism. Currently, treatment strategies involve early intervention programs that focus on techniques that target all areas of development (Bryson, Rogers, & Fombonne, 2003). A few of the most common interventions are applied behavior analysis (ABA); Picture Exchange Communication System (PECS); Social Communication, Emotional Regulation and Transactional Support (SCERTS); school-based treatment and education of autistic and communication handicapped children (TEACCH) method; and speech and occupational therapy (Autism Speaks, 2009). In addition to these interventions, antipsychotic medication may also be prescribed to children with ASD to treat severe symptoms such as aggression and self-injury.

Often, several interventions are combined to create an individualized and integrated treatment program for the child. ABA is a popular early-intervention strategy based on principles that emphasize being rewarded for good behaviors to correct problem behaviors (Autism Speaks, 2009). PECS is a type of treatment whereby individuals with minimal verbal ability use picture cards to communicate. This technique can improve communication skills, which can also lead to improvements in spoken language (Autism Speaks). The SCERTS model is a framework that focuses on promoting communication initiated by the child. It combines strategies from other intervention approaches, such as ABA (Autism Speaks). TEACCH is an education program that is adapted to the child's needs based on general guidelines. TEACCH is unique in that the focus is on structuring children's environments to accommodate them while also teaching them to behave in an appropriate manner (Autism Speaks).

Many more schools are also creating specialized programs to accommodate students with autism spectrum disorders. Instead of students with ASD being placed in segregated classroom environments alongside children with intellectual disabilities, they are increasingly being included in regular classroom settings. Advocacy by parents of children with ASD and increased knowledge about the disorder have caused educators to realize the importance of meeting these students' needs. In addition, private schools catering to children with developmental disabilities and special needs are becoming more and more available to families, who may decide that inclusive education is not appropriate for their child (Bryson et al., 2003). Families may also opt to home school their child due to the social demands and sensory overload often associated with traditional classroom settings (Jones, 2002). Although there is debate as to whether inclusive versus segregated education is better for children with ASD due to factors related to teacher expertise, social exposure, and relative costs, the fact that parents now have a choice in their child's schooling options reflects the growing number of accommodations available.

EDUCATIONAL STRATEGIES

- Educate parents, teachers, and students about autism spectrum disorders through a workshop or information session. Create brochures describing the disorders and the challenges that these students face.
- Implement social skills workshops in schools for children with autism. Emphasize the social challenges of children with autism and go over strategies to make socialization easier for these students.
- Teach educators effective classroom strategies for managing children with autism, especially in an integrated classroom context. For example, train educators to provide clear instructions and a structured routine for the child.
- Identify appropriate referral sources for families of children with autism.
- Organize parent and/or teacher support groups.

DISCUSSION QUESTIONS

1. What are the possible implications for the interpretation and treatment of a child's disorder if he or she is diagnosed? How does a diagnosis affect the child's special services in the school?

2. Should daycare workers and teachers be required to learn about autism spectrum disorders if they have a child or children with ASD in their classes? If so, what do they need to know to be able to help the child?

3. Should programs be in place in the schools for children to learn about ASD and other neurodevelopmental disorders? How might this both create and reduce stigma associated with these disorders?

4. When is it appropriate to start medicating children with autism? What are the risks and benefits of this type of treatment, especially for children who receive medication at school?

RESEARCH SUMMARY

- Autism may have many genetic and nongenetic causes. In some instances, autism is a feature of an identifiable genetic condition; however, the specific genes that may be responsible for the majority of cases are still unknown.
- Researchers are optimistic that within the next decade, improved genetic technologies may help in the discovery of specific genetic pathways.
- Research in this area can lead to an increase in the understanding of the differences between autism spectrum disorder subtypes, as well as facilitate early identification of ASD and intervention both at home and at school.
- Earlier and more intensive intervention—ideally before the age of 2 or 3—typically leads to better outcomes for children with autism.
- No single treatment or intervention is appropriate for all children with autism. Several interventions are typically combined to create an individualized and integrated treatment program for the child.

RESOURCES

Brock, S. E., Jimerson, S. R., & Hansen, R. L. (2006). *Identifying, assessing, and treating autism at school.* New York: Springer.

Edwards, A. (2002). *Taking autism to school.* St. Louis, MO: JayJo Books.

Fein, D., & Dunn, M. (2007). *Autism in your classroom: A general educator's guide to students with autism spectrum disorders.* Bethesda, MD: Woodbine House.

Jones, G. (2002). *Educational provision for children with autism and Asperger syndrome.* London: David Fulton.

The following Web sites offer comprehensive information about autism spectrum disorders:

Autism Speaks: www.autismspeaks.org

Autism Society: www.autism-society.org

Kids Health "Autism": http://kidshealth.org/kid/health_problems/brain/autism.html

HANDOUT

THE GENETICS OF AUTISM

Autism is a complex neurodevelopmental disorder characterized by impairments in the areas of social interaction, speech development, and range of interests and activities. Autism is the most severe manifestation of a broad spectrum of disorders known as autism spectrum disorders (ASD) that share these essential features but vary in their degree of severity and/or age of onset.

What are the known genetic causes of autism spectrum disorders?

	Type	Cause	Prevalence in ASD
Single-Gene Causes	Rett syndrome	Mutation on MECP2 gene	1–5%
	Fragile X syndrome (FXS)	Mutation on FRX1 gene	2–5%
Autosomal Dominant Disorder Causes	Tuberous sclerosis (TSC)	Mutation on TSC1 and/or TSC2 gene	1–4%
Autosomal Recessive Disorder Causes	Smith-Lemli-Opitz syndrome (SLO)	Mutation on DHCR7 gene	<1%
	San Filippo syndromes	Enzymatic defects	<1%
	Phenylketonuria (PKU)	Enzymatic defects	unknown
	Adenylosuccinate lyase deficiency	Metabolic defects	<1%
	Cohen syndrome	Mutations on COH1 gene	unknown
Chromosomal Duplication Causes	Angelman syndrome	Duplication of chromosome 15q11–13	1–5%
	Prader-Willi syndrome (PWS)		
Chromosomal Deletion Causes	Smith-Magenis syndrome	Deletion of chromosome 17p11.2	unknown
	Phelan-McDermid syndrome	Deletion of chromosome 22q13.3	
			TOTAL: 10–15%

What are some of the treatments and interventions for ASD?

Type of Intervention	Description
Applied Behavior Analysis (ABA)	Program whereby positive behaviors are encouraged by using rewards and consequences
PECS (Picture Exchange Communication System)	Technique that uses picture cards to help children make requests for items and activities
SCERTS (Social Communication, Emotional Regulation and Transactional Support)	Framework that integrates various techniques and focuses on promoting communication initiated by the child
TEACCH (Treatment and Education of Autistic and Communication Handicapped Children)	Technique that structures the child's environment to accommodate him or her while also teaching the child to behave in an appropriate manner

6

The Biology of Shyness*

Paul C. McCabe, Sarah E. Groark, and Brian Dalpiaz

Larissa is a 7-year-old, second-grade student who lives with her mother. Her teacher, Mrs. Bennett, reported to her mother that Larissa "is extremely quiet, very hesitant to participate in class, and rarely initiates interaction with her peers." Larissa's mother notices similar behavior at home. Larissa has only a couple of friends, whom she rarely seeks out. Her mother also reports that Larissa seems to catch colds frequently, sometimes causing her to miss school. Recently, Larissa's inhibited behavior has hindered her reading progress at school. Mrs. Bennett insists that Larissa is a capable reader but reports that she appears nervous when asked to read aloud. At these times, Larissa sometimes cries and has difficulty speaking at all. Larissa's mother has noticed similar behavior when Larissa is in new social situations.

The psychologist at Larissa's school met with Mrs. Bennett and Larissa's mother to discuss possible intervention strategies to encourage Larissa's social and academic confidence. As a group, they agreed on several strategies. Larissa would be placed in a much smaller reading group to reduce her anxiety and fear of reading aloud. To improve her social skills, the teachers will create situations for Larissa to engage in nonverbal play with peers (e.g., building blocks, LEGOs, arts and crafts). Finally, Mrs. Bennett agreed to provide more "low-stress" opportunities for Larissa to participate in class (e.g., by handing out papers).

After several months, both Larissa's mother and her teacher noticed improvement in her social interactions. She gradually began playing with others during playtime. In her small reading group, Larissa was able to read aloud. With encouragement from Mrs. Bennett, Larissa continues to exhibit more social and academic confidence.

---

*Adapted from Holden, B., & McCabe, P. C. (2005). The biology of shyness: The role of the amygdala. *Communiqué, 33*(7), 40–43. Copyright by the National Association of School Psychologists, Bethesda, MD. Use is by permission of the publisher. www.nasponline.org

INTRODUCTION

Shyness is a common behavior observed in children. Biological factors can contribute to a shy temperament. Biology and social experiences interact either to reinforce or reduce social anxiety in children. Shyness has an impact on development and academic performance. Therefore, interventions to address shyness within the classroom and home are useful to prevent unnecessary delays related to excessive inhibition.

BACKGROUND

Shyness, also known as "inhibited temperament," is associated with a number of emotional, behavioral, and cognitive outcomes that may be detrimental for children (Crozier & Hostettler, 2003). Research focusing on the biological bases of shyness has conceptualized individual differences in behavior and academic performance as a function of development. The amygdala has been identified as one of the neural regions in the brain that is important for at least two processes related to affect and emotionality. One of the processes is the identification of the emotional significance of a stimulus in the environment. The other process is the production of affective states and emotional behaviors (Phillips, Drevets, Rauch, & Lane, 2003). School psychologists and educators can benefit children by being aware of the research examining the neurodevelopmental differences among shy and noninhibited children when guiding assessment and intervention efforts.

The Role of the Amygdala

To understand the emotional processing of children with inhibited temperaments, an understanding of the function of the amygdala is necessary. The amygdala has been implicated as a primary neural structure in encoding emotional responses. Located within the limbic system on the temporal lobe of the brain, the amygdala is an almond-shaped structure that plays a primary role in coordinating reactions in response to perceived threats and mediating emotional responses. Bilateral lesions of the amygdala in monkeys result in significant changes in social behavior, including social disinhibition and impaired fear conditioning (Phillips et al., 2003). On the other hand, stimulation of the amygdala in animals leads to increases in levels of corticosterone and autonomic signs of fear and anxiety. In humans, findings of lesion effects in the amygdala are mixed. For example, there are some reports that lesions result in emotional blunting and reduced fear conditioning (Phillips et al.). However, other studies report no differences in behavior (Anderson & Phelps, 2002).

The amygdala has been identified as playing an important role in the processing of emotional information. For this reason, the amygdala has been associated with several psychological, physiological, and behavioral disorders. For example, right and total amygdala volumes were found to be significantly larger in individuals with general anxiety disorder (De Bellis et al., 2000). Stein (1998) has suggested that the amygdala, or dysfunction of the amygdala, plays a part in the development of social phobia. Furthermore, twin studies have determined that the amygdala plays a role in the heritability of inhibited and uninhibited behavior (Robinson, Kagan, Reznick, & Corley, 1992).

Researchers have found that individuals with inhibited temperaments will have increased amygdalar activity in response to novel stimuli. Schwartz et al. (2003) found that stimuli symbolic of overt threat may not be necessary to activate the amygdala. For inhibited individuals, novel facial stimuli with neutral expressions activate the amygdala more than familiar faces. This conclusion is consistent with the theory that individuals with inhibited temperament perceive novel or unfamiliar people and objects as potential threats (Schwartz et al.).

Further evidence of the amygdala's role in inhibited and shy behavior can be found in Robinson and colleagues' (1992) twin study. After independent observations of children in standardized laboratory situations, the authors were able to make specific conclusions. They concluded that shy, wary, and avoidant behaviors in response to unfamiliarity are partially due to genetic influences. In this study, the authors noted that the excitability of the amygdala can be influenced by a variety of chemicals. They further noted that these substances are under some genetic control and have some genetic or heritable variation in humans. Furthermore, recent research indicates that a specific gene is strongly associated with childhood behavioral inhibition and is related to increased amygdalar and insular cortex activation—two limbic brain structures involved in emotional processing (Smoller et al., 2008).

Amygdala and Cortisol Levels: The HPA System

In addition to using neurological assessments, researchers have discovered that by sampling children's saliva at different times of the day, cortisol levels can be recorded. Cortisol is the end product of one of the stress-sensitive systems in the brain known as the hypothalamic-pituitary-adrenocortical (HPA) system (Zimmermann & Stansbury, 2004). The amygdala is one of the major functioning parts of this system. Under stressful situations, this system produces cortisol. When cortisol is elevated, it allows the body to respond to challenging conditions by activating energy sources and affecting memory, learning, and emotions so that the person can manage the stressful situation (Zimmerman & Stansbury).

As long as the HPA system is turned off quickly after activation, its function and the subsequent increase in cortisol is adaptive and beneficial. However, sustained activation of the HPA can have physiological costs. Prolonged high levels of cortisol can cause a weakening of the immune system as well as an increase in corticotropin-releasing hormone (CRH) in the central nucleus of the amygdala (Schmidt, Fox, Rubin, & Sternberg, 1997; Schulkin, Gold, & McEwen, 1998). This increase in CRH may intensify fearfulness in children and further predispose them to develop a framework of thoughts and behaviors that leads them to expect fear (Schmidt et al.).

Psychological and Immune Correlates of HPA Activation

One of the triggers of the HPA system is uncertainty, and uncertainty is one of the primary characteristics of children with inhibited temperament.

Inhibited children show signs of wariness and fear when faced with novel or unfamiliar faces, people, and situations. Inhibited children are said to have a low threshold for uncertainty and are avoidant and/or fearful of unfamiliar events (Kagan & Snidman, 1999). Zimmermann and Stansbury (2004) studied cortisol levels in shy children and found that that level of shyness predicted cortisol elevation in response to a stranger approach situation. Interestingly, the authors found that shy children regulated their cortisol production after the threat had passed. That is, 15 minutes after the initial stranger approach situation, the cortisol levels of the majority of children had decreased to baseline. This finding suggests that it is not the regulation of cortisol that is the primary concern for shy children but rather the more frequent activation of the HPA system. In other words, these children had developed a cognitive-perceptual framework that anticipated fear and subsequently triggered their HPA systems more frequently than in their peers.

Heightened and/or frequent activation of the HPA and the concomitant increase in the level of cortisol may affect children's health as well. Shy children complain of feeling unwell with symptoms such as feeling sad, lacking an appetite, being irritable, and experiencing insomnia significantly more than their non-shy peers (Chung & Evans, 2000). The resultant higher cortisol levels in shy children may serve an immunosuppressant function; that is, it lowers their immune functioning. As a result, shy children may suffer more illnesses and require longer recovery from illnesses than their non-shy peers (Chung & Evans). Shy children are more likely to miss school days because of illness, which may serve to compound their shyness and reinforce withdrawal behaviors.

Shyness is also associated with increased risk for psychopathology. For example, Kagan and Snidman (1999) found that children who show an inhibited temperament are at a slightly higher risk for the development of an anxiety disorder. Researchers have argued that there are many similarities between shyness and social phobia. Shy children also have lower self-esteem than their non-shy peers as early as 4 years of age (Kemple, 1995).

The combination of biological temperament and social history determines the sensitivity with which an event activates limbic structures, such as the amygdale, and the ensuing emotional response (Kagan & Snidman, 1999). Although children's temperament remains largely immutable, strategies can be employed to prevent exacerbation of inhibited temperament and reinforcement of anxiety responses.

IMPLICATIONS FOR EDUCATORS

With an estimated 15% to 20% of 1- to 2-year-old children showing a pattern of inhibited behavior (Robinson et al., 1992), the need for early identification and intervention is apparent. Although teachers report great concerns for students with emotional and behavioral difficulties, excessive shyness was one of the behaviors that elicited the least concern from teachers (Poulou & Norwich, 2000). Many young children exhibit periods of shyness or hesitation but are able overcome their hesitation and engage in typical social activities. However, a small percentage continue to exhibit severe behavioral inhibition even after an adjustment period. School psychologists and educators may need to take a proactive and preventive role in helping to identify and ameliorate the effects of severe behavioral inhibition in children.

Many excessively shy children will need help overcoming their inhibitions, particularly if they must surmount biological underpinnings that serve to trigger and maintain their behaviors. Their withdrawn behaviors and heightened physiological arousal in novel yet not overtly threatening situations are no more explicable to them than the physiological arousal experienced by typical peers when faced with great peril. Educators should be aware of the biological, environmental, and sociocultural factors implicated in shyness and treatments that focus on these areas.

Therapeutic interventions for shyness can mirror those used for social anxiety disorder, given the amount of overlap between the two. Recent evidence suggests that cognitive behavioral interventions with pharmacotherapy are particularly effective in reducing withdrawal behaviors and increasing participation ("Beyond Shyness," 2003). School psychologists can serve a vital role in helping to coordinate interventions, collecting data, monitoring progress, and collaborating with teachers. School psychologists and educators can work together to identify ways to increase participation and social successes while minimizing chances for social failure or embarrassment. Behavioral treatments, such as systematic desensitization, may require in vivo exposure to the feared stimulus, which for many children requires direct exposure to their fears in the classroom. Another technique for increasing social competence is a peer-mediated intervention, where peers are trained to initiate, model, and reinforce appropriate social behavior (Greco & Morris, 2001). Obviously, these techniques require careful and delicate orchestration in which the school psychologist and educator play an important role.

The educational team can also coordinate and collect information regarding behavior and functioning in the home and school environments. Gathering information from home and school environments through parent and teacher reports can help pinpoint settings and tasks in which the child is succeeding, as well as those that are more problematic (Henderson & Fox, 1998). This can help direct and narrow intervention strategies. Rating scales targeting temperament, behavioral, and emotional problems are particularly useful, especially those that use complementary parent and teacher forms.

School psychologists and educators can also identify those behaviors that deviate from developmentally appropriate reactions to novelty exhibited by most children. The approach-withdrawal dimension of temperament suggests that it is common and often adaptive for children to express guardedness when in unfamiliar circumstances (Henderson & Fox, 1998). However, this behavior applies only to situations of novelty and should dissipate with the passage of time. Excessive and protracted guardedness, even in familiar settings, suggest that alternate explanations of behavior are necessary, which may include inhibited temperament or social phobia, among other explanations. A more extensive psychoeducational evaluation may be necessary to isolate the behaviors and their related causes.

Although improvements in behavior and social participation may be achievable through intervention and monitoring, the literature is generally unequivocal in concluding that shyness is a lifelong temperament.

Accordingly, psychologists and educators must work with inhibited youngsters and their parents to foster an atmosphere of acceptance. Shy children should be encouraged to accept their natural gifts and challenges and come to terms with their heightened sensitivity and physiological arousal that may be triggered more often than in their non-shy peers. Educators and parents of inhibited children should also learn to identify when a child is enduring periods of intense anxiety related to social situations and find ways to reduce that anxiety gradually through carefully planned interventions. The educational team can help advocate acceptance of shyness as behavioral trait but not as a disabling trait.

EDUCATIONAL STRATEGIES

- Develop an atmosphere of acceptance in the classroom. Normalize shyness and depict it positively through fictional portrayals or having students share stories of times when they felt shy.
- Provide shy children opportunities to participate in classroom activities that do not require speaking, such as shutting the door, turning on/off the lights, handing out materials, and so on.
- Provide support for the child by checking in with him or her regularly and rewarding small improvements.
- Avoid forcibly pressing shy children into situations that they are actively refusing, as this will almost always exacerbate their fears as well as diminish their trust in you. Rather, gradual exposure with encouragement and rewards for progress is the most effective strategy to increase participation and build trust.
- Encourage peer relationships by capitalizing on the interests and strengths of the child and pairing him or her with children who have similar interests.
- Provide models of effective communication behavior and teach communication skills.
- Watch for warning signs of increasing anxiety/avoidant behavior and peer problems (e.g., bullying).

DISCUSSION QUESTIONS

1. There is strong evidence that shyness is a largely heritable, lifelong temperament. How should this evidence inform the way educators approach this issue?

2. What classroom interventions might reduce HPA activation and cortisol production in shy children? What specifically would be effective about these interventions?

3. How might an educator differentiate between developmentally appropriate levels of shyness and more maladaptive inhibition/anxiety?

4. How can parents and the school collaborate to increase the social competence of a child with excessive shyness?

5. What steps can educators take to increase acceptance of shy behavior among different age groups (elementary, middle, and high school)?

RESEARCH SUMMARY

- Shyness appears to have a robust biological basis, which helps to explain why shyness is considered a stable temperament that persists through life.
- The amygdala is a component of the limbic system in the brain, and it participates in the release of cortisol in the event of stress.
- In shy children, an overactive amygdala produces an excess of cortisol, causing a heightened and prolonged stress response; this response leads shy children to anticipate both stressful and novel situations as upsetting and frightening.
- Uncertainty is one of the primary triggers of stress for shy children. Lessening their uncertainty reduces their cortisol production, making them less primed to expect (and to respond to) what they perceive to be a fearful stimulus.
- The physiological response to uncertainty for a shy child can become reinforced over time and be triggered without warning, so the child may become fearful without knowing why. Gradual exposure to the feared stimulus can help the child overcome the fear.
- Excessive shyness, and the anxiety accompanying it, can disrupt attention, memory, learning, emotions, and immune responses.

RESOURCES

Online

A Healthy Me! This Web site by Blue Cross Blue Shield of Massachusetts includes articles by Anne Krueger on shyness in children of various ages:

- Ages 1–3: www.ahealthyme.com/topic/shyness1to3
- Ages 3–6: www.ahealthyme.com/topic/shyness3to6
- Ages 6–12: www.ahealthyme.com/topic/shyness6to12
- Ages 12–16: www.ahealthyme.com/topic/shyness12to16

Center for Effective Parenting, "Shyness" by Kristen Zolten, MA, and Nicholas Long, PhD: www.parenting-ed.org/handout3/Specific%20 Concerns%20and%20Problems/shyness.htm

Family Village: www.familyvillage.wisc.edu/general/social-skills .html. University of Wisconsin—Madison site lists links to social skills resources.

Free Spirit Publishing: www.freespirit.com. This site has information and resources to deal with a wide range of social issues.

Shake Your Shyness: www.shakeyourshyness.com. Site by Licensed Clinical Psychologist Renée Gilbert, PhD, contains information for parents and teachers.

Shykids.com: www.shykids.com. Comprehensive site for parents, teachers, teens, and kids.

The Shyness Institute, from *Encyclopedia of Mental Health* by Lynn Henderson and Phillip Zimbardo: www.shyness.com/encyclopedia .html

South Australia Children, Youth and Women's Health Service, Parenting and Child Health, "Shyness": www.cyh.com/HealthTopics/ HealthTopicDetails.aspx?p=114&np=141&id=1948

TeensHealth by the Nemours Foundation, "5 Ways to Shake Shyness": http://kidshealth.org/teen/your_mind/emotions/shy_tips .html

University of New England Psychology Department, "Helping Young Children Overcome Shyness": www.une.edu.au/bcss/psychology/ john-malouff/shyness.php

Books

Adelman, L. (2007). *Don't call me shy: Preparing shy children for a lifetime of social success.* Austin, TX: LangMarc.

Brozovich, R., & Chase, L. (2008). *Say goodbye to being shy: A workbook to help kids overcome shyness.* Oakland, CA: Harbinger.

Kervatt, G. G. (1999). *The silence within: A teacher/parent guide to working with selectively mute and shy children.* Oak Ridge, NJ: Author

Laney, M. O. (2005). *The hidden gifts of the introverted child: Helping your child thrive in an extroverted world.* New York: Workman.

Markaway, B., & Markaway, G. (2005). *Nurturing the shy child: Practical help for raising confident and socially skilled kids and teens.* New York: St. Martin's.

Swallow, W. K. (2000). *The shy child: Helping children triumph over shyness.* New York: Warner Books.

HANDOUT

SHYNESS IN CHILDREN

What Is Shyness?

- Shyness is a term used to describe individuals' discomfort, cautiousness, fear, and lack of confidence or skills in social settings, despite the desire to be social.
- Shyness is a common personality trait and can range in intensity from mild cautiousness to extreme avoidance and panic. Excessive shyness, however, has been linked with some long-term psychological consequences.

Why Are Some Children Shy?

- Biology—there is a great deal of evidence suggesting people are born predisposed to shyness and may exhibit shyness traits throughout their lives.
- Lack of social experience
- Previous experiences that were negative or frightening
- Poor social skills

Some Good Things About Being Shy

- Shy children are often attentive and motivated students.
- Shy children often lack aggressive behaviors and therefore may be preferred by adults and children.
- Shy children are often good listeners.
- Shy children are often more sensitive to others' needs.

Things to Watch for With Shy Children

- Lack of friends or a "best friend"
- Signs of depression and/or anxiety
- Avoidance of school and other group activities
- Complaints of stomachaches and headaches at times when social interactions are required—the child's shyness may be manifested as physical pain

How to Help Shy Children

- Accept the whole child; don't criticize the child for his or her shyness.
- Don't label them as "shy"—they may take it as a criticism and feel less confident.
- Show empathy; secure bonds with adults increase social competence.
- Encourage taking risks and socializing with new peers; set goals and keep track of progress.
- Resist overprotecting them; children need to learn strategies to cope with new situations on their own.
- Discuss emotions with the child. Children with a greater understanding of their emotions will understand the feedback from peers better.
- Encourage the child to participate in a sport or extracurricular activity that interests him or her and will increase his or her social encounters.
- Model appropriate social behavior.

Take slow steps forward and take care not to push too hard. Do not force the child into a situation that she or he is actively refusing, as this may worsen the fear.

7

Families of Children With Genetic Disorders

Jennifer E. Bruce, Sara Quirke, and Steven R. Shaw

Cassie, a student in fifth grade, is a typically developing 10-year-old female with average academic functioning and no behavioral problems in the class. Cassie has three siblings: 14, 12, and 2 years old. Cassie's parents have been concerned about the development of their youngest child, Laura, for the past year. Laura has not reached the developmental milestones expected for a child her age. She is behind in all areas of development, including motor, language, and cognitive development. They have taken Laura to numerous doctors' appointments in pursuit of a diagnosis but have had no success. The doctors agree that she is behind in these areas but have been unable to provide a concrete diagnosis.

Near the end of the academic year, Cassie's mother came in for a parent-teacher interview. At this appointment, Cassie's mother informed the teacher that Laura was tested a few weeks ago for a rare genetic disorder. Laura tested positive for a syndrome called 22q13 deletion syndrome, or Phelan McDermid syndrome (PMS). She explained that this syndrome causes chronic medical conditions (e.g., chronic diarrhea, seizures), intellectual disabilities, behavior problems (e.g., autistic-like stereotypic behaviors), and physical disabilities. Cassie's mother was upset about the long-term implications of the diagnosis yet was relieved that she finally knew the cause of their daughter's slow developmental progress.

Cassie's mother decided to confide in the teacher about the diagnosis to seek answers regarding her family's future. She is worried about how her other children will react to having a sibling with a disability. Will she be able to give them the attention they need while caring for a child with a severe disability? In addition, she does not know if her marriage will be able to withstand the stress of the extra caretaking responsibilities, medical appointments, and advocacy that will be needed to ensure the best life for her child. She does not know whom to talk to and hopes that Cassie's teacher will be able to answer her questions or, at the very least, point her in the direction of someone who may be able to help her.

INTRODUCTION

Advances in the genetics and diagnoses of developmental disabilities have lead to significant improvements for children. Interventions can begin earlier, prognoses are more accurate, understanding of genetic disorders is improved, and the stage is set for future research to identify how best to improve education and management of problem behaviors for specific disorders. Previously, the causes of developmental disabilities were not clearly identified. Not knowing the cause, prognosis, or exact nature of the developmental disabilities was always stressful for families. Even with the improvements in understanding, major challenges and risk factors for the quality of life persist for families of children with developmental disabilities.

Families of children with genetic disorders are at risk for negative outcomes. Financial stressors; behavioral, academic, and social outcomes of siblings; marital discord and divorce; and job stress all occur at higher rates in families of children with genetic disorders than in families with typically developing children. These negative outcomes for families in turn lead to worse outcomes for children with genetic disorders than for children in families who have a better quality of life. Many affected families can avoid these negative outcomes and grow stronger. Resilient families tend to have affected children who respond better to school-based interventions. Improved understanding of families of children with genetic disorders is likely to lead to positive educational experiences for affected children and their siblings.

BACKGROUND

Most families living with a child with a disability did not have any prior knowledge about disorders or disabilities. They may only have had stereotypical notions of disability conceptualized by society. These ideas can be negative and inaccurate. Thus, families that do not have experience with disability may have a distorted view and be poorly prepared to cope with a child who presents with such a disorder. Therefore, hearing the news that a child has a disorder can be devastating and traumatic (Seligman & Darling, 2007).

Asking Questions of Professionals

After a child is diagnosed with a disorder, parents face the task of gathering and understanding multiple sources of information regarding the diagnosis and recommended intervention methods on their own (Baker-Erickzen, Brookman-Frazee, & Stahmer, 2005). In addition, parents have many and diverse sources of information available to choose from, often increasing stress and anxiety (Guralnick, 2000). Parents may find it difficult to get the information they need from professionals. Professionals report that they present the diagnostic information gradually and in response to parents' reactions to the information; however, parents would rather receive the information all at once. Parents also prefer that professionals show more caring and emotion during the diagnostic process (Byrnes, Berk, Cooper, & Marazita, 2003). Because parents and professionals have different goals concerning diagnosis, it is important for parents to take advantage of the time they have with the professional by being inquisitive about their child's condition and prognosis and by being assertive in obtaining the information.

Managing Emotional Trauma

The period following diagnosis has been described as a grieving process or one of ambiguous loss (O'Brien, 2007). *Ambiguous loss* stems from family stress theory, which proposes that stress is a result of changes in a family and that severe stress results from changes that are characterized by ambiguity (Boss, 2006). When the child's diagnosis is suffered as an ambiguous loss, parents experience conflicting emotions, such as fear and hope, frustration and joy, and helplessness and determination (O'Brien). The conflicting emotions arise from the ambiguity of the situation, such as the lack of clarity of the diagnosis; the difficulty in predicting the child's outcome; day-to-day changes of the child's behaviors that affect family relationships; and the typical appearance of the child (especially in autism), which raises expectations regarding behavior and functioning. All of these factors contribute to distress in the family. Thus, the postdiagnosis period is an important time to provide the support necessary to enable parents to move toward accepting and adapting to their child's disability (Mansell & Morris, 2004).

Parents caring for a child with a disability over the life span are subjected to stress and poor mental health due to the burden of care required (Seligman & Darling, 2007). Families with a child with a disability require some level of social support to maintain both their child's health and their own health. Sources of support include family and friends; however, it may be difficult to tell other family members and friends that a child has a disability due to negative reactions, misunderstandings, and lack of knowledge. Parents may find understanding friends in other parents who are also caring for a child with a disability. Support groups where families can share information and talk about their children can be helpful. Support groups serve to lessen feelings of loneliness and isolation, provide role models, provide information, and provide examples of families and situations to which they can compare themselves. Family members who have been enrolled in ongoing support groups frequently develop bonds with other families. These sources of support may help parents to cope with their child's disability, in turn helping them to maintain their own physical and mental health.

Stressors Faced by Families of Children With Genetic Disorders

Parents of children with disabilities face the same yet more exaggerated stressors as families with typically developing children. In addition to these exaggerated stressors, they also face pressures that are only experienced by families of a child with a disability (Cohen, 1999). Roles change, lives are reorganized, caregiving demands increase, and resources often become strained (Dellve, Samuelsson, Tallborn, Fasth, & Hallberg, 2006). These changes may cause stress and instability in the family unit.

Families must come to terms with the differences between their child and typically developing children. This difficult undertaking may involve grieving the loss of the child they had originally imagined raising (Longo & Bond, 1984). In addition, parents are forced to manage the day-to-day hassles of their child's condition. These may include medical needs, educational needs, therapies, and many other caretaking responsibilities (Longo & Bond). Not only are parents taking care of the needs of their child with a disability, but they are also balancing the needs of other family members.

Parents are often required to educate and advocate in schools and the community at large (Tarleton & Ward, 2007). Parents are often the expert on their child's disorder and, therefore, have to teach family and friends, educational professionals, therapists, and organizations about their child's needs. In cases of rare disorders, even the child's physician may not know as much as the parent and, thus, benefits from the parent's expertise (Minnes & Nachshen, 1997).

Mothers of Children With Genetic Disorders. Mothers are placed at an increased risk for mental and physical illness when parenting a child with a disability. Women of children with disabilities report lower levels of happiness, self-esteem, and self-efficacy than women of children without disabilities. They are also more likely to show signs of psychological distress than mothers of typically developing children (Baker & Blacher, 2002). The literature is clear that the mental health of mothers of children with disabilities is threatened due to the increase in stress and strain of having a child with a disability.

Furthermore, when compared to fathers of children with a disability, mothers show more parental stress, as well as higher physical and emotional strain (Dellve et al., 2006). Reasons for this may be that traditional gender roles become stronger for parents of children with a disability, as mothers tend to take on the responsibility of being the primary person in charge of the child's medical needs, behavior, and education (Dellve et al.). This may contribute to an additional strain on mothers when compared to fathers (Gray, 2003).

Fathers of Children With Genetic Disabilities. There is little research on fathers' response to disability in the family. The reason for this may be because mothers continue to be primary caregivers, especially when a child has a disability (Dellve et al., 2006). When both parents are considered, fathers tend to report lower levels of stress and fewer mental health problems (Olsson & Hwang, 2001).

Even though mothers experience higher rates of stress, fathers are not free from negative outcomes of having a child with a disability. Both mothers and fathers report symptoms of depression and lower marital adjustment when their child has severe behavior problems (Baker, Blacher, & Olsson, 2005). Fathers who score high on incompetence show high levels of stress and, in turn, score negatively on overall life satisfaction (Dellve et al., 2006). As has been shown, fathers, although not as severely as mothers, experience difficulties due to having a child with a disability.

Marital Stress in Families of Children With Genetic Disabilities. Studies of marital stability in families of children with disabilities show mixed results. Many studies indicate lower levels of marital satisfaction and higher rates of divorce and separation (Witt, Riley, & Cairo, 2003), while others find no differences in marital satisfaction (Seltzer, Greenberg, Floyd, Pettee, & Hong, 2001). Some marriages are strengthened, others damaged by having a child with a disability. Given these varied results, one can assume that marriages are affected differently, depending on many external factors that are not always measured by the investigator.

About 6% more marriages of parents of children with disabilities end in divorce, compared to marriages of parents with children who are typically developing (Mauldon, 1992). Although a significant result, this is not as large as expected based on earlier assumptions. Divorce occurs slightly more frequently in families who have a child with a disability, but this does not directly indicate that all parents of children with a disability will end their marriages. Even though the marriage is increasingly stressed, some families are able to withstand the strain and adapt to having a child with a disability.

Given equivocal findings on marital stress, researchers have examined why some relationships are strengthened while others are damaged. One hypothesis is that the extent of maladaptive behavior by the child is linked to lower marital satisfaction. Another proposition is that parents of children with disabilities who experience more daily hassles also report lower marital satisfaction (Stoneman & Gavidia-Payne, 2006). Probably both child maladaptive behavior and daily hassles require more time and energy and, therefore, put more strain on the marital relationship.

Siblings of Children With Genetic Disabilities. Contradictory evidence exists concerning the effect of living in a family as a sibling of a child with a disability. Siblings in this type of family situation are deemed a population at risk for psychological issues (Sharpe & Rossiter, 2002). Siblings have higher adjustment difficulties and more emotional symptoms and behavior problems with friends in comparison to children without a sibling with a disability (Giallo & Gavidia-Payne, 2006). The increased responsibility of the sibling for the care of a brother or sister with a disability places an undue amount of stress on the child. Likewise, the increased amount of parental attention required by the child with a disability minimizes the amount of attention that the sibling receives.

Increased Responsibilities of Siblings. The roles of family members change when a child with a disability enters the family due to stress and the increased need for resources. Parents caring for a child with a disability have an increased amount of responsibility in comparison to families without a child with a disability. They must make an extra effort to provide appropriate care for their child. This may entail a number of activities, including making frequent visits to the hospital, providing accommodations in the home, implementing and monitoring special diets, and involving the child in treatment and therapy. In such a situation, parents rely on their other children to help lessen the burden of care, even if the children are ill prepared to assume such a role (Siegel & Silverstein, 1994). This action leads siblings to adapt to the situation by acquiring an excessive sense of responsibility, which can result in a loss of the experiences of childhood.

Strengths in Families of Children With Genetic Disorders

To determine the positive changes in family dynamics, Stainton and Besser (1998) asked parents of children with a disability this question: "What are the positive impacts you feel your son or daughter with an intellectual disability has had on your family?" Through this process with parents, the researchers were able to identify seven positive core themes that parents felt their child with the disability was responsible for contributing to their family.

1. A source of joy and happiness

2. A reminder of what is important in life and a forced reassessment of priorities

3. An expanded personal, social, and community network

4. A source of family unity

5. An increase in tolerance and understanding, not only in the area of disability but in the acceptance of all human differences

6. A source of personal growth and strength

7. A lesson to community members about acceptance and the potential of children with disabilities

Stainton and Besser made it clear that children with disabilities bring more than struggles to the lives of their families. Along with the struggles, they provide many joys, strengthen relationships, and improve character.

The majority of families express feelings of joy, love, acceptance, satisfaction, optimism, and strength from parenting a child with a disability. Few parents have difficulty identifying the diverse rewards of having their child. Many times, satisfaction is mentioned more often than negative experiences, and caregivers find the experience of raising a child with a disability rewarding (Grant, Ramcharan, McGrath, Nolan, & Keady, 1998). These positive functions may act as a mechanism for adaptation to the stressors and strains of raising a child with disabilities (Hastings, Allen, McDermott, & Still, 2002). Interestingly, mothers who report higher levels of caregiving demand for their child with a disability also report more growth and maturity (Hastings et al.). A child with severe disabilities poses a high level of challenge and, therefore, provides mothers with the opportunity to grow personally and develop a mature outlook on the world. This is further evidence that having a child with a disability, even with severe demands, can have positive outcomes for the caregiver.

Family Resilience. During the past decade, researchers have begun to study resilience concerning family systems (Patterson, 2002). *Resilience* is the study of why some families facing adversity function well, while others in a similar situation do not (Bayat, 2007). The term *protective factors* distinguishes individuals who cope well from those who experience serious problems, even though they live in similar situations (Werner & Smith, 1992). Realizing these strengths enables families to build on them and better manage their stress (Lietz, 2006).

Researchers have studied families with children who have disabilities to determine these resiliency factors. Three main factors that promote resilience: (a) open discussions and consultations with family; (b) positive bonds between the parents; and (c) continuous and intensive educational, therapeutic, and psychological supports. They also found that families who had positive feelings toward their child, toward coping, and toward family relationships were more able to adapt in a resilient manner. Parents with a large support system cope better. Having many supportive family members, friends, and organizations and adequate financial support decreases the strain experienced by families with a child with a disability.

Positive Changes in Sibling Development. Siblings of children with a disability experience more stressors compared to siblings of typically developing children (Giallo & Gavidia-Payne, 2006). Evidence also supports the idea that siblings of children with disabilities are well adjusted psychosocially and report low levels of loneliness (Kaminsky & Dewey, 2002). They have high self-concepts and are well-adjusted academically and behaviorally. They also have the same level of self-esteem and competence as children with typically developing siblings.

Children who have siblings with a disability have increased assertiveness, helpfulness, and resilience and less self-centeredness. By helping with the care of a sibling, social competence and self-esteem are fostered in these children. Siblings of children with a disability when compared to typically developing siblings describe greater affection as well as less competition and quarrelling in their relationships (Kaminsky & Dewey, 2002). These siblings are more prosocial and nurturing toward the affected sibling than siblings of typically developing children are toward each other.

EDUCATIONAL STRATEGIES

- Attempts to change children's behavior require extensive cooperation and support from families. However, stressors, family disruption, and emotional issues can interfere with this process.
- Developing and encouraging parent support groups helps to promote parent resiliency and build resources for parents. School-based parent support groups can be effective in reducing parent stressors.
- Afterschool programming for children with disabilities eases time pressures and burdens on parents and families.
- Siblings also have positive outcomes from being in support groups. However, the outcomes of siblings with disabilities are often more positive than commonly thought. Educators can work with siblings to help develop supports for the child with a disability while at school.

DISCUSSION QUESTIONS

1. How would you describe the positive changes in family dynamics after a child is diagnosed with developmental disabilities?

2. What suggestions would you make regarding a parent's fear about the strength of his or her marriage?

3. How does one know if the degree of responsibility assigned to the sibling of a child with a disability has become excessive?

4. Have the parents been monitoring their children to observe any negative effects of the sibling's responsibilities?

5. As a teacher, how can you take steps to learn about families of the students in your class, including which students may have a sibling with a disability? If there are such children in the class, have their mood and behavior been interpreted appropriately in light of their situation at home?

RESEARCH SUMMARY

- Most families living with a child with a disability did not have any prior knowledge about disorders or disabilities. They may only have had stereotypical notions of disability conceptualized by society. These ideas can be negative and inaccurate. Thus, families that do not have experience with disability may have a distorted view and be poorly prepared to cope with a child who presents with such a disorder.
- The uncertainty of the future of a child with a disability creates significant family stress.
- Parents of children with disabilities have slightly higher divorce rates than parents of typically developing children.
- Although there are some risk factors, there are also positive outcomes for siblings of children with disabilities. This includes increased assertiveness, helpfulness, and resilience; less self-centeredness and competitiveness; and greater affection.
- Some families have social, family, and financial resources that make them resilient to the stressors of having a child with disabilities.

RESOURCES

Genetic Alliance: www.geneticalliance.org

National Organization for Rare Disorders: www.rarediseases.org

University of Kansas Medical Center, Genetics Education Center: www.kumc.edu/gec/support/grouporg.html#specific. List of links to organizations that provide information and support groups for genetic and rare conditions.

HANDOUT

HELPING FAMILIES WITH A CHILD WITH A DISABILITY

When first learning that their child has a disability, parents face many challenges:

- Coming to the realization that the child has a disability
- Obtaining complete diagnostic information from professionals
- Learning about the disability and dispelling stereotypes
- Managing a mixture of emotions

Many stressors are involved with having a child with a disability. The list that follows includes just some of the many changes that may cause stress and instability to the family unit.

- Role changes in the family
- Reorganization of lives of all family members
- Increase in caregiving demands, including dealing with day-to-day hassles of the child's condition (e.g., medical needs and educational needs and therapies, to name a few)
- Strain on family resources
- Coming to terms with the differences in your child when compared to a typical child
- Grieving the loss of the child they had originally imagined raising
- Balancing the developmental needs of other family members
- Becoming experts in your child's disability and providing education and advocacy in your community

Fathers and mothers experience parenting a child with a disability differently.

- Women have lower levels of happiness, self-esteem, and self-efficacy than men.
- Women are more likely than men to show signs of psychological distress.
- When compared to fathers of children with a disability, mothers show more parental stress, as well as higher physical and emotional strain.
- Both mothers and fathers report symptoms of depression and lower marital adjustment when their child has severe behavior problems.

Marital strain in families of children with disabilities occurs slightly more frequently than in marriages that have children that are typically developing. Parents of children with disabilities are more satisfied with their marriages when

- their children have fewer maladaptive behaviors;
- their families have fewer daily hassles; and
- fathers use problem-focused coping strategies that actively confront stressful problems.

Siblings of a child with a disability are also affected. Parents must realize the effect of placing added responsibility on and devoting less attention to their other children. They must monitor the mental health of their other children.

Families can experience positive effects from having a child with a disability.

- Feelings of joy, love, acceptance, satisfaction, optimism, and strength
- Increased sense of purpose and a change in priorities
- An expanded personal, social, and community network
- Family unity
- Increase in tolerance and understanding
- Personal growth and strength
- Perseverance and an ability to challenge authority

Acquired Disorders of Childhood

8

Prenatal Alcohol Exposure*

Biological and Behavioral Outcomes

Erica J. Deming and Paul C. McCabe

Tomás is an 8-year-old student diagnosed with fetal alcohol effects (FAE). His physical symptoms include small eye openings, flattening of the cheekbones, and an indistinct ridge between the upper lip and nose. Tomás presents with borderline cognitive abilities both verbally and perceptually. He demonstrates difficulty with abstract thinking and reasoning, as well as with generalizing information from one learning situation to the next. He requires a great deal of repetition and concrete examples to accompany new concepts. Socially and emotionally, Tomás also struggles. He is not accepted by his peer group and is often ridiculed by his peers due to his physical differences. He does not read social situations well and often behaves inappropriately. In addition to having difficulty navigating social situations, Tomás also frequently struggles to anticipate and understand the consequences of his behaviors.

Tomás resides with his biological mother and younger sibling, and his sibling also displays some symptoms of a fetal alcohol spectrum disorder. Tomás's mother reports behavioral difficulties in the home and has recently begun seeking community-based family counseling. She has been forthcoming with Tomás's pediatrician and school personnel regarding Tomás's exposure to alcohol *in utero*.

Tomás is not eligible for special education services, based upon the most recent psychoeducational testing. A functional behavior assessment and behavioral intervention plan have recently been implemented to address inappropriate behaviors present in the school setting. In the classroom, Tomás's desk is placed near the teacher. Visual cues on his desk remind him of

*Adapted from Deming, E. J., & McCabe, P. C. (2003). Prenatal alcohol exposure: Biological and behavioral outcomes. *Communiqué, 32*(2), 16–18. Copyright by the National Association of School Psychologists, Bethesda, MD. Use is by permission of the publisher. www.nasponline.org

appropriate ways to seek teacher attention. A daily home-school notebook is used to provide consistency between Tomás's home and school environments. Additionally, Tomás participates in a weekly social skills building counseling group with his peers. School personnel have reached out to Tomás's mother to assist her in seeking additional resources for her family, including a community-based program for children like Tomás.

INTRODUCTION

Children exposed to moderate to heavy amounts of alcohol *in utero* often present with a host of behavioral and learning needs. Research points to a continuum of exposure and related effects, ranging from moderate to heavy alcohol exposure with subtle neurobehavioral implications to heavy alcohol exposure with significant anatomical, learning, and behavioral implications. Children who have been exposed to alcohol *in utero* represent a large population, often unknowingly underserved.

BACKGROUND

Approximately 30 years ago, Jones and Smith discovered a pattern of neurological deficits associated with mothers who consumed alcohol during pregnancy (Jones, 1986). To date, researchers and medical professionals have identified a continuum of alcohol exposure and related effects, including fetal alcohol syndrome (FAS), fetal alcohol effects (FAE), alcohol-related birth defects (ARBD), and alcohol-related neurodevelopmental disorder (ARND). Educators have been working with the fetal alcohol spectrum disorders (FASD) population for several decades, namely those children with FAS and FAE, and are typically knowledgeable about FASD-related physiological, behavioral, and academic symptomatology. However, they may not be as aware of the subtler yet real consequences of alcohol-related birth defects (ARBD) or alcohol-related neurodevelopmental disorder (ARND).

Although the diagnostic criteria for fetal alcohol syndrome is clear, reliable identification and diagnosis of additional FASDs are unclear for a number of reasons, making it difficult to establish prevalence rates. A continuum of symptom presentation exists for FASD, making it difficult to determine the exact amount of exposure to alcohol of a particular child. In addition, limits of recollection and self-report on behalf of the mother make it difficult to identify all cases of FASD. FAS occurs in approximately 0.5 to 2 per 1,000 live births in the United States. However, cases of FASD (which includes FAS, partial FAS, ARBD, and ARND) occur in an estimated 1 in 100 live births (Schonfeld, Paley, Frankel, & O'Connor, 2006). Furthermore, some populations, such as Native Americans, may have much higher prevalence rates (Teeter & Semrud-Clikeman, 1997). Additional risk factors include previously having a child with FAS; having a low socioeconomic status; identifying as Black/African American, American Indian/Native American, or Alaska Native; being a smoker; being unmarried; having a history of drug use; having a history of physical or sexual abuse; experiencing psychological stress; and having a mental health disorder(s) (Floyd, O'Connor, Bertrand, & Sokol, 2006).

Neuroanatomical Effects of Prenatal Alcohol Exposure

The neuroanatomical effects of prenatal alcohol exposure depend on the stage of neural development when the growing fetus is exposed to alcohol. The first critical developmental period occurs when the neural tube and crest are forming. In humans, this occurs during the first trimester of pregnancy. Mice that were exposed to alcohol at this stage demonstrated major neural tube deficits and severe facial feature distortions similar to those of human children with FAS (Guerri, 1998).

The next critical prenatal developmental level occurs during the second trimester, when the central nervous system, excluding the cerebellum, begins to differentiate. The brain's neurons, too, begin to migrate and specialize, and synaptic connections are established. Alcohol exposure during this time negatively affects the proliferation of neural cells, especially in the neocortex, hippocampus, and sensory cortices (Guerri, 1998).

The final critical period of prenatal development occurs during the third trimester, when the brain undergoes a tremendous growth spurt. It is important to consider that the growth spurt continues after birth, until the child is approximately 2 years of age, which suggests that some of the detrimental effects of prenatal alcohol exposure during the third trimester may be ameliorated. During the third trimester, the synaptic connections become more fully formed, preparing the fetus with the means to sustain life outside the womb. Other activities during this developmental stage include rapid growth in the cerebellum and the formation of astroglial and oligodendroglial cells, which are insulating cells that play a major role in signal propagation in the brain.

Alcohol's Effect on the Neocortex, Hippocampus, Cerebellum, and Neurotransmission

Neocortex. The neocortex, consisting of the left and right hemispheres and the motor, sensory, visual, and auditory cortices, is evolutionarily the most recent part of the human brain. It constitutes a great majority of brain volume and serves to integrate and make sense of daily activities. As with all areas of the brain, prenatal alcohol exposure can have a severe effect on the neocortex. Exposure to alcohol has the potential to decrease brain volume by as much as 13%, reduce the number of neurons by 33%, and reduce the volume of supportive glial cells by as much as 36% (Guerri, 1998). At the most basic level, negative effects of prenatal alcohol exposure include less proliferation and migration of neural cells and decreased, aberrant, or redundant formation of synapses.

Sowell et al. (2002) reported on the neocortical structures of adolescents who experienced prenatal alcohol exposure. Comparing 21 adolescents exposed to alcohol to a comparison group exhibiting normal development, researchers found abnormal hemispheric placements. For instance, they found that portions of the temporal and parietal lobes were shifted backwards in the left hemisphere. In addition, gray matter was asymmetric, with more volume in the posterior inferior temporal lobes, possibly interfering with language functioning.

Hippocampus. Several of the central symptoms associated with fetal alcohol exposure are memory and attention deficits. This observation has led researchers to study the effects of prenatal alcohol exposure on the hippocampus, as this structure is associated with memory organization and storage. Again, the extent of damage, especially concerning the hippocampal structures, is determined by the stage of development at exposure as well as by the concentration of exposure. Studies have shown that moderate alcohol consumption decreases pyramidal cells, neurons that transmit information to other parts of the central nervous system, but causes hypertrophy, or increased growth, in other areas. Krahl, Berman, and Hannigan (1999) administered alcohol to rats at different stages of gestational development and then compared the hippocampal structures of the group that received the teratogen at early in gestation to another that received it later. They found more severe effects in the earlier exposed group, suggesting that the negative effects of prenatal alcohol exposure on the hippocampus may peak during early prenatal development.

Cerebellum. Behavioral symptoms of prenatal alcohol exposure sometimes involve deficient motor skills and poor coordination. Autopsies performed on children exhibiting fetal alcohol effects have discovered decreased size and malformation of the cerebellum and complete agenesis, or lack of development, of the cerebellar vermis, which is the tissue that connects the hemispheres of the cerebellum (Guerri, 1998; Teeter & Semrud-Clikeman, 1997). In addition, studies with rats have shown decreased cerebellum size, directly correlated with the time at which the brain was exposed to alcohol. In most cases, the damage to this area occurs when alcohol is consumed in the third trimester. The behavioral effects of the cerebellar malformation are typically motor coordination difficulties, fine motor dysfunction, and gait irregularities.

Neuronal Level. Numerous studies have concluded that fetal cell death commonly follows maternal alcohol consumption. Glial cells, which provide support to neurons, are often abnormally produced or destroyed by alcohol exposure. In particular, astrocytes, comprising approximately 50% of brain cells, are reduced in numbers by as much as 36% in the sensory cortices (Guerri, 1998). The death of astrocytes or astroglia, which are responsible for maintaining neuronal metabolism among other duties, can affect myelination and neuron migration, thereby disrupting neural transmission.

Research efforts have examined the action of neurotransmitters, specifically gamma-amino butyric acid (GABA), at various neuron receptors in the brain, mainly the N-methyl-D-aspartate (NMDA) receptor (Olney, Farber, Wozniak, Jevtovic-Todorovic, & Ikonomidou, 2000). Alcohol interferes with the activity of GABA and NMDA receptors during synaptogenesis, leading to apoptotic neurodegeneration (cell death by suicide). Furthermore, researchers determined that the minimum amount of alcohol required to trigger this neurodegeneration was approximately 200 mg/dL for 4 consecutive hours; when this concentration was maintained over 4 hours or more, the neural death progressed. This concentration is equivalent to a blood alcohol content level of 0.20, which is twice the legal limit for operating a motor vehicle in many states. On average, a 120-pound individual would need to consume around seven servings of alcohol to reach this level. This finding could partially explain why many children born to alcoholic mothers have reduced brain weights.

Typical Anatomical Features of Children With Fetal Alcohol Exposure

One of the most prominent anatomical features associated with FASD is atypical facial features. These are often the first indication that further assessment is warranted. Facial abnormalities include microcephaly (small head size), deficient eye formation causing abnormally small eye openings, a short nose, flattening of the face or cheekbones, a small upper lip, and an indistinct ridge between the upper lip and nose (Jones, 1986). Associated features may include a fold of skin in the corner of the eye, low nasal bridge, smaller than normal jaw, and misshapen ears. Facial features are typically more distinct on the left side of the face, and most abnormalities can be directly linked to brain malformation during prenatal development. These features tend to become less apparent during puberty (Teeter & Semrud-Clikeman, 1997).

Neurobehavioral Effects of Prenatal Alcohol Exposure

The most prevalent neurobehavioral effects of prenatal alcohol exposure are cognitive deficits. Numerous studies have demonstrated a high rate of delays and intellectual disabilities in this population of children. Prenatal alcohol exposure is one of the leading causes of intellectual disabilities (Green, 2007). Related to cognitive deficiencies, these children typically have poor adaptive skills, especially in the social domain (Teeter & Semrud-Clikeman, 1997).

Although most children with FASD display some level of cognitive deficit, a large majority do not have intellectual disabilities. Variability in intellectual functioning is large, ranging from low to average. However, even children with FASD who score within the average range on traditional intelligence tests are likely to display deficits not commonly identified through traditional psychoeducational testing, such as in executive functioning. These deficits often result in daily functioning difficulties, including difficulty with planning and sequencing, inhibition, and lack of cognitive flexibility (Green, 2007). Schonfeld and colleagues (2006) studied executive functioning deficits in children with FAS, partial FAS, and ARND and found significant impairment across all groups. Although these children may not qualify for special education services, they nonetheless may require additional educational services.

Attention problems have also been associated with this population, and children with FASD often appear very similar to their nonexposed peers who have attention deficits (Coles, 2001). Children with FAE exhibit earlier-onset, inattentive subtypes, often with comorbid psychiatric and medical conditions (O'Malley & Nanson, 2002). Children with FAE also may have complex learning disabilities, including mixed receptive-expressive language disorders, working memory problems, and, often, mathematics disorders. Children with FAE have more difficulty with planning tasks that involve the prefrontal cortex. In addition, deficits have been noted on tasks that involve puzzles, highlighting deficits in planning and working memory (Kodituwakku, Handmaker, Cutler, Weathersby, & Handmaker, 1995). Studies investigating the impact of prenatal alcohol exposure and a child's ability to sustain attention over time suggest the most pronounced deficits in tasks that require not only sustained attention but also executive functioning tasks, such as recall of information and response inhibition (Jacobson & Jacobson, 2002). Jacobson and Jacobson report less correlation between FAS and hyperactivity.

Although the most typical effects of prenatal alcohol exposure are cognitive deficits, some researchers suggest that maladaptive social behaviors in infancy, childhood, adolescence, and adulthood may also result from alcohol exposure in the womb. Attachment concerns, as well as state regulation deficits (the ability to control one's arousal level), have been found in studies with both human and animal subjects, although for humans this finding is complicated by environmental factors. In addition, behavior checklists completed by parents and teachers have found various social skill deficits in FASD adolescents. As individuals with FASD enter adulthood, they are more likely to experience trouble with the law, exhibit inappropriate sexual behavior, suffer from depression, entertain suicide, and exhibit parental neglect of their own children (Kelly, Day, & Streissguth, 2000). As with cognitive and other behavioral deficits associated with this population, research suggests that children across the FASD spectrum are at equal risk for the development of maladaptive social skills and mental illnesses (O'Connor et al., 2002; Schonfeld et al., 2006).

Mediating the neurobehavioral effects of prenatal alcohol exposure is the complex transactional relationship between the child's individual differences and the family environment. Although children are born equipped with many of the innate mechanisms that carry them through life, environmental factors also foster or deplete the potential for success. Many FASD children come from unstable, chaotic, or stressful home environments. Studies investigating the relationship among prenatal alcohol exposure, increased child behavior difficulties, and maternal stress suggest that the behavioral effects of prenatal alcohol exposure extend to the family unit by increasing maternal stress levels (Paley, O'Connor, Kogan, & Findlay, 2005). Only 9% of children with fetal alcohol syndrome involved in a longitudinal study resided with both biological parents, and 33% of the children were given up for adoption or left at the hospital after birth (Streissguth et al., 1991).

IMPLICATIONS FOR EDUCATORS

Prenatal alcohol exposure is one of the leading causes of preventable birth defects and cognitive impairments in children. Therefore, it is essential that educators are aware of the diagnostic signs and intervention strategies with this population. Our role in assisting children consists of providing both prevention and intervention to children and families. In some instances, teachers and school personnel are in a role to educate the parent community about the harmful effects of alcohol exposure during pregnancy. This is most likely to occur with parents who are already members of the school community, as well as through outreach programs that target parents in the broader community. For many parents or future parents, especially teenagers, education about the harmful effects of consuming alcohol during pregnancy may be the best prevention. We are also in a position to educate parents who might already have a child with FASD so that they may be better equipped if they have another child.

Working with families that have a child or children with FASD is a twofold process. It consists of (1) identifying the child who may have been exposed to alcohol and (2) consulting with the school team and the parents to develop and implement an educational plan to assist the child. Identifying the child can be difficult, as children with FASD can be very heterogeneous in their symptom presentation and many do not show the physical characteristics associated with full FAS. However, significant neurocognitive effects may still be present in the child with FASD, and the absence of physical markers does not preclude the possibility of prenatal alcohol exposure (Mattson, Riley, Gramling, Delis, & Jones, 1998). Identification is further complicated by the social taboo associated with prenatal alcohol consumption, as few parents are willing to admit to their alcohol consumption during pregnancy. Therefore, a thorough background review, including comprehensive medical and developmental history and in-depth parent interview, are often necessary to ascertain the degree of prenatal alcohol exposure.

Although some children with FASD may be eligible for special education services due to significant cognitive delays or learning disabilities, a large majority will be ineligible to receive such services, despite moderate learning and behavioral needs. In these cases, it becomes the responsibility of the general education teacher, parent, and other school professionals to make appropriate environmental modifications in the classroom. Resources may include behavioral plans, school-based counseling or other social-emotional interventions, and any remedial educational opportunities that are available. Furthermore, children with FASD often require services through adolescence and adulthood, depending on the severity of their needs, highlighting the need for transition planning.

Identification of FASD is of primary concern in the education field, and prevention efforts are worthwhile. We are called upon to serve as scholars, advisors, and tacticians and to balance carefully advocacy and prevention with acceptance and tolerance. Only with a delicate balance of support, compassion, and gentle yet firm insistence, grounded in the latest science, will school personnel be most effective in increasing awareness of FASD and preventing its future occurrence.

EDUCATIONAL STRATEGIES

- School personnel are in a position to provide both prevention and intervention support for children and families who are at risk for having children with FASD or who are already impacted by FASD.
- Personnel working with at-risk adolescents or families may be able to provide education about the detrimental effects of consuming alcohol during pregnancy.
- Children with FASD often present with cognitive and behavioral needs, including cognitive impairments, learning disabilities, poor adaptive skills, planning difficulties, sequencing problems, cognitive inflexibility, attention difficulties, language disorders, working memory delays, and maladaptive social behaviors.

- For school personnel who suspect a child may have FASD, the process of serving that child is often twofold, consisting of (1) identifying the child that may have been exposed to alcohol and (2) consulting with the school team and parents to develop and implement an educational plan to assist the child.
- Although some children with FASD may be eligible for special education services, a large majority are not. In those cases, school personnel are often called upon to make environmental modifications. Appropriate resources may include behavior intervention plans, school-based counseling, and remedial educational opportunities such as tutoring.

DISCUSSION QUESTIONS

1. What do educators need to look for when they suspect fetal alcohol spectrum disorder (FASD)? What are appropriate "first steps" for teachers to take when FASD is suspected?

2. Alcohol use during pregnancy has a longstanding social stigma and, as a result, often goes unreported by parents. How can educators, psychologists, and counselors develop effective relationships between school personnel and families to promote open and honest communication?

3. Children with FASD often present with deficits in executive functioning, such as difficulties with planning and sequencing. How might these difficulties present in the classroom? What classroom interventions can teachers use to address these areas of need?

4. Children with FASD often present with externalizing behaviors that interfere with their daily functioning. What interventions are appropriate for these behaviors, and what factors should be taken into account when considering medication for this population?

5. How does FASD align with the current special education system? What symptoms of FASD would warrant special education services? What are the limitations of the special education system in meeting the needs of children with FASD?

RESEARCH SUMMARY

- Individuals with fetal alcohol spectrum disorders (FASD) represent a highly heterogeneous population, with symptoms ranging from subtle behavioral/learning needs to marked physical, behavioral, and intellectual impairments.
- Fetal alcohol syndrome (FAS) occurs in approximately 0.5 to 2 per 1,000 live births in the United States. However, cases of FASD occur in an estimated 1 in 100 live births (Schonfeld et al., 2006).
- The type and degree of impairment is highly dependent upon the stage of fetal brain development when alcohol exposure occurs. Much of the research is limited to animal studies.

- Research has provided information about the impact of alcohol exposure on different areas of the brain, including the neocortex, hippocampus, and cerebellum. Behavioral symptoms range from intellectual impairment, memory and attention-related deficits, and deficient motor skills.
- Physical features associated with FASD include small head size, small eye openings, short nose, flattening of the face or cheekbones, small upper lip, and indistinct ridge between the upper lip and nose.
- Neurobehavioral features associated with FASD include cognitive impairment, poor adaptive skills, executive-functioning difficulties, attention problems, and maladaptive social behaviors.

RESOURCES

Larkby, C., & Day, N. (1997). The effects of prenatal alcohol exposure. *Alcohol Health & Research World, 21,* 192–198. Available October 1, 2009, at http://pubs.niaaa.nih.gov/publications/arh21-3/192.pdf

The Centers for Disease Control dedicates a portion of its Web site to Fetal Alcohol Spectrum Disorders: www.cdc.gov/ncbddd/fas/.

HANDOUT

EFFECTS OF PRENATAL ALCOHOL EXPOSURE ON CHILDREN

Consumption of alcohol during pregnancy can be detrimental to the growth and development of an unborn baby. Presently, research has not identified any safe level of alcohol consumption for expectant mothers; therefore, *avoiding any alcohol throughout all stages of pregnancy is advised.*

Children who have been exposed to moderate to heavy amounts of alcohol *in utero* often present with various learning and behavioral needs. Deficits associated with prenatal alcohol exposure include the following:

- Cognitive impairments (including intellectual disabilities)
- Facial abnormalities
- Growth retardation
- Behavioral difficulties, including hyperactivity, inattention, and impaired social-emotional functioning

Researchers and medical professionals have identified a continuum of alcohol exposure and related effects, including fetal alcohol syndrome (FAS), fetal alcohol effects (FAE), alcohol-related birth defects (ARBD), and alcohol-related neurodevelopmental disorder (ARND).

When a child presents with profound impairments, including when a child has been diagnosed with intellectual disabilities as a result of heavy prenatal alcohol exposure, special education services are often implemented. However, the learning and behavioral needs of many children who have been exposed to alcohol *in utero* are not significant enough to qualify them for special education services; nonetheless, they have distinctive educational and behavioral needs. These children may be underserved due to lack of awareness about their prenatal alcohol exposure, limited awareness about interventions suitable for this population, or lack of resources. Parents play a vital role in recognizing the needs of these children, providing an accurate account of alcohol usage during pregnancy, and advocating for appropriate educational services.

- Inform your child's pediatrician about alcohol consumption during pregnancy so that appropriate diagnoses/referrals can be made. It is especially important to include information about when alcohol consumption occurred during the pregnancy, frequency of consumption, and estimated amounts of alcohol consumed.
- Be aware that alcoholic beverages are often served in larger vessels or contain a higher alcohol percentage than we expect, thereby increasing alcohol intake. For example, although you may be served one glass of wine, the amount of alcohol in the glass could be equivalent to two or more servings, depending on vessel size and alcohol level. It is recommended that *all alcohol be avoided throughout pregnancy*, as it is unclear what constitutes a safe level of consumption and measuring actual alcohol intake is difficult.
- Talk to your child's teacher about the child's exposure to alcohol, including any related diagnoses (fetal alcohol syndrome, fetal alcohol effects). If your child has cognitive and/or behavioral needs, he or she may require special education services. Pediatricians, parents, or school staff can initiate further evaluations if needed.
- As a parent of a child with fetal alcohol exposure, consider your own level of psychological support and mental health. For some parents, participation in individual psychotherapy can help improve overall mental health, enhance coping skills, foster acceptance of their child's condition, and prevent future fetal alcohol exposure.

9

Prenatal Exposure to Antidepressants*

Paul C. McCabe and Caryn R. DePinna

Maya facilitates weekly parenting groups. The group meets and discusses parenting techniques, such as what to expect from children of specific ages and parenting children with special needs. One of the members of the group is Mrs. W, who has twin 4-year-old boys with significant behavior problems. Mrs. W comes to the group on a regular basis and is very involved. After a meeting, Mrs. W discloses to Maya that she is expecting her third child. When Maya congratulates Mrs. W, she observes that Mrs. W seems upset and worried. When asked, Mrs. W discloses that she has been diagnosed with depression and has been treated with antidepressants for the last few years. She also expresses concern about taking medication while she is pregnant, as well as the consequences of going off the medication during her pregnancy. Maya refers Mrs. W to her doctor and to a community agency that conducts group counseling. Maya also volunteers to help Mrs. W find information about the risks of taking antidepressants during pregnancy.

After speaking with her doctor and reviewing some research with Maya, Mrs. W learns that antidepressants can have adverse effects on infants in some cases and no effect in others. Mrs. W is still unsure about what she should do and decides to visit her psychiatrist with questions. Mrs. W discusses her history of depression, including its severity, and the type of medication she has been prescribed, the dosage, and the research available on it. Ultimately, Mrs. W decides to stay on her medication throughout her pregnancy.

Consider the following: How can educators support women who are faced with this dilemma? What information can educators provide parents, and what can be done to support children of depressed parents in school?

*Adapted from Johnson, K. E., & McCabe, P. C. (2004). The effects of prenatal exposure to antidepressants. *Communiqué, 32*(8), 41–43. Copyright by the National Association of School Psychologists, Bethesda, MD. Use is by permission of the publisher. www.nasponline.org

INTRODUCTION

The National Institute of Mental Health (NIMH) estimates that at any given time, 9.5% of the U.S. population suffers from a depressive disorder and two thirds of those suffering are women (NIMH, 2008). Depression occurs in 7% to 15% of all pregnancies (Evans, Heron, Francomb, Oke, & Golding, 2001). In one study of African-American and Latina women, half (51%) reported elevated depressive symptoms (Zayas, Cunningham, McKee, & Jankowski, 2002). As medication has become the treatment of choice for depression, the need to examine the effects of antidepressants on prenatal development has become increasingly urgent. Researchers estimate that 30% to 33% of pregnant women use psychotropic medications (Arnon, Shechtman, & Ornoy, 2000; Barki, Kravitz, & Berki, 1998). The literature available on the effects of prenatal exposure to antidepressants is inconclusive, and more research is required to understand the effect that antidepressants have on human development. The U.S. Food and Drug Administration (FDA) has not approved any psychotropic medications for use during pregnancy and lactation (Stowe, Strader, & Nemeroff, 2001) and has published public health advisories warning doctors and patients about the possible risks of taking antidepressants during pregnancy (FDA, 2006).

BACKGROUND

The physiological changes that women experience during pregnancy have an effect on the absorption of antidepressants. These changes include an increase in the extent to which material is digested; increased absorption of medication (because material moves more slowly through the digestive system); and increased metabolism, which quickens the rate at which medication is broken down (Stowe et al., 2001). All of these factors affect the amount of medication absorbed into the mother's system. The passage of psychotropic drugs through the placenta is well documented; therefore, any antidepressants in the mother are present in the fetus as well (Hendrick, Stowe, Altshuler, & Hwang, 2003).

Physiological features of the fetus also may place it at increased risk. The developing fetus has a higher cardiac output, greater blood-brain barrier permeability (increasing the likelihood the antidepressants can move into the developing central nervous system), decreased plasma protein and plasma protein-binding affinity, and decreased hepatic enzyme activity (Baum & Misri, 1996; Iqbal, 1999; Stowe et al., 2001). The central nervous system develops throughout pregnancy and continues to develop after birth. For this reason, psychotropic drugs may pose a special threat, as they target the neurotransmitters of the central nervous system (Baum & Misri).

Once the baby is born, the level of antidepressants present in breast milk is also a concern. According to Stowe and colleagues (2001), a neonate's liver is less able to remove medications from its body, and medications may stay in an infant's system longer than for more mature people. Currently, the research available on the effects of breast-feeding while taking antidepressants is mixed. Some research studies have reported symptoms including colic, fever, hypotonia, poor sleeping habits, poor feeding, irritability, seizures, and decreased growth rate in babies nursed with affected milk (Brent & Wisner, 1998; Kristensen et al., 1999). However, other studies report no adverse affects (Blier, 2006; Gentile, 2006).

Types of Antidepressants

Selective Serotonin Reuptake Inhibitors (SSRIs). Serotonin is one of the three neurotransmitters implicated in depression. Inefficient serotonin transmission across the synapse between neurons contributes to depressive symptoms. After one neuron releases serotonin into the synaptic cleft, some serotonin is received by surrounding neurons, and the rest is reabsorbed back into the original neuron to be recycled. SSRIs slow this reabsorption process so that more serotonin remains in the synaptic cleft to be received by other neurons. This promotes serotonin transmissions, leading to more electrochemical firing of successive neurons and typically elevating mood. SSRIs include medications such as fluoxetine (Prozac), paroxetine (Paxil), sertraline (Zoloft), citalopram (Celexa), and escitalapram (Lexapro).

Further research is needed in the area of prenatal exposure to SSRIs. Past and present research is equivocal, and some results are troubling. Animal studies indicate that SSRIs can have adverse effects (Altshuler et al., 1996); however, no such long-term studies have been conducted with humans. In humans, SSRI exposure is related to perinatal effects such as jitteriness and irritability, as well as lower gestational age, lower birth weight, smaller head circumference, lower Apgar scores, difficulty feeding, difficulty breathing, and increased rate of spontaneous abortions (Arnon et al., 2000; Barki et al., 1998; FDA, 2006; Misri, Kostaras, & Kostaras, 2000). Also a rare condition called persistent pulmonary hypertension, a serious and life-threatening condition in newborns, is six times more common in babies whose mothers took an SSRI after the 20th week of pregnancy (FDA).

Tricyclic Antidepressants (TCAs). Tricyclic antidepressants work by blocking the reuptake of both norepinephrine and serotonin at nerve endings. Thus, excess norepinephrine and serotonin are not absorbed back into the transmitting neuron and can instead facilitate the efficacy of norepinephrine and serotonin transmission. Examples of tricyclic antidepressants include amitriptyline (Elavil), amoxapine (Asendin), clomipramine (Anafranil), desipramine (Norpramin), doxepin (Sinequan, Adapin), imipramine (Tofranil), nortriptyline (Pamelor, Aventyl), maprotiline (Ludiomil), and protriptyline (Vivactil; Stowe et al., 2001).

Further research is needed on the effects of prenatal exposure to TCAs. Current research is mixed but seems to indicate that TCAs are free of teratogenic effects, such as congenital malformations and developmental delays (Altshuler et al., 1996; Simon, Cunningham, & Davis, 2002). However, there is some evidence that minor problems, such as decreases in gestational age, birth weight, head circumference, and Apgar scores, as well as perinatal symptoms, such as withdrawal and anticholinergic effects (blocking of acetylcholine, an important neurotransmitter), increase with TCA exposure (Altshuler & Szuba, 1994; Arnon et al., 2000; Barki et al., 1998; Iqbal, 1999).

Monoamine Oxidase Inhibitors (MAOIs). Monoamines include a group of three molecularly similar neurotransmitters: serotonin, norepinephrine, and dopamine. Low levels of these neurotransmitters are known correlates of depression. Once a neuron has released these neurotransmitters into the synapse, the enzyme monoamine oxidase works to clean up the excess neurotransmitters in preparation for the next neuronal firing. MAOIs inhibit the work of monoamine oxidase, so more monoamines remain in the synapse to be absorbed by postsynaptic receptors. This increases the efficacy of transmission and is associated with elevated mood.

However, MAOIs also have a dangerous side effect. Although MAOIs block the removal of serotonin, dopamine, and norepinephrine, they also block the removal of tyramine, which affects blood pressure. Excess tyramine can lead to an increase in blood pressure that causes the blood vessels in the brain to burst, resulting in death. Patients on MAOIs must adhere to a strict diet, avoiding foods that increase tyramine levels, such as cheese, fermented foods, sausage, and alcoholic beverages. Examples of MAOIs include isocarboxazid (Marplan), phenelzine (Nardil), and tranylcypromine (Parnate; Stowe et al., 2001).

MAOIs are the least researched of the three major groups of antidepressants. Available research seems to agree that MAOIs are risky during pregnancy, both to the mother and the child, and should be discontinued until after birth (Altshuler & Szuba, 1994; Barki et al., 1998; Iqbal, 1999).

Untreated Depression

Numerous studies exist on the risks of untreated depression in pregnant women. There is some evidence that maternal stress and stress hormone concentrations have an adverse effect on fetal brain development (Stowe et al., 2001). Several studies show that maternal depression has a negative effect on maternal-infant attachment and child development (Stowe et al.). Discontinuing antidepressants can also create problems, such as suicidal ideation and withdrawal (Einarson, Selby, & Koren, 2001). In one study, women who stopped taking their antidepressant medications during pregnancy were five times more likely to have a relapse of depression during the pregnancy than those mothers who continued to take their antidepressant medications (Cohen et al., 2006; FDA, 2006). Doctors must weigh the benefits of medicating the mother against the possible risks to her and her child. Some doctors prefer to keep pregnant patients on their medications, gradually cutting back in the third trimester. For women who decide to stop taking antidepressants upon becoming pregnant, a gradual step-down is recommended to reduce the risk of withdrawal.

Conclusion

The research on the effects of prenatal exposure to antidepressants is growing but still incomplete. Current results are equivocal, with older studies claiming no teratogenic effects and more recent research claiming otherwise. Researchers have raised some concerns, especially with perinatal effects such as withdrawal and anticholinergic symptoms (fever, flushing, dilated pupils, central nervous system disorders, drowsiness, difficulty breathing, delirium, coma, abnormal heart rhythm) during the first month of life. There is a need for longitudinal research examining the impact of prenatal exposure to antidepressants from birth to age 18 years. Given the certainty of placental passage of antidepressants and the fragility of the developing central nervous system, the long-term effects of prenatal exposure to antidepressants are perhaps the most important. The possibility of increased risk of developing depression in adolescence or early adulthood has not been addressed. The majority of research at present discusses the immediate effects on and possible risks to pregnancy and newborns without examining long-term effects.

IMPLICATIONS FOR EDUCATORS

Although most educators will not be involved with helping expectant mothers choose whether or not to take an antidepressant during pregnancy, it is nevertheless important that educators are familiar with the effects of depression on mothers and their offspring. A school is not only a place where children come to learn but also an informational and referral resource for children and their families. Educators, including teachers, psychologists, guidance counselors, and school social workers, can be a resource for expectant mothers and families in their schools. For many families, schools are the only resource available, and parents will look to educators for advice on a variety of child-rearing topics, including prenatal health care decisions. Educators should be informed on the research related to these topics, as well as knowledgeable about referral sources where parents can find the answers they seek.

Schools are increasingly becoming involved in community health and mental health initiatives because of ease of access for the populations being served; availability of trained professionals; and the common objectives among educational, medical, mental health, and community partners. For example, many schools routinely offer prenatal care services for expectant teens because the teens are already in school and schools can incorporate parent training, child development, and infant care into the expectant mothers' class schedules. One study examined the effectiveness of school-based prenatal care versus hospital-based prenatal care and found that mothers who utilized school-based prenatal care were 3 times less likely to deliver a low-birth-weight child than those mothers who attended hospital-based prenatal care. The mothers receiving hospital-based prenatal care were 1.5 times less likely to receive comprehensive prenatal care (Barnet, Duggan, & Devoe, 2003). This finding suggests that schools may be in a better position to provide a full range of prenatal care to teen mothers, as well as a broad range of educational and health resources to all expectant mothers. The availability of health care resources will enable expectant mothers who are depressed to make more informed decisions about whether or not to use antidepressants during pregnancy.

EDUCATIONAL STRATEGIES

- Facilitate open communication and good rapport between parents and educators so parents are comfortable seeking resources and information from school.

- Become knowledgeable about community resources and services and pass this information along to parents who are seeking this information.
- Provide appropriate behavioral and academic interventions to children who have had any type of pre- or postnatal complications or early developmental delays.
- Help expectant mothers who appear depressed or report depressive symptoms to find the medical and mental health support they need during the pregnancy.
- Work with the school to evaluate expectant mothers' access to prenatal care in the community and determine if the provision of prenatal care services in the school is feasible and likely to lead to more comprehensive care.

DISCUSSION QUESTIONS

1. As the research shows, the effects of prenatal exposure to antidepressants are unclear. What are the possible risks of medicating during pregnancy verses not medicating?

2. Pregnant women with depression who stop taking antidepressants are five times more likely to have a relapse of depression during the pregnancy, yet these medications pose potential health risks to the developing fetus. How can teachers, psychologists, and administrators support women and their families who are faced with this dilemma?

3. Battling depression while raising children is a heavy burden for many mothers. Stress, frustration, and other negative behaviors may develop. How can schools help families cope?

4. Should schools play a larger role in facilitating health care delivery in communities, especially in those communities where health care access is difficult or unobtainable?

RESEARCH SUMMARY

- The National Institute of Mental Health estimates that 9.5% of the U.S. population suffers from a depressive disorder and that two thirds of those suffering from depression are women.
- Depression occurs in 7% to 15% of all pregnant women.
- During pregnancy, physiological changes in the mother cause an increase in her metabolism rate. Psychotropic medications, if taken, can be passed more easily from the mother to the fetus.
- Prenatal exposure to antidepressants may cause effects in the newborn such as these:
  - Jitteriness
  - Irritability
  - Early delivery
  - Low birth weight
  - Smaller head circumference
  - Lower Apgar scores

    o Withdrawal symptoms

    o Difficulty breathing and persistent pulmonary hypertension

- Prenatal exposure to antidepressants may increase the rate of spontaneous abortion.
- Untreated depression can have adverse effects on pregnant women, and discontinuing antidepressants can cause suicidal ideation and withdrawal. Women who discontinue antidepressants when pregnant are five times more likely than women who continue medication to suffer relapse of depression during the pregnancy.
- The present research findings suggest that adverse affects present in newborns related to prenatal exposure to antidepressants; however, the long-term effects are unknown.

RESOURCES

Medline Plus: www.nlm.nih.gov/medlineplus/depression.html. This Web site, part of the National Institutes of Health, offers in-depth information and resources about depression.

National Alliance on Mental Illness, "Pregnancy Pointers for Women with Psychiatric History": www.nami.org/Content/ContentGroups/ Helpline1/Pregnancy_Pointers_for_Women_with_Psychiatric_History .htm. This article focuses specifically on psychiatric medications and pregnancy.

National Institute of Mental Health, "Women and Depression: Discovering Hope": www.nimh.nih.gov/health/publications/depression-what-every-woman-should-know/complete-publication.shtml. NIMH is also part of the National Institutes of Health. This article focuses on women and depression.

HANDOUT

INFORMATION ABOUT PRENATAL EXPOSURE TO ANTIDEPRESSANTS

- Research on prenatal exposure to antidepressants is mixed. Past research has suggested that there are few to no adverse effects. However, more recent research reports more significant and potentially life-threatening risks.
- Current research suggests that prenatal exposure to antidepressants may result in the following effects:
  o Low birth weight
  o Early delivery
  o Low Apgar scores
  o Increased risk of spontaneous abortion
  o Increased risk for bodily and cardiovascular malformations in the infant
  o Difficulty breathing and persistent pulmonary hypertension in the infant
- Numerous studies have examined the risk of untreated depression in pregnant women. There is some evidence that maternal stress and stress hormone concentrations have an adverse effect on fetal brain development. Discontinuing antidepressants can also create problems such as suicidal ideation and withdrawal. Also, women who discontinue antidepressants during pregnancy are much more likely to suffer a relapse of depressive symptoms.
- Doctors and expectant mothers must weigh the benefits of medication against the possible risks. Some doctors prefer to keep pregnant patients on their medications, gradually cutting back in the third trimester. For women who decide to stop taking antidepressants upon becoming pregnant, a gradual step-down is recommended to reduce the risk of withdrawal.
- Due to the inconclusiveness of the research, women who are depressed and pregnant are strongly recommended to seek medical advice about treatment options during their pregnancy.

10

Celiac Disease and Youth*

Implications for Educators and Allied Professionals

Jessica B. Edwards George, Jessica A. Hoffman, and Debra L. Franko

Meghan, a 13-year-old Caucasian female, was recently diagnosed with celiac disease (CD) after a few months of gastrointestinal symptoms, including abdominal pain, diarrhea, and nausea. She missed approximately 4 weeks of school because of doctors appointments for evaluation and testing and feeling too ill to attend. Initially, Meghan and her parents were relieved to hear that she had CD and "not cancer or some other awful disease." They were delighted to know that Meghan's symptoms would get better if she adhered to the gluten-free diet (GFD). The family mobilized around Meghan to assist her in this major lifestyle change.

Before being diagnosed, Meghan was described as being a star student and a social butterfly with an infectious sense of humor. Since beginning the GFD, Meghan's gastrointestinal symptoms have been alleviated, but over the past month, she has become increasingly irritable, oppositional, and angry toward others, especially her mother, whom she blames for giving her CD. She has begun isolating herself in her bedroom and refusing to go to activities with her friends. Her parents report that she uses gastrointestinal symptoms as an excuse to get out of chores and other responsibilities. Meghan reportedly threatens that she will cheat on her diet if she does not get what she wants. Meghan's family states that she demands to be the center of attention at family gatherings and throws tantrums or has meltdowns if all family members do not accommodate

*Adapted from Edwards George, J. B., Blom-Hoffman, J., & Franko, D. L. (2006). Celiac disease and children: Implications for psychologists and educators. *Communiqué, 34*(8), 38–40. Copyright by the National Association of School Psychologists, Bethesda, MD. Use is by permission of the publisher. www.nasponline.org

her dietary needs. Meghan frequently expresses the wish that everyone should have to follow a GFD like her. She often states, "My life is falling apart."

At school, Meghan's grades and social network have begun to suffer. She has not begun to re-engage in academics after her long absence. Meghan refuses to eat school lunches or bring a lunch from home for fear of feeling different. She states that her friends tease her with gluten-containing treats and she responds with verbal aggression. For example, Meghan has been overheard saying, "That's fine. Keep eating gluten. You'll be fat from it one day and I'll be thin." Some of her friends at school have stopped asking her to join them in social activities as Meghan typically declines or, according to her friends, is miserable.

INTRODUCTION

Diagnoses of celiac disease (CD) are on the rise in the United States, affecting more and more children and adolescents in their daily eating routines both at home and at school. CD has effects on academic performance and social development. Educators can assist children and families in adjusting to concerns related to CD while in school.

BACKGROUND

Celiac disease, also known as celiac sprue, nontropical sprue, gluten-sensitive enteropathy, and gluten intolerance, is a chronic, immune-mediated disease of the intestine, triggered by the ingestion of gluten proteins in genetically susceptible individuals (Cárdenas & Kelly, 2002). Gluten is a water-insoluble protein component of wheat and other grains, such as rye and barley (Devlin, Andrews, & Beck, 2004). CD is primarily characterized by chronic inflammation of the surface of the small intestine in response to gluten. This inflammation is caused by an inappropriate response to gluten that activates immune cells (T cells). The inflammation leads to intestinal injury with loss of the intestinal villi, malabsorption of nutrients, and other clinical symptoms (Schuppan, 2000). Simply put, the body of an individual with CD turns against itself. The immune system is misguided and targets healthy, normal tissues, typically in the small intestine, as if it were fighting an infection. CD is a chronic disease and can manifest at any age following the introduction of gluten into an individual's diet. The clinical manifestations are diverse due to the complex relationships among genetic, environmental, and immunogenic factors (Cárdenas & Kelly).

Prevalence

CD was once considered a rare disease that affected mostly children of Northern European ancestry and caused mainly gastrointestinal symptoms. However, CD is now known to be common among people of all ages in many parts of the world. Thus, CD is more prevalent than previously believed, and more children with CD than previously thought are in school environments (Green & Jabri, 2003; Treem, 2004). A recent large prevalence study conducted in the United States found the overall prevalence of CD in individuals without evident risk factors to be 1 in 133 (Fasano et al., 2003). Despite this prevalence rate, it is believed that fewer than 5% of those with CD have been diagnosed (Talley, Valdovinos, Petterson, Carpenter, & Melton, 1994).

Symptoms

The clinical presentation of CD in pediatric populations is diverse and varies by child, contributing to difficulties in making an accurate diagnosis. CD has been coined a "clinical chameleon" because of the wide range of symptoms that children can manifest (Fasano, 2003). Children may present with typical, atypical, or silent forms of CD (Catassi & Fasano, 2002), which can range from abdominal cramping, bloating, fatigue, canker sores, and irritability to neurological effects, hair loss, weight loss, stunted growth, osteoporosis, and muscle wasting.

Diagnosis

A diagnosis of CD is usually made by testing an individual's blood for specific antibodies followed by biopsy of the small intestine via endoscopy to look for the characteristic intestinal injury. A second biopsy to confirm that the intestinal injury improves after the individual is treated with a GFD is confirmatory of the diagnosis but not always required (Cárdenas & Kelly, 2002).

Treatment: The Gluten-Free Diet

The prescribed treatment for CD is to maintain the gluten-free diet for life to avoid damage to the intestinal villi, thus preventing symptoms and some of the associated conditions and diseases. By following a diet that replaces gluten-containing foods with gluten-free, nutrient-dense grains, seeds, legumes, and nuts, children with CD can lead normal, healthy lives (Dennis & Case, 2004). The gluten status of food is not always apparent, as gluten is added to seemingly "safe" foods that do not naturally contain it (e.g., candies, soy sauces, salad dressings, shredded cheeses, toothpastes, mouthwash, prescription and nonprescription medications, and vitamins). Educators, school nurses, and school psychologists must be aware of the foods that children with CD can and cannot eat. This is best accomplished by collaborating with the family to understand the child's diet and dietary restrictions. If one is unsure as to whether the child can have a certain food, then the child's family, pediatrician, or nutritionist should be consulted. Occasions when this can be an issue include classroom-based nutrition education activities involving food tasting, school trips that include meals and snacks, and classroom celebrations where gluten-containing food is frequently served.

Issues in Treatment of Celiac Disease

Complications and Consequences of Untreated Celiac Disease. Adherence to the GFD is important because of the short-term and long-term complications and consequences of CD. An elevated frequency of intestinal T-cell lymphoma and an increased risk of other malignancies, such as esophageal and throat cancer and non-Hodgkin's lymphoma, have been found in individuals with untreated CD (Corrao et al., 2001). There is also a strong association between CD and other conditions/diseases, such as type 1 diabetes, rheumatoid arthritis, liver disease, Sjögren's syndrome, Addison's disease, congenital heart disease, cystic fibrosis, thyroid disease, lupus, Down syndrome, Turner syndrome, and Williams syndrome (Collin et al., 1994). Early diagnosis and adherence with the GFD is important for optimal health, and it appears to reduce the risk for a subset of uncommon but aggressive forms of malignancy and associated disease and conditions.

Dietary Adherence. Adhering to the GFD can be extremely challenging for individuals with CD regardless of age. Rates of adherence in adolescent populations vary from 56% to 83% (Kumar et al., 1988; Mayer, Greco, & Troncone, 1991). Individuals diagnosed with CD at a young age are reported to have the highest rates of adherence, while those diagnosed as adolescents have the most difficulty adhering to the GFD (Pietzak, 2005). In addition, females tend to adhere more to the GFD than males (Ciacci et al., 2003).

Barriers to Dietary Adherence. Correctly following the GFD is not easy. Children with CD may inadvertently or purposely ingest gluten for a number of reasons. In a survey conducted by the Canadian Celiac Association with biopsy-confirmed adults and children with CD, 45% of the adults surveyed indicated that they found the GFD to be very difficult to moderately difficult to follow (Crannery, Zarkadas, Graham, & Switer, 2003; Rashid et al., 2003). Wheat and wheat-based food products are staples in North American diets. An increasingly hectic lifestyle has contributed to a greater reliance on packaged convenience foods and more meals eaten away from home. These convenience meals often contain gluten and, thus, make navigating mealtime more complex for individuals with CD. Logistical problems (e.g., child not having access to GF food at school or gluten being added to otherwise "safe" foods in processing) and psychological barriers (e.g., child feels deprived by not being able to ingest gluten-containing products, such as birthday cake or snack treats, or child wants to eat what other kids are eating) make adherence to the GFD difficult.

Eighty-five percent of adults and 90% of children surveyed by the Canadian Celiac Association reported that just finding GF foods was a major barrier in adhering with the diet (Crannery et al., 2003). Another serious challenge to maintaining the GFD is unclear labeling. Eighty-five percent of adults surveyed said that it is a struggle to determine if foods are GF (Crannery et al.). Although gluten is a common ingredient in many foods, ingredient lists often make it difficult for individuals to determine if a food product is truly GF. School psychologists and educators must be aware of the additional burdens and stressors created when following the GFD on both the family and the child.

Comorbidity in CD. Comorbid psychological difficulties, such as reactive anxiety and depression, are common in children and adults with CD (Addolorato et al., 2001; Ciacci, Iavarone, Mazzacca, & DeRosa, 1998) and are further barriers to adherence with the GFD (Edwards George et al., 2008; Pietzak, 2005). In a meta-analysis of the effect of depression and anxiety on adherence with medical treatment, DiMatteo, Lepper, and Croghan

(2000) found that individuals with depression are three times less likely to adhere to medical treatment recommendations than patients without depression. Many children experience psychological reactions to being placed on a restrictive diet (e.g., feeling deprived, angry, anxious, or sad/depressed), which have been found to complicate adherence further. Children with CD may also display increased irritability, separation anxiety from parents, emotional withdrawal, and behaviors commonly displayed by children with autism (Pietzak, Catassi, Drago, Fornaroli, & Fasano, 2001). Educators and allied professionals need to be aware of the affective components of CD; carefully monitor children for depression, anxiety, and other behavioral presentations; and make recommendations for support when appropriate.

IMPLICATIONS FOR EDUCATORS

Strategies to Support Students With CD

A global approach that combines medical, dietary, and psychological support in treating and educating youth with CD may prove to be the most effective. In this approach, youth are the center of a complex, interacting system that includes their family, school, medical providers, and so on.

Support the Child With CD. Be supportive and understanding of the difficulties associated with adhering to the GFD. Children on a GFD need to learn how to cope with being surrounded by others eating foods that they cannot eat. As such, children need to be able to discuss their feelings associated with this restriction. It is important to assist and support children in expressing their emotions regarding their diet and disease by reinforcing that it is normal to feel upset, angry, and/or sad. School should be an environment where unpleasant emotions can be expressed and coping strategies can be learned.

Support the Adults. Have an open and honest relationship with the family of a child with CD. The child and the family are typically the best sources of information on CD and the GFD and the best resources to ensure the safety and happiness of the child while in school. Be sensitive to the fact that raising (and educating) children can be exhausting and this can be heightened for those raising (and educating) a child with severe dietary restrictions. Adults often need to talk about their frustrations and feelings regarding their role in helping a child with CD, whether to a parent, psychologist, or educator.

Dietary Adherence. Maintaining proper nutrition is essential for any child, but this is especially the case with CD. Youth with CD have strict dietary restrictions that they must adhere to in order to avoid symptoms and long-term consequences. Adhering to the GFD at school can be extremely difficult for youth. Allowing access to alternative gluten-free (GF) foods for all youth in the classroom, not just for the child with CD, at special events and holidays may assist in reducing the burden and may alleviate feelings of being different. It can be heartbreaking for a child to be unable to eat special treats on special occasions, such as birthdays or holidays.

Parents of children with CD may need assistance to communicate the child's dietary needs to school food services. Educators and allied professionals can assist families by serving as liaisons between students with CD and their families and school food services. For example, food service employees must know the implications of cross-contamination of GF food in the food-prep environment for a child with CD and clean all utensils and work surfaces that have been exposed to gluten-containing foods. This is especially important for children who participate in free breakfast or lunch programs, as they may not have access to GF foods at home; obtaining them may be too great a financial hardship for the family. Moreover, schools are frequently able to grant special dietary accommodations for children with CD, such as having access to a microwave to heat lunch brought from home, as children with CD do not have the same convenient choices that typical children have for brown-bag lunches.

Managing Pain. Many youth with CD experience pain, be it dull or sharp, chronic or acute, or abdominal or joint. It is especially important to attend to pain in children who have been diagnosed recently and have not yet responded to the GFD. In addition, youth with CD can experience intense pain when GFD lapses occur. Furthermore, many children suffer in pain for years before being officially diagnosed and treated. Pain management and relaxation strategies can be taught to youth and their families; these may include diaphragmatic breathing, cooling and warming techniques, progressive muscle relaxation, and imagery.

Toileting Needs. An urgent need to use the bathroom, excess gas, and fecal soiling/incontinence can be common in youth with CD, especially if they are newly diagnosed or experience a lapse in the GFD. Enduring these symptoms can be embarrassing and at times traumatic for children, especially adolescents. Families and educators must be sensitive to this embarrassment and flexible regarding special toileting needs. Access to a private bathroom at school, standing permission to leave the classroom quickly to use the bathroom, and a place to store extra clothing can be helpful in reducing stress around toileting in school.

School Absenteeism. Absenteeism is a common problem associated with any chronic illness, and CD is no exception. For example, frequent illness, doctor appointments, diagnostic tests, and frequent fatigue and/or pain may affect a child's ability to get up, go to school, and concentrate. Such absences are common both when the child and family do not know what is wrong and as the diagnosis of CD is being pursued. Some children with CD may develop a negative attitude toward school due to perceived academic deficits, inability to engage in sports or activities due to symptoms such as fatigue, lack of flexibility from teachers and school personnel around mealtimes and toileting, and decreased time spent with peers. At times, youth with CD may refuse to go to school; this situation should be handled in collaboration with the child's educators. If the child's school performance is slipping, then a catch-up plan should be developed. It might include supplementary tutoring, individualized instruction, or a Section 504 plan (with accommodations to help the child adjust to the learning environment).

Psychological Treatment and Evaluation. For the majority of youth with CD, formal psychotherapy is not needed. However, for some youth who experience severe emotional disturbance or for families who are eager to find effective ways of helping their child or adolescent to cope with the disease, referral to a psychologist or counselor can be useful. Typically, the child's primary physician or pediatric gastroenterologist should be able to assist in finding the proper therapist. In addition, many medical centers have pediatric psychologists who are trained to provide behavioral and mental health interventions to youth in medical settings. They are typically available to educate families about the psychological, emotional, and social effects of physical symptoms and illnesses on children and to assess children's emotional and behavioral functioning. They also provide treatment services with the goals of enhancing children's and families' adjustment to a medical diagnosis; helping children and families follow a treatment regimen, such as adhering to the GFD or making changes in their routines; and teaching children skills for coping with stress and for managing pain. Educators have a unique perspective on a child's adjustment to living with a chronic disease and can be a first line for referral to a mental health professional.

EDUCATIONAL STRATEGIES

- The primary focus of CD management is adherence to a GFD.
- Be knowledgeable and mindful of GF snacks and foods in the classroom and cafeteria.
- Be aware of nonfood items that contain gluten (e.g., clay, paste, crayons), which may affect children with CD.
- Considerations must be made for toileting needs as appropriate.
- School absenteeism is a common issue that may need to be addressed via a Section 504 plan or other formal plan.
- Adjustment issues and behavior changes are common. A plan to promote positive changes in behavior needs to be put into place if this is an issue.
- Communicate any changes in behavior, including in academic performance, to the parents.

DISCUSSION QUESTIONS

1. How might educators and allied professionals facilitate the adjustment of students diagnosed with celiac disease?

2. Some children with celiac disease demonstrate behavioral challenges in home and at school. How might educators and allied professionals assist teachers and parents with changing maladaptive behaviors and replacing them with more adaptive behaviors? How might the principles of cognitive therapy be used?

3. What are some things that parents can do to enlist school professionals' help with coping with the diagnosis of CD and maintaining a gluten-free diet for their child?

4. How does the age of a student with celiac disease contribute to the presentation of symptoms and treatment? How do adolescents differ from younger children in regards to treatment and diet adherence?

RESEARCH SUMMARY

- Celiac disease is an underdiagnosed condition caused by intolerance to gluten. The body's immune system responds to gluten as if it were an infectious agent, causing damage to the gastrointestinal tract.
- Symptoms can include bloating, irritability, cramping, fatigue, weight loss, neurological symptoms, and others.
- The GFD is the only treatment for CD. It typically greatly reduces symptoms and leads to healing of the intestines.
- The GFD is difficult to maintain, especially for school-age children.
- Significant secondary effects of celiac disease may affect school performance and social interactions. These include school absenteeism, pain management, toileting needs, adherence to the strict dietary regimen, irritability, behavioral difficulties, and impact on family dynamics.

RESOURCES

Green, P., & Jones, R. (2006). *Celiac disease: A hidden epidemic.* New York: HarperCollins.

Hassett, S. (2009). *Living with celiac disease.* Bloomington, IN: Xlibris.

Shepard, J. E. D. (2008). *The first year: Celiac disease and living gluten-free; An essential guide for the newly diagnosed.* Cambridge, MA: DaCapo Press.

Tessmer, K. (2009). *Tell me what to eat if I have celiac disease.* Franklin Lakes, NJ: New Page Books.

The following Web site contains information about celiac disease and gluten-free diets: Celiac.com: www.celiac.com

HANDOUT

CELIAC DISEASE: HELPFUL HINTS FOR EDUCATORS

Having a child with celiac disease (CD) will affect some aspects of school and home life. Increased patience and understanding is important in executing the necessary changes for the child with CD and everyone else involved.

What is celiac disease, and who has it?

CD is a chronic, immune-mediated disease of the intestine triggered by the ingestion of gluten proteins. CD primarily is characterized by chronic inflammation of the surface of the small intestine in response to gluten, a water-insoluble protein component of wheat and other grains, such as rye and barley. In the United States, the prevalence of CD has been estimated to be 1 in 133 individuals. Although the rate of diagnosis is increasing in the United States, it is estimated that fewer than 5% of those with CD are currently diagnosed. Thus, having a child with CD in your family or classroom is becoming more and more likely.

What are the symptoms of CD?

The clinical presentation of CD in youth is diverse and varies by child, but it typically includes chronic diarrhea, weight loss, stunted growth, and abdominal distention. It is important to have open communication with the child's caregivers regarding the child's specific symptoms and how to identify when the child might have been exposed to gluten.

How is celiac disease treated?

The only accepted treatment for CD is lifelong adherence to a gluten-free diet (GFD), which requires the avoidance of all products derived from wheat, barley, and rye (and oats*). Complete avoidance of gluten-containing foods is exceedingly difficult, perhaps explaining in part why adherence to GFD is estimated to be only 45% to 80%.

Whose responsibility is the GFD?

Ultimately, it is ideal for the student with CD to take full responsibility for managing the GFD in school, but this of course depends on the developmental level of the child and the recency of the diagnosis. Educators can be helpful in assisting the child with CD in developing self-management skills. For example, adults can read food labels together with the child and identify suspect ingredients, making decisions together about whether or not a food is safe. Remember the goal is to provide the child with adequate information to help him or her to gain confidence and knowledge about living with CD and maintaining the GFD.

How does having a child with celiac disease affect the classroom?

- *Attendance.* Attendance can be an issue for a child with CD. It may take some time for symptoms to ameliorate after beginning the GFD. In addition, if or when lapses in the GFD occur, the resulting

---

* In some individuals with CD, the protein in oats (avenins) can trigger an immune response similar to that provoked by gluten. In addition, oats grown and processed in North America may be cross-contaminated with wheat, barley, and rye. Oats may need to be avoided by those newly diagnosed with CD until it can be clearly demonstrated that the CD is well controlled.

symptoms may send a child home from school. Medical appointments with gastroenterologists and nutritionists are also typical reasons for tardiness or absence.

- *Toileting needs.* Special restroom privileges may be needed for a child with CD at school due to an increased urgency to use the toilet. Having a special code for "running" to the restroom and placing the child's seat near the door may help in such circumstances.

- *Snacks and the cafeteria.* Many popular snack items contain gluten. The caregivers of a child with CD should be able to provide a supply of gluten-free snacks and a list of appropriate snacks if snacks from home are not available. Having a "stash" of gluten-free snacks in the classroom is helpful. Food service staff in the cafeteria should be educated about the disease to ensure safe food options for the child with CD. Educators can assist in reminding the child not to swap food or touch other foods, and they can clean table surfaces of residue that might contain gluten to avoid cross-contamination.

- *Miscellaneous items.* Many miscellaneous nonfood items may contain gluten and should be avoided due to the potential for contamination. For instance, popular brands of clay, crayons, and paints may contain gluten and may make their way into a child's body. Substitutions for craft projects that involve pasta and cereal will also be needed. Stickers and envelope glue that need to be licked can contain hidden gluten and should be avoided when working with young children. Theatrical makeup used in school plays, such as lipstick, can also include gluten. Remember this rule of thumb: "When in doubt, contact the child's caregiver."

11

Postpartum Depression and Its Relationship to Behavior Problems in Children

Danielle Parente and Paul C. McCabe

Vanessa is a 37-year-old mother with a daughter who is now 8 months old. Although it has been 8 months since the delivery, Vanessa has been experiencing feelings of restlessness and irritability, crying spells, lack of energy, overeating, and withdrawal from friends and family. Recently, she has been feeling so sad that she does not even feel like caring for the baby; she feels an overwhelming lack of confidence in her parenting skills. At first, Vanessa's husband thought it was normal for her to have "mood swings" after giving birth due to hormonal changes. However, he decided to contact the physician when her symptoms did not appear to improve over time.

Vanessa has been quietly suffering with depressive symptoms yet is resistant to telling her physician. After several efforts by her husband, she finally agreed to explain the symptoms to the doctor. The physician diagnosed her with postpartum depression (PPD) based on the symptoms she described. The physician explained that although the "baby blues" are common after giving birth, they do not last as long as PPD. She was diagnosed with PPD because her symptoms have persisted for 8 months.

The doctor recommended that Vanessa receive assistance with caring for the baby and house chores. In addition, daily counseling and a support group were implemented to help educate Vanessa about PPD and associated symptoms. Antidepressants are another option in alleviating the symptoms of PPD; however, her physician was reluctant to prescribe them initially because she is breast-feeding. Vanessa complied with the treatment and showed noticeable improvement in her behavior and mood. She responded well to the talk therapy and was relieved to discover other mothers who were experiencing the same feelings. Vanessa gained a sense of connectedness and no longer felt alone in her fight against PPD. Additionally, the baby showed improvement in sleep patterns and overall disposition.

INTRODUCTION

The development and long-term outcome of children whose mothers have experienced postnatal depression is an issue of considerable importance. Research has shown that depression occurring in the first few months post-partum is associated with an increased risk for both behavioral and emotional problems in children. The incidence of postpartum depression (PPD) in Western societies is approximately 10% to 15%. Its cause is multifaceted (Grace, Evindar, & Stewart, 2003). Because mothers primarily constitute infants' social environment and mediate their experiences with the external world, it is important to elucidate how PPD impacts child development and may contribute to emotional and/or behavioral problems in children.

BACKGROUND

Maternal depression is one of many correlates to behavior problems in children. Other correlates include negative mother-partner interactions, caregiver environments, parenting styles, and family conflict. Nevertheless, a number of studies directly link maternal depression to behavioral problems in children (Elgar, Curtis, McGrath, Waschbusch, & Stewart, 2003).

West and Newman (2003) conducted a study that examined how mild parental symptoms of depression and anxiety could be predictive of temperament and behavior patterns in preschool-age children. The results revealed that mild parental depression was linked to increased levels of internalizing and externalizing behavior problems in the children, as well as difficulty with attention and emotion regulation. Mild parental anxiety was also linked to child behavior problems, but it was more associated with children's temperamental difficulties in attention and emotion regulation. However, another study examining depressed women with disruptive children, nondepressed women with disruptive children, and nondiagnosed women and children found that disruptive children displayed overall negative behavior regardless of the mothers' clinical status (McFarland & Sanders, 2003).

Phillips and O'Hara (1991) investigated the effects of postpartum depression on behavior problems in a 4½-year follow-up study. Of the 90 mothers who had participated in the earlier study, 70 were evaluated for later maternal depression. Most of the mothers were Caucasian and married. The women who experienced postpartum depression were found to have experienced depression during the past 4½ years; however, parent-rated scores of children's behavior problems were close to normal, despite previous maternal PPD. PPD was directly related to subsequent maternal depression but not child behavior problems. Only concurrent depression is related to child behavior problems later in preschool (Grace et al., 2003).

Cicchetti, Rogosch, and Toth (1998) examined how maternal depression influences child development and how contextual risks mediate the relationship between maternal depression and child behavioral problems. The authors expected that offspring of mothers with a major depressive disorder (MDD) would exhibit more maladaptive developmental outcomes than offspring of mothers with no history of a psychiatric disorder. These children were also predicted to be more likely to have behavior problems (Cicchetti et al.). The hypothesis was that toddlers with depressed mothers would be exposed to contextual risks, such as marital discord, family conflict, lower levels of social support, and higher stress. This study was designed as a matched comparison group to evaluate (a) the extent to which contextual risk contributed to insecure attachments and child behavior problems in concert with maternal depression and (b) the extent to which contextual risk could provide an explanatory mechanism linking maternal depression and these child developmental outcomes.

The participants were a subset of a larger longitudinal study on the effects of maternal depression on child development. Results indicated that when children of depressed mothers were compared with those of the nondepressed mother group, there were significant differences in total behavioral problems and marginally significant group differences in internalizing behaviors but no differences in externalizing behaviors (Cicchetti et al., 1998). In addition, when contextual risk factors were measured, the relationship between total number of behavior problems and maternal depression disappeared, but the effect of maternal depression on internalizing child behavior remained.

Murray and colleagues (1999) conducted a 5-year longitudinal study to investigate the development of 5-year-old children with mothers with and without PPD. Maternal and teacher reports were used to rate child behavior, and mother-child interaction was rated with time-sampled videotape. Results indicated that the child's behavior with the mother, presence of behavior disturbance at home, and quality of social play at school were related to the presence of PPD in the home, even when accounting for maternal depression and parental conflict. The child's relationship with his or her mother was related to the quality of their attachment at 18 months, and current conflicts between the mother and the child's father were predictive of the quality of behavior the mother exhibited to her child. The authors concluded that while maternal behavior varies depending on changes in the environment, the child's exposure to PPD in the first months of life may have a lasting effect on the child's psychological functioning.

Elgar and colleagues (2003) examined the relationship between maternal depressive symptoms and child adjustment problems over a 4-year period. The study used cross-lagged panels that involved three cycles of data and utilized the National Longitudinal Survey of Children and Youth (NLSCY). The results indicated that maternal depression doubled the rates of each child problem area (e.g., hyperactivity, aggression, and emotional problems). Although maternal and child symptoms were found to be correlated, differences between cross-lagged correlations showed that maternal depression tended to precede child hyperactivity and aggression and to follow child emotional problems.

Another research team conducted a longitudinal study using growth-mixture modeling to organize classes of depressed mothers over the course of their depression. Their children were assessed from infancy through 6.5 years on behavioral and physiological measures. Results indicated that the children of chronically depressed mothers had elevated externalizing behavior problems, poorer social competence, reduced frontal lobe activation, and abnormal respiratory and heart rhythm. Those children whose mothers had milder depression or depression that was abating were more likely to exhibit increased hyperactivity and inattention compared to children of nondepressed mothers (Ashman, Dawson, & Panagiotides, 2008).

Maternal Depression and Childhood ADHD

Research on maternal depression and behavior problems in children has also examined brain activity, maternal depression and children with attention deficit/hyperactivity disorder (ADHD), marital conflict, and the effects of behavioral problems on the mothers' functioning. A study conducted by Dawson and colleagues (2003) examined behavior problems and brain electrical activity in 3-year-old children of mothers with and without a history of depression. The findings revealed that children of depressed mothers had lower brain activation in the parietal and frontal areas of the brain than children of nondepressed mothers. In addition, children of chronically depressed mothers also had higher levels of externalizing behavior problems.

Another study examined the relationship between maternal depression and parenting as a predictive measure of children with ADHD later developing a conduct disorder (Chronis et al., 2007). They found that maternal depression predicted later conduct problems in children with ADHD. However, early positive parenting skills had a resiliency effect and predicted fewer conduct problems. Similarly, a study of Korean mothers with ADHD children found that those mothers who used corporal punishment on their children were more likely to suffer from depression (Shin & Stein, 2008). The use of harsher forms of discipline is predictive of later behavior and conduct problems, and it appears that children with ADHD are particularly susceptible to negative parenting behaviors when their parents suffer from depression.

Child-Family Dynamics

Franck and Buehler (2007) explored the mediating role of adolescents' perceptions of triangulation (e.g., parents bringing the child into the middle of disputes). Their study included marital hostility, as well as mothers' and fathers' depressive affect and the effect it has on behavior in children. The findings revealed that triangulation was related to adolescent internalizing but not to externalizing problems. Mothers' depressive affect was related to adolescent internalizing behaviors. In contrast, fathers' depressive affect was related to both internalizing and externalizing problems.

Garstein and Sheeber (2004) examined (a) how child behavior problems are related to disrupted family functioning and lowered maternal self-efficacy and (b) how these outcomes mediate the relations between initial levels of child behavior problems and subsequent maternal symptoms of depression. They found that mothers whose children who exhibit behavior problems and interfere with family functioning tend to have feelings of incompetence and are at risk for increasing depressive symptoms.

Another study examined the transactional relationship between boys' externalizing behaviors and mothers' depressive symptoms over time. The disruptive and antisocial behaviors of boys ages 5 to 15 were compared to maternal depression using a parallel processing model with cross-lagged associations. The model indicated reciprocal effects between parent and child such that maternal depression predicted behavior problems in the boys and disruptive and antisocial behaviors exhibited by the boys predicted exacerbated maternal depression. Also, notable transition periods (age 5–6 years old as the child started school and again at 11–12 years old at the emergence of adolescence) had strong effects, suggesting that these may be particularly challenging ages for depressed mothers and their children (Gross, Shaw, & Moilanen, 2008).

IMPLICATIONS FOR EDUCATORS

The effects of maternal depression on children are not limited to behavioral problems. Maternal depression may also contribute to a child's poor peer relationships, difficulty in school, grade retention, and dropping out of school. Schools need to be proactive and get involved in supporting families by providing information and resources about maternal depression and child development. Awareness programs can be implemented in school or the community to assist families in receiving necessary education and support. Many parents are unaware of the effects that maternal depression can have on their children. Educators can help families seek out the proper care to treat depression, behavior problems in children, and family conflict.

Educators can play an important role in identifying mothers experiencing maternal depression. Educators are more likely to be in contact with parents on an ongoing basis than health care professionals. Parent-teacher conferences can be a forum to discover how parents are coping with their child's behavior, as well as overall family dynamics. Schools can provide educators with professional development opportunities that strengthen their skills in assessing maternal depression, child mental health, and the impact of community on families' mental health. Early identification of maternal depression coupled with comprehensive family intervention services can help to minimize the adverse consequences of maternal depression, childhood behavior problems, and family conflict.

Support groups have been shown to reduce depressive symptoms. In addition to providing support, they reduce the stigma of mental health problems and the services intended to ameliorate them. Educators can work with the communities they service and help identify or advocate for programs that provide screening and referrals, health education workshops, and home visitation for maternal depression. For example, the Caribbean Women's Health Association in New York City organizes the Community Mom's Program. This program is designed for immigrant women who are pregnant and parenting children from birth to age 2 (Knitzer, Theberge, & Johnson, 2008). In Boston, a program called Family Connections implemented at Head Start and Early Head Start sites is designed to build competency among the staff to engage with parents on issues of depression, adversity, parenting skills, and seeking services for children and families in emotional distress (Knitzer et al.).

Programs like these are successful because they help identify children and families in crisis (when they may otherwise have been overlooked or have failed to seek help on their own). Since educators spend a significant amount of time with children and their families, it makes sense to equip educators with the skills needed to identify, intervene with, and refer children and their families who are experiencing depression and conflict. Early identification of parental depression, family conflict, and child behavior problems can help families obtain the support they need and prevent exacerbation of problems.

EDUCATIONAL STRATEGIES

- Disseminate information to other educators and parents that childhood behavioral problems are not limited to ADHD but can be a result of maternal depression, caregiver environments, parenting styles, and family conflict.
- Implement schoolwide programs for educators and parents designed to prevent childhood behavioral problems and provide support to overwhelmed families.
- Perform outreach and education to expectant mothers and new mothers to prepare them for potential depressive symptoms, address the stigma associated with depression, and provide resources from which they can seek help.
- Create a list of maternal depression symptoms to help educators identify and assist families in obtaining appropriate care.
- Create workshops that provide parents with information about parenting skills, child development, and mental health issues before and after childbirth.
- Build a comprehensive network of community service providers to strengthen mental health services for both expecting and postpartum families.

DISCUSSION QUESTIONS

1. Is screening for maternal depression prior to birth helpful in determining the development of postpartum depression?

2. What resources can expectant mothers use to educate themselves on parenting and postpartum depression? What can health care providers do to assist mothers in obtaining this information?

3. How might early interventions for postpartum depression affect a child's development both emotionally and psychologically?

4. How might behavioral interventions for problematic child behaviors eventually improve depressive symptoms in the mother?

5. What role can educators play when behavioral problems are exhibited in the classroom? How can educators support mothers who are depressed with their child's behavior problems?

6. What types of psychological services can schools provide for children living with a parent who suffers from a mental illness? How can these services enhance the child's learning and psychological development?

RESEARCH SUMMARY

- The incidence of postpartum depression in Western societies is approximately 10% to 15%. Its cause is multifaceted.
- Evidence suggests that children reared in families with parental depression and family conflict are more likely to develop both internalizing and externalizing behaviors.
- The quality of attachment between mother and infant has implications for the long-term adjustment of the child. This attachment process can be hindered when the primary caregiver is suffering from depression.
- There appears to be a reciprocal relationship in which maternal depression exacerbates child behavior problems and the worsening behavior aggravates the parent's depressive symptoms.
- Maternal depression is linked to increased levels of both internalizing and externalizing behavior problems in children, as well as difficulty with attention and emotion regulation.
- For children with ADHD, parenting styles and maternal depression are predictive of developing a conduct disorder.

RESOURCES

FamilyDoctor.org, "Postpartum Depression and the Baby Blues": http://family doctor.org/online/famdocen/home/women/pregnancy/ppd/general/379 .html

Mental Health America (formerly the National Mental Health Association): www.mentalhealthamerica.net

National Institute of Mental Health: http://science.education.nih.gov/supplements/ nih5/Mental/default.htm. NIMH, part of the National Institutes of Health, publishes this curriculum supplement, which includes links to resources for teachers about mental illness and its treatment.

Postpartum Education for Parents: www.sbpep.org

Postpartum Support International: http://postpartum.net

WomensHealth.gov, "Depression During and After Pregnancy": www.4women .gov/faq/postpartum.htm. This Web site is produced by the National Women's Health Information Center, part of the U.S. Department of Health and Human Services.

HANDOUT

IDENTIFYING AND TREATING POSTPARTUM DEPRESSION

Postpartum depression can happen any time within the first year after childbirth. A mother may experience a number of symptoms, including sadness, lack of energy, trouble concentrating, anxiety, and feelings of guilt and worthlessness. The difference between postpartum depression and the "baby blues" is that postpartum depression often affects a woman's well-being and lasts for a longer period of time.

Some of the treatments for postpartum depression (PPD) include psychotherapy and medication such as antidepressants. Psychotherapy involves talking to a psychologist or social worker to learn how to change the way depression makes you think, feel, and act. Antidepressants can also be considered to treat symptoms of depression, but care should be taken when the mother is breast-feeding. When taking medication, it is important to follow the instructions from the physician, as well as instructions that come with the medications.

The diagnostic signs of PPD include the following:

- Feeling restless, irritable, sad, hopeless, and overwhelmed
- Crying a lot and having no energy or motivation
- Eating too little or too much on a regular basis
- Sleeping too little or too much on a regular basis
- Loss of interest or pleasure in activities that were previously enjoyable
- Withdrawal from friends and family
- Physiological symptoms, such as headaches, chest pains, heart palpitations, or hyperventilation

The U.S. Department of Health and Human Services reports that fatigue after delivery, disrupted sleep pattern, and insufficient rest often keep a new mother from regaining her full strength for weeks after delivery, which may contribute to PPD. Other factors that may contribute to PPD are hormonal changes in the mother's body. Two hormones that increase during pregnancy are estrogen and progesterone. After childbirth, these hormones rapidly drop back to prepregnancy levels. This rapid change can contribute to PPD. Postpartum depression needs to be treated in consultation with a physician. Counseling, support groups, and, in some cases, medication can relieve symptoms and improve the overall well-being of the mother and child.

Untreated depression may cause additional psychological and physical stress not only for the mother but for the entire family. Symptoms such as lack of energy, trouble concentrating, and irritability can render the mother unable to nurture, care for, and show affection to her child. This may lead to feelings of guilt and loss of confidence in parenting ability and may interfere with the attachment process between mother and child. Untreated maternal PPD can also affect the infant by causing delays in language development and emotional bonding with others; increasing behavioral problems, sleep problems, and distress; and lowering activity level. If you or someone you know is suffering from PPD, tell a loved one or call your doctor right away.

12

Pediatric Responses to Asthma*

An Overview for Educators

Adrienne Garro

Louis is a 13-year-old sixth grader with moderate, persistent asthma who attends a public middle school. He was diagnosed with asthma at age 5 and experiences almost daily symptoms of coughing, wheezing, and shortness of breath. Louis has been prescribed short-acting relief medication (Proventil inhaler) and controller medications (Flovent and Singulair) to prevent and treat his symptoms, but he does not use these on a consistent basis. Louis's parents report that he is a difficult and oppositional teenager who often refuses to follow directions because he "thinks he knows it all." Louis was retained in second grade due to poor academic progress, particularly in reading. He was evaluated by the child study team in third grade and found to have a number of academic weaknesses, but these were not significant enough to warrant special education classification.

Louis continues to struggle academically and reports that he "hates school with the exception of lunch, gym, and recess." He is described by his teachers as bright and kind but also frequently sullen and moody. Louis enjoys sports, especially football and basketball, but he often needs to stop or limit his participation in these activities, as well as gym and recess, due to his asthma symptoms.

*Adapted from Garro, A. (2008). Health-related quality of life in pediatric asthma: An overview for school psychologists. *Communiqué, 36*(8), 33–37. Copyright by the National Association of School Psychologists, Bethesda, MD. Use is by permission of the publisher. www.nasponline.org

Consider the following: What additional assessment information should be gathered to understand better the impact of asthma on Louis's functioning? As an educator, what recommendations would you make to Louis's family to help improve management of his asthma at home? What steps or strategies can be implemented to improve Louis's functioning in his school and community?

INTRODUCTION

As the most common chronic illness of childhood, affecting almost 9% of all children, asthma is encountered on a regular basis in schools. Although educators are often aware of the basic symptoms of asthma (e.g., shortness of breath, wheezing, etc.), they are often less aware of the psychological and emotional responses to this illness and its implications for students' everyday functioning. The impact of pediatric asthma can be better understood by examining health-related quality of life (HRQOL). HRQOL entails the multiple effects of a health condition upon a person, including the experience of symptoms and the impact of the condition and its treatment on everyday activities (Schipper, Clinch, & Powell, 1990). HRQOL in students with asthma can be enhanced through a number of educational and psychosocial strategies.

BACKGROUND

When examining the effects of pediatric asthma and HRQOL, it is important to consider three domains: (a) the experience of symptoms, (b) the impact of these symptoms and asthma treatments on everyday activities, and (c) the psychosocial implications of this illness. These three domains are inextricably linked with one another, and all are influenced by a wide array of factors.

Experience of Symptoms

With respect to symptoms, cases of asthma are categorized according to four levels of severity (National Heart, Lung, and Blood Institute [NHLBI], 2007):

1. Intermittent: Characterized by episodes of symptoms twice a week or less, nighttime symptoms twice a month or less, and no symptoms and normal lung functioning between episodes.

2. Mild persistent: Characterized by episodes of symptoms more than twice a week but no more than once per day, nighttime symptoms more than twice a month, and asthma attacks that may affect everyday activities.

3. Moderate persistent: Characterized by daily episodes of symptoms, nighttime symptoms more than once per week, exacerbations twice a week or more that may last days, and asthma attacks that may affect activity and sleep.

4. Severe persistent: Characterized by episodes of symptoms throughout the day on most days, frequent nighttime symptoms, and physical activity that is likely to be limited.

Some researchers and practitioners have begun to utilize new systems of asthma management. Yawn, Brenneman, Allen-Ramey, Cabana, and Markson (2006) emphasized the importance of incorporating measures of asthma control and patients' responses to treatment, such as reports of symptom severity and frequency, assessment of everyday limitations due to asthma episodes, and reports of the need to use rescue medications. School clinicians and educators can play key roles in these systems of management by assisting in medication monitoring, educating other school personnel about medication side effects, and ensuring that students with asthma receive appropriate accommodations and services. These may include use of medical devices (e.g., peak flow meter), individual and/or family counseling, assessment of leisure functioning and development of appropriate recreational activities, parent training, and school health and/or medical services.

In examining the experience and frequency of asthma symptoms, known as asthma morbidity, it is important to consider the role of sociodemographic factors. For example, low socioeconomic status and living in poverty have been found to be associated with greater asthma prevalence and morbidity (CDC, 2009). Negative health outcomes from asthma have also been linked with single-parent households, younger maternal age, and lower parental education levels (Grant, Lyttle, & Weiss, 2000). Asthma is more likely to strike children living in urban areas due to greater exposure to pollutants and trigger factors, higher levels of radiation from heated surfaces such as rooftops, and decreased vegetation coverage in comparison to more suburban and rural regions. The combination of poverty and urban environment is especially detrimental and contributes to increased rates of hospitalization and emergency department visits (Kimes et al., 2004). Consequently, school professionals who are employed in poor and/or urban areas are more likely to serve students who suffer from serious and/or uncontrolled asthma. These students are likely to require greater surveillance and monitoring with respect to their physical health and psychosocial functioning.

In addition to the above factors, race/ethnicity appears to play a key role in asthma HRQOL. Some research indicates that the prevalence and morbidity of asthma are higher among African-American and Puerto Rican children in comparison to White children (Lara, Akinbami, Flores, & Morgenstern, 2006). Students from these backgrounds with asthma, especially those who have other risk factors, are more likely than others to experience negative HRQOL and require monitoring of their symptoms and screening for asthma-related psychosocial problems.

Impact on Student Functioning

When it comes to the impact of pediatric asthma on everyday functioning, the past decade has seen a number of positive changes. Many of these are attributable to improved recognition and treatment, including disease management programs and school- or home-based educational programs. Such programs teach children and adolescents with asthma, as well as their families, to identify symptoms early, use medications appropriately, and recognize and reduce exposure to asthma triggers and risk factors (e.g., dust, pollen, cigarette smoke). In addition, a wide variety of medications, ranging from quick-acting inhalers (e.g., Atrovent) to long-term combination drugs (e.g., Advair), are efficacious in combating symptoms and improving lung functioning.

Other good news related to HRQOL is that many youth with asthma, especially in the mild to moderate range, are able to function satisfactorily in school. Annett, Aylward, Bender, Lapidus, and DuHamel (2000) found that most children with asthma do not experience permanent neurological damage related to loss of oxygen. Results from several studies (e.g., Johansen, 2004) indicate that most students with asthma demonstrate academic achievement that is comparable to that of their healthy peers.

Despite this progress, many children and adolescents with asthma continue to experience poor HRQOL, including reduced participation in physical and recreational activities (e.g., extracurricular sports, gym class), disrupted social interactions, and reduced involvement with peers. Many students with asthma experience higher rates of school absenteeism compared to healthy peers (Shohat, Graif, Garty, Livne, & Green, 2005). These absences can result in disruptions in learning and/or decreased involvement in academic activities.

As is the case with other chronic illnesses, HRQOL in asthma is also related to indirect effects of the disease as well as its treatment. For example, a number of students with asthma experience fatigue, which may be attributable to a current episode of reduced lung functioning or an episode that occurred at night and disrupted sleep (Lenney, 1997). In addition, while a wide array of effective asthma medications are now available, students taking these medications must also deal with possible side effects, such as headache, throat irritation, and hoarseness from inhaled corticosteroids; mood changes and decreased or blurry vision from oral corticosteroids; or headache, nausea, and diarrhea from leukotriene modifiers (ALA, 2009).

Psychosocial Implications

The psychosocial implications of pediatric asthma are manifold. For clinicians and educators, it is important to emphasize that each child's or adolescent's psychological response to the illness is unique and needs to be considered in the context of demographic and environmental factors. These unique responses notwithstanding, the research literature indicates that asthma does impose stress and psychosocial challenges on children and adolescents. For example, research by McQuaid, Kopel, and Nassau (2001) and Klinnert, McQuaid, McCormick, Adinoff, and Bryant (2000) found higher levels of behavioral difficulties in children with asthma compared to healthy children. The above studies and other research (e.g., Alati et al., 2005) indicate that children and youth with asthma are particularly at risk for internalizing problems such as anxiety and depression. The relationship between asthma and these difficulties is complex and reciprocal. Students with asthma may experience anxiety because they worry about asthma attacks and the effects on their daily lives; at the same time, anxiety and distress can increase the likelihood of an attack and exacerbate symptoms.

Some research indicates that a person's current asthma status is associated with the condition's psychosocial impact. For example, Halterman and colleagues (2006) found that greater asthma severity is associated with higher likelihood of behavioral difficulties. Other studies have found that it is not severity but rather variables such as the general health of the child or parent and family functioning that better explain differences in psychological functioning and HRQOL (Calam, Gregg, & Goodman, 2005). Although it is apparent that parent and family factors are related to HRQOL in pediatric asthma, the specific mechanisms are unclear. It is possible that these variables affect HRQOL and other asthma outcomes through asthma management strategies practiced at home (e.g., adherence to medication regimens; Klinnert, McQuaid, & Gavin, 1997) and/or through psychophysiological pathways (Wright, Rodriguez, & Cohen, 1998).

IMPLICATIONS FOR EDUCATORS

Given the high prevalence of pediatric asthma, educators are likely to encounter students with this condition on a regular basis. Collaboration among families, schools, medical professionals, and students themselves is vital to effective asthma management. Educators not only need to be aware of students' individual asthma symptoms but also knowledgeable regarding other factors that can impact the course and progression of the illness. These include severity level, subtypes, and patterns of symptoms (e.g., seasonal variations). In addition, school professionals can make valuable contributions when it comes to assessing the impact of asthma on students' everyday functioning and quality of life. This can be done through the use of surveys, such as the Adolescent and Child Health and Illness Profiles (Starfield et al., 1995), or through semistructured interviews. In assessing HRQOL, clinicians and educators should obtain a comprehensive picture of functioning that takes into account additional risk factors (e.g., poverty, low availability of appropriate health care), as well as student and family strengths and resources. Results from such assessments can be used by educational teams to gauge the impact of asthma on different areas of school functioning and to develop appropriate accommodations and interventions.

Educators must be competent in determining and providing appropriate services, accommodations, and interventions for students with asthma. It is essential to consider each student individually and not use a cookie-cutter approach. Each student with asthma should have an individual asthma action plan that specifies his or her symptoms and management. Due to possible side effects, students who take medication on a regular basis may require specific school-based accommodations, such as medication monitoring. Those with severe asthma may be eligible for a classification of "other health impaired" and receive special education and related services. Students with less severe asthma may be eligible for accommodations under Section 504, since their disease constitutes a physical impairment that significantly limits one or more major life activities. More recently, research and clinical practice have highlighted links between pediatric asthma and obesity (Figueroa-Muñoz, Chinn, & Rona, 2001). Due to the challenges posed by the combination of these conditions, it is important for school clinicians to collaborate with teachers and families to develop nutritional counseling as well as appropriate exercise and weight management programs.

School professionals can also fulfill important roles with respect to counseling and behavioral interventions in pediatric asthma. Because students with asthma are at higher risk for anxiety disorders and depression, early detection and screening may prevent the development of these problems. If students are already experiencing depression or anxiety, then school psychologists and other professionals can conduct individual or group counseling to help them understand and cope with stressors and emotions related to their disease. Although the use of specific counseling techniques with students with asthma has not been widely studied, preliminary research suggests that the teaching of active coping strategies, such as relaxation combined with guided imagery and writing about stressful experiences, can be effective in enhancing psychological as well as physical well-being (Peck, Bray, & Kehle, 2003).

EDUCATIONAL STRATEGIES

- Educate students, teachers, and other school professionals and staff about asthma symptoms and management. Schools can obtain free asthma toolkits online to help develop asthma education programs (e.g., American Lung Association: www.lungusa.org/site/pp .asp?c=dvLUK9O0E&b=22590).
- Work collaboratively with families and students themselves to ensure appropriate asthma management in schools. All students with asthma should have asthma action plans that are readily accessible to teachers, school nurses, and other relevant school professionals.
- Medication monitoring is essential for all students with asthma, not only to ensure that their illness is being treated effectively but also to observe potential side effects and maximize participation in school activities.
- Develop a coordinated plan to facilitate positive adjustment for students who miss school for extended periods due to asthma. Such a plan should help these students to progress academically and maintain connections with peers and recreational activities. Information regarding school reintegration plans can be found online (e.g., U.K. Department for Education and Skills: www.dcsf .gov.uk/research/data/uploadfiles/RR598.pdf).
- Students with asthma, especially those from high-risk backgrounds, should be screened for anxiety and depression on a regular basis.
- School clinicians who are appropriately trained can develop positive coping skills in students with asthma through the use of relaxation and guided imagery techniques as well as appropriate recreational activities.

DISCUSSION QUESTIONS

1. What types of child, family, and school factors have an effect on quality of life in pediatric asthma? How do these factors contribute positively or negatively to quality of life?

2. How might different types of asthma medications affect a student's functioning in school? What are the potential positive and negative effects from these medications?

3. How can educators assess the impact of asthma on students' functioning?

4. How can educators work collaboratively with families and health care providers to improve management of pediatric asthma?

5. Besides medication, what other interventions can be beneficial in improving outcomes for pediatric asthma?

RESEARCH SUMMARY

- Asthma is the most common pediatric chronic illness, affecting almost 9% of all children ages birth to 17.

- Asthma prevalence and morbidity are higher among African-American and Puerto Rican children. In addition, poverty and living in urban areas are associated with more negative asthma outcomes.

- Quality of life has improved for many children with asthma due to advances in medication and the development of educational management programs. Despite these advances, pediatric asthma, especially more severe and/or uncontrolled asthma, continues to present significant health and psychosocial challenges, including disruptions in school functioning, activity limitations, and greater risk for anxiety disorders and depression.

- Schools can most effectively address pediatric asthma by working collaboratively with families, students, and medical professionals; comprehensively assessing the impact of the illness on student functioning; and adopting an individualized approach to intervention.

- Students with asthma can benefit from educational interventions that teach them to recognize and manage symptoms. Some students will also benefit from interventions that teach active coping strategies.

RESOURCES

Dozor, A. J., & Kelly, K. (2004). *The asthma and allergy action plan for kids: A complete program to help your child live a full and active life.* New York: Simon & Schuster.

Lewis, J., Allen, T., Bryant-Stephens, N. A., Pawlowski, S. B., & Jablow, M. M. (Eds.). (2004). *The Children's Hospital of Philadelphia guide to asthma: How to help your child live a healthier life.* Hoboken, NJ: John Wiley & Sons.

The American Lung Association Web site offers extensive information about asthma, including its specific impact on children, monitoring and treatments, and current research: www.lungusa.org/site/c.dvLUK9O0E/b.33276/k.D288/Asthma.htm

HANDOUT

PEDIATRIC RESPONSES TO ASTHMA

The most effective approach to reducing the burden of a child's asthma involves both prevention and intervention. Most importantly, families need to follow the medication regimen prescribed by their child's health care provider, make sure that he or she has a complete health history of their child, and discuss the positive effects and potential side effects of asthma medications. Many effective medications are available to control, treat, and even prevent asthma attacks. The table below lists some of the most commonly used medications for pediatric asthma.

Type of Medication	Possible Side Effects
Inhaled bronchodilators: Can be short-acting relief or longer-acting controller medications.	Increased heart rate, nausea, vomiting, nervousness, headache, palpitations, sleeplessness, tremors, shaking feeling
Anti-inflammatories: These long-term control medications to prevent attacks must be taken regularly to be effective.	Side effects vary depending upon the specific type of medication.
a. Corticosteroids: Can be oral or inhaled. (These are different from the performance-enhancing steroids taken by some athletes.)	a. For corticosteroids, side effects range from increased thirst and appetite, skin rash, and insomnia for the oral form to dry mouth, cough, and headache for the inhaled form.
b. Leukotriene modifiers: This is a newer class of medications; they are taken orally.	b. For leukotriene modifiers, they include headache, nausea, diarrhea, and infection.
c. Other anti-inflammatories: May be oral (e.g., Tilade) or inhaled (e.g., Intal).	c. For other anti-inflammatories, they include coughing, shortness of breath, skin rash/itching, headache, sore throat, and nausea.

Families should keep a record of all medications that the child is taking that includes the name of the medicine; its purpose, dosage, and frequency of administration; and side effects that the child experiences, if applicable. In addition, the following steps can be taken to manage a child's asthma effectively and improve his or her quality of life.

- Families, teachers, and other professionals need to maintain clear communication and take a collaborative approach to asthma management. Many states require schools to implement asthma action plans, which are written plans that recognize signs of asthma attacks, take specific steps based on symptoms and peak flow readings, manage medications, and organize contact information for the student.
- Reduce or, if possible, eliminate a child's exposure to triggers that may cause or aggravate asthma symptoms.
- Educate yourself and others regarding specifics about a child's asthma, including severity level; subtypes (e.g., exercise-induced), if applicable; and patterns of symptoms, including seasonal variations.
- Educate children, using developmentally appropriate language, about their asthma and ways that it can be managed.
- Investigate asthma intervention programs that may be offered in your community. Examples include asthma summer camps, which provide medical supervision and recreational and educational activities; group-based educational programs, such as Open Airways for Schools; and asthma toolkits, which provide planning activities and other tools for schools to collaborate with families and health organizations.

13

Food Allergies and Intolerances

What Educators Need to Know

Doris Páez and Gillian W. Thomas

Ellen is a 7-year-old student entering second grade. She has a positive history of severe allergic reactions, including anaphylactic shock in reaction to peanuts. Ellen had a near-fatal reaction to peanut butter at age 4. Even being in the proximity of peanuts or peanut shells triggers a reaction that includes hives and difficulty breathing. Processed foods not containing nuts often share kitchen equipment that comes in contact with nuts; this trace amount of nuts also creates significant breathing problems for Ellen. Fried foods, too, commonly use peanut oil and create serious problems for Ellen.

In addition, at age 7, Ellen once suffered anaphylactic shock in response to a bee sting. Her parents, upon recognizing the symptoms, used the injectable epinephrine prescribed for her peanut allergies. She responded quickly.

Ellen's parents are well practiced in managing her severe allergies. Ellen's mother takes Ellen out of school during lunch period. They often eat a home-prepared lunch in a local park. Ellen knows to leave the class when birthday treats are passed around, as cakes and cookies may contain trace amounts of peanuts. Ellen's parents drive her several miles to school because they have concerns about peanut exposure on the school bus.

Ellen is not judged to be old enough or responsible enough to carry injectable epinephrine during the school day. Ellen's teacher received training in how to deliver injectable epinephrine and has the kit in her desk. When Ellen leaves the classroom for music or physical education, the injectable epinephrine kit is passed to the appropriate teacher, who is also trained in the use of the kit. Ellen wears a waist pack with the injectable epinephrine while at recess or in the community. She wears a medical alert bracelet describing her conditions with directions for the injectable epinephrine. Rarely is her kit more than a few feet away.

Ellen often feels isolated from her peers, as common social experiences during mealtime and recess are limited by her need to avoid any exposure to peanuts. Birthday parties, sleepovers, and eating in restaurants are also challenging for Ellen. Playing outside can be dangerous due to bee sting allergies. The result is that Ellen does not have the same social experiences as most second-grade students. Ellen's parents have concerns about her social skills and ability to make friends. Therefore, they frequently invite students to Ellen's home, where Ellen can be in a safe, peanut-free environment. However, Ellen has developed severe anxiety concerning possible exposure to peanuts or bees. She often quizzes classmates on whether they have eaten peanut butter in the last day before she will play with them. To many of her classmates, this behavior is odd and serves to isolate Ellen further.

For Ellen, peanut allergies have become as debilitating medically and socially as many chronic illnesses. For Ellen's family, friends, and school, her peanut allergies are a focal point of their relationship with Ellen.

INTRODUCTION

The most highly publicized and researched health issues for children, adolescents, and their adult supervisors are food allergies. The number of children diagnosed with food allergies has doubled in the past 10 to 20 years (Sicherer, 2006). This is partly due to increased awareness, but there is also evidence that allergies are more common than in the past. Between 2% and 8% of the children in the United States have food allergies (LeBovidge et al., 2006). In the school-aged population, approximately 2.2 million children have food allergies. One in every 17 children under the age of 3 has food allergies. An estimated 50 percent of people with food allergies may experience anaphylaxis or a serious allergic reaction that is rapid in onset and may cause death. The Food Allergy and Anaphylaxis Network (FAAN) reported that anaphylaxis accounts for 50,000 emergency room visits each year (2008b) and that more than 150 people die annually from anaphylaxis (2008a).

The food allergy epidemic has had a profound impact on the functioning of all persons (e.g., classmates, friends, parents, teachers, coaches) surrounding children and adolescents. It has increased the need for education, communication, and vigilance. Society is becoming increasingly aware that all the places in which children and adolescents learn and develop healthy social relationships outside of their homes (e.g., child care centers, schools, afterschool programs, summer camps) could be potentially life threatening and should be made safer (Lyons & Forde, 2004).

BACKGROUND

What Is a Food Allergy?

Many children experience adverse reactions at least once to food at some time in their lives, and many parents or adult supervisors may mistakenly believe that these children have food allergies. However, a food allergy is one of a number of adverse reactions that a child can have to food. Researchers distinguish between *food intolerances* and *food allergies*. A diagnosis of food allergy usually is made on history alone, but blood tests and skin-prick testing are usually used to support the diagnosis. A food allergy is an abnormal immunologic response to food proteins that can produce acute, life-threatening reactions and/or chronic disease that affects daily life. Intolerances are reactions to food that do not involve the immune system, such as lactose intolerance. Food poisoning is also a form of intolerance.

Although food intolerance is gradual and variable, food allergies are rapid, highly visible reactions that are readily linked to a food. The symptoms of a food-allergic reaction range from mild to moderate skin, respiratory, and gastrointestinal symptoms to life-threatening anaphylaxis or anaphylactic shock. The most commonly affected body part is the skin. Hives is the most common skin symptom. The skin can become red and itchy, and sometimes a rash develops. Swelling of the skin may be noticed on the lips and eyelids. The gastrointestinal tract is the next most likely affected system, with symptoms including itchy mouth, stomachache, nausea, vomiting, diarrhea, and cramps. Mild respiratory symptoms may include a stuffy or runny nose and are not necessarily dangerous.

A number of different foods trigger reactions. Allergic reactions have been linked to almost 200 foods and beverages (Hannaway, 2007). Milk, eggs, peanuts, tree nuts, fish, shellfish, soy, and wheat account for 90% of all food allergic reactions (Vickerstaff, 2007). Other foods that trigger reactions include seeds (e.g., sesame, sunflower), spices (e.g., nutmeg, coriander, paprika), fruits, and vegetables. Allergic reactions often vary across development. Children over the age of 3 years commonly have no reaction or less severe reactions to food triggers that did cause reactions at a younger age.

How Can an Allergy Cause Death?

Life-threatening anaphylaxis, or anaphylactic shock, occurs when breathing or blood circulation is impaired. Because of chemicals released into the bloodstream, blood pressure falls. The heart may beat faster in an attempt to circulate blood to vital organs. Mild respiratory symptoms include coughing or throat clearing that is not associated with an itch in the throat. Obvious and potentially dangerous breathing symptoms, which may signal throat closing, include hoarseness, difficulty swallowing, high-pitched sounds with breathing, repetitive cough, wheezing, or struggling to breathe. Other symptoms of a child having difficulty breathing can include chest pulling with each breath, flaring nostrils, or rapid breathing pattern.

How Do Food Allergies Develop?

There are various theories of how food allergies develop. From a biological perspective, food allergies develop when the immune system attacks harmless food proteins. This abnormal response of the immune system produces acute symptoms. The human immune system is extremely complex, given its challenging task of protecting the body from a wide range of harmful invaders. The immune system defends the body from harmful bacteria, viruses, and parasites. These germs can enter the body through various ports; for example, germs can enter through inhalation, ingestion, or broken skin. To complicate matters, many harmless bacteria are needed to maintain adequate health. The immune system must be able to identify whether to ignore or attack invaders. The allergic reaction is triggered when the antibody IgE identifies an allergen as harmful and mast cells release chemicals, such as histamine, that produce inflammation. Mast cells reside primarily in the skin, intestines, and respiratory tract; thus, allergy symptoms include rashes, gastrointestinal distress, and breathing difficulties.

Other causes of food allergies include foods ingested prenatally by mothers and foods ingested by breast-feeding mothers. In addition, the "hygiene hypothesis" states that current hygiene practices (i.e., oversterilization of environments and overuse of antibacterial agents) may be altering immune system responses (Hannaway, 2007; Isolauri, Huure, Salminen, & Impivaara, 2004; Sicherer et al., 2003). Additional research is needed to provide support for these hypotheses.

Does Food Allergy Management Differ by Developmental Stage?

Developmentally specific areas need to be addressed for food-allergic children and adolescents. School-age children tend to develop allergies to different foods than those affecting infants and young children. Most of the cases of cow's milk and egg allergies identified in infancy resolve spontaneously prior to age 3. In contrast, the allergies identified in school-age children tend to be lifelong. Food allergy management varies as children progress from infancy to young adulthood.

For the child or adolescent with food allergies, proceeding from the safe confines of a home to the outside world can be daunting (Hannaway, 2007). Daycare centers are considered challenging sites to manage allergies because of the lack of an on-site nurse and the potential for accidental exposure to food allergens via shared toys and eating areas and lessons involving manipulation of foods. Similarly, schools do not always have a nurse on-site, and exposure to food allergens can take place in the classroom, gym, auditorium, and cafeteria. Other sites, such as afterschool programs and camps, can also be problematic. Although school cafeterias and eating centers are the most likely place for life-threatening allergic reactions, they are not the only places where food allergies occur. In a study conducted in Massachusetts, 19% of life-threatening allergic reactions occurred outside the school building, such as on the playground, while traveling to and from school, or on field trips (McIntyre, Sheetz, Carroll, & Young, 2005).

To assist with social interactions and communication, many commercial products are available that target different developmental ages. For younger children, these include T-shirts identifying food allergies to wear on outings and disposable placemats. Older children may wear medication identification jewelry, such as personalized medical bracelets and necklaces, and restaurant cards indicating special needs and precautions are available for older children to present to restaurant staff. There are also products designed to facilitate the carrying and protection of the auto injector. The American Academy of Pediatrics (AAP) 2009 *Guidelines for the Administration of Medication in School* indicates that children should be given permission to carry certain medications, such as "albuterol for asthma," as long as the physician and parents have stated in writing that the child can assume this responsibility.

What Social-Emotional or Behavioral Issues Are Associated With Food Allergies?

The possibility that food allergies are the cause of a child's learning, social-emotional, or behavioral difficulties needs to be considered. First, a behavior may be directly linked to an allergy. School personnel should carefully observe behaviors, particularly of younger children, in the context of food and other allergens. Consideration should be given to consulting with families about seeking medical testing or making appropriate referrals if a food allergy is suspected.

Living with food allergies can also create such high levels of stress, anxiety, depression, and social activity avoidance for children that it leads to psychosocial adjustment problems. Family members may also experience social-emotional problems as the result of the food allergies of one or more of the children in the family (Bollinger et al., 2006). The psychological well-being of identified food-allergic children should be carefully monitored and may require professional evaluation. Anxiety, depression, and anorexia/bulimia have been identified in children and adolescents with food allergies at higher rates than in the rest of the population (Bollinger et al.).

It is unusual for personnel addressing psychological needs to consider a child's diet. However, the link between behavior and diet make food a necessary part of the food allergy discussion. First, some children and adolescents with food allergies and their families follow various types of elimination diets. Elimination diets can be simple (e.g., avoid only the food allergen) or complex. These diets can actually exacerbate or fuel a condition such as malnutrition, anorexia, or bulimia. Indeed, it is recommended that children and adolescents with food allergies be screened for these disorders prior to food elimination diets (Rakel, 2007). Before an elimination diet is implemented, the individual must be properly tested and a food allergy confirmed. A thorough medical history, commonly obtained by an allergist, must precede testing. After allergens are positively identified, they should be eliminated from the diet if an immediate or dangerous type of allergic reaction is likely to result. Selection of foods to be eliminated from the diet depends on the history of allergic reactions, the disorder of the child, and the test results. Because avoidance of food allergens is the only form of treatment for food allergies, elimination diets are used to varying degrees for all food-allergic children.

Although high rates of food allergies have been found among children with autism, there is no evidence that food allergies cause autism (Stern et al., 2005; Szpir, 2006; Williams, Dalrymple, & Neal, 2000). In recent years, it has been suggested that food allergies play a role in causing or worsening autism. Specifically, gluten (a wheat protein) and casein (a milk protein) have been blamed for worsening symptoms in children with autism. These food proteins break down into smaller proteins (peptides), which are hypothesized to function like narcotics in children with autism, thereby worsening their behavioral changes. Reports that children with autism spectrum disorders have abnormal immune function have not been substantiated (Stern et al.).

What Is the Status of Research on Causes and Treatments?

Research is currently underway on anti-IgE (antibody) therapy, immunotherapy, and oral desensitization. Clinical trials are being conducted using injections of anti-IgE antibody proteins. Immunotherapy involves injecting diluted doses of an allergen over several years to program the immune system to be less responsive to the allergen. While this type of therapy has been conducted in some form since 1911, derivatives of specific proteins are the latest evolution. For example, according to Hannaway (2007), a modified peanut protein vaccination is currently being studied. Similarly, oral desensitization involves increasing tolerance of allergens by placing small amounts of allergens under the tongue at regular intervals. Preliminary results indicate that gradually presenting trace amounts of offending foods (e.g., peanuts, milk, eggs) leads to increasing tolerance. However, definitive data regarding tolerable amounts are not currently available. Moreover, it appears that some combination of these three research areas may be the most promising treatment option (Hannaway, 2007). More research in this area is needed. Research will also be needed to demonstrate the effects of specific interventions, such as implementation of policies and school staff education.

IMPLICATIONS FOR EDUCATORS

The physical and psychological well-being of food-allergic children requires proactive planning, communication, and vigilance (Sicherer, Munoz-Furlong, Murphy, Wood, & Sampson, 2003). Guardians, caretakers, and other adults who come into contact with food-allergic children can employ several proactive actions and emergency responses.

Create a Core Team

Although all professionals working with a child or adolescent with food allergies must be knowledgeable about the various aspects of allergies, a core team of individuals who may be involved with affected children should be identified at service sites (e.g., schools, camps, sites of extracurricular activities). At the school, this team can be comprised of a school nurse, school psychologist, teacher, principal, food service and nutrition manager, and counselor. Once the team is established, they should begin working with the parents and the student, if age-appropriate, to institute a prevention plan and an emergency plan. It is also highly recommended that additional school staff members be educated on the food allergy emergency plan (also referred to as a food allergy action plan).

Food Allergy Emergency Plan

At the onset of preparing the food allergy emergency plan, the school staff should be knowledgeable about the federal and state laws, as well as the local school district policies, that apply. The next phase includes a review of the student's health records submitted by parents and health care providers. The health records should inform the action plan so that the child will not be unnecessarily excluded from a school activity because of his or her food allergy. Food allergens should be eliminated from the student's meals, educational tools, arts and crafts projects, and incentives. The food allergy plan should clearly indicate the treatment steps, dosage and location of medications, emergency call list, and list of school staff members trained to address a food allergy emergency. Thereafter, a team member should ensure that the document is appropriately filed and distributed.

The National Association of School Nurses has found essential components missing in school food allergy emergency plans when compared to the Food Allergy and Anaphylaxis Network's (FAAN) food allergy action plan. Plans were void of such things as emergency contact information, medication administration instructions, and health history information (Powers, Bergren, & Finnegan, 2007). Additionally, district transportation administrators should be included in either the planning or distribution of the food allergy action plan so that personnel under their supervision can be properly advised of and educated about children and food allergies.

Storing of Medications

School personnel need to coordinate with the school nurse to be certain that medications are properly stored and available in accordance with the health care provider's standing order for emergency medications, including epinephrine. Emergency medications are preferably stored in an easily accessible central location to which designated school personnel have access. Students may be allowed to carry their emergency medications on their persons if doing so is age-appropriate and permitted by both local and state regulations (Ben-Shoshan et al., 2008).

It is essential that all teachers and school staff who interact with the student on a regular basis can recognize symptoms of an allergic reaction. The teachers who work with the child also need to be knowledgeable about what to do in case of an emergency. Likewise, school bus drivers need to be trained to recognize symptoms of an allergic reaction and know what action to take. Support personnel who may have only occasional or passing contact with food-allergic students (e.g., educator, school psychologist, social worker, guidance counselor, and adjunct teaching personnel) should also receive training. Moreover, itinerant school personnel, contracted workers (e.g., maintenance workers), and temporary personnel (e.g., substitute teachers) who provide services to many schools within a district or provide school services intermittently should be briefed regarding children with food allergies in the school building.

If a first responder is not the designated and/or trained staff member, then that individual should (a) ensure that the emergency medical system is activated (e.g., call 911), (b) locate the school nurse or designated/trained staff member to initiate the emergency action plan, and (c) check the child's breathing status and pulse. Personnel should be trained on options for treatment, including decision rules for administering epinephrine. Delaying epinephrine administration once a life-threatening symptom is evident can contribute to fatal outcomes (Ben-Shoshan et al., 2008).

Label Literacy

Despite passage of federal food labeling legislation, not all food labels and restaurant menus have complied with requirements for simpler language on labels. Therefore, school personnel and other caretakers benefit from instruction on hidden sources of food allergens in all products (not just food) and food label reading discussions. The U.S. Food and Drug Administration, Center for Safety and Applied Nutrition, provides excellent food label literacy materials at its Web site (www.cfsan.fda.gov/~dms/lab-cat.html).

Empowering Children With Food Allergies and Their Peers

School- or community-based counseling for the social-emotional experiences encountered by the diagnosed child, parents/guardians, or siblings should be made available. Support groups for all members of families are now available in every state and can be accessed via medical providers and the FAAN Web site (www.foodallergy.com). Schools should consider establishing guidance programs and support groups for children with food allergies. Food allergies, like any chronic medical problem, can lead to increased frustration and can be made worse by stress. Adults should monitor times of heightened stress for children and adolescents (e.g., high-stakes testing) and provide ways to relieve this stress (Freund & Ryaunier, 2003).

Because of the potentially life-threatening implications for a child with food allergies, school personnel and other caretakers sometimes contribute to heightened stress when a student with a food allergy has been assigned to their classroom. They may harbor fears and frustrations related to the precautions and vigilance required. Strategies to provide emotional support for school personnel directly involved with a child with food allergies should be considered. Emotional support can come in the form of tangibles, such as providing the classroom with additional adult supports for specific activities. Support may also be in the form of opportunities to express their concerns about the food allergy.

Assessing the impact of a food allergy via school- or clinic-based intervention teams should also be considered. For example, any member of a family can be administered a measure such as the Food Allergy Impact Scale (Bollinger et al., 2006). This questionnaire has 32 items for the caregiver of a child with food allergies to complete. The caregiver rates the impact of the child's food allergy on a 7-point scale (from *not at all* to *very much*) for eight aspects of daily family activities: meal preparation, family social activities, caregiver-supervised child social activities, autonomous child social activities, school activities, family relations, caregiver stress and free time, and employment and finances.

EDUCATIONAL STRATEGIES

- Health classes should include information regarding the recognition and treatment of life-threatening allergic reactions.
- Educators should ensure that a copy of the signed medical statement from the physician outlining appropriate meal substitutions is available.
- All staff members should know where emergency medications, such as epinephrine, are stored and how they should be administered in case a student has an allergic reaction in the school cafeteria or elsewhere in the school.
- Parents and cafeteria staff should forward food allergy information to educators and relevant staff members in case there are questions about any special diet.
- All school personnel should be trained in reading labels and reviewing menus. Avoid cross-contact of foods, which occurs when two foods come into contact with each other, causing their proteins to mix. A good way to avoid this is to use separate utensils and wash them thoroughly with warm, soapy water.
- Work with a registered dietician, school lunch staff person, or other qualified nutrition specialist to manage dietary substitutions at school and on field trips.

DISCUSSION QUESTIONS

1. What are the schools' responsibilities concerning keeping the school environment free from foods that cause common allergies and intolerances?

2. Some schools do not have school nurses. Who should be the primary medical contact with parents and medical professionals in these situations?

3. How can school personnel assist children with food allergies to develop social skills, including managing peer pressure, related to making good food choices?

4. What is the best method of having parents communicate their child's allergies and intolerances to school personnel? What is the best method of educating school personnel about management and crisis issues concerning food allergies?

RESEARCH SUMMARY

- Food allergies account for more than 150 deaths annually (FAAN, 2008a).
- Food allergies develop when the immune system attacks harmless food proteins.
- Life-threatening anaphylaxis, or anaphylactic shock, occurs when breathing or blood circulation is impaired. The heart may beat faster in an attempt to circulate blood to vital organs.
- Obvious and potentially dangerous breathing symptoms that may occur with throat closing include hoarseness, difficulty swallowing, high-pitched sounds with breathing, or struggling to breathe. Symptoms of a child having difficulty breathing can include chest pulling with each breath, flaring nostrils, or a rapid breathing pattern.
- School-age children tend to develop allergies to different foods than those affecting infants and young children. Most of the cases of cow's milk and egg allergies identified in infancy resolve spontaneously prior to age 3. In contrast, the allergies identified in school-age children tend to be lifelong.
- Social-emotional or behavioral issues associated with food allergies are anxiety, depression, and adjustment problems.

RESOURCES

Canadian Society of Allergy and Clinical Immunology. (1995). *Anaphylaxis in schools and other child care settings.* Retrieved October 1, 2009, from http://www.csaci.ca/index.php?page=360

Hannaway, P. J. (2007). *On the nature of food allergy: A complete handbook on food allergy for patients, parents, restaurant personnel, child-care providers, educators, school nurses, dieticians and health-care providers.* Marblehead, MA: Lighthouse Press.

International Food Information Council. (2004). *School foodservice and food allergies: What we need to know.* Retrieved October 1, 2009, from http://www.ific.org/publications/other/allergysheet.cfm?renderforprint=1

Stevens, R. R. (2002). Section 504 plan outline for children with severe food allergies. Retrieved October 1, 2009, from www.allergysupport.org

In addition, the National Agricultural Library of the U.S. Department of Agriculture provides a "Resource List on Food Allergies and Intolerances for Consumers" at www.nal.usda.gov/fnic/pubs/bibs/gen/allergy.pdf.

HANDOUT

SUCCESSFULLY MANAGING FOOD ALLERGIES IN CHILDHOOD

The following are general recommendations offered by the Canadian Society of Allergy and Clinical Immunology and the International Food Information Council for when the child with food allergies is at school or a school-related function. These recommendations apply to all personnel having responsibility for the care of children (e.g., school staff, educators, coaches, afterschool workers, and school bus drivers).

- Information and identification sheets (photographs, allergens to avoid, management plan) for children with life-threatening allergies should be readily available.
- The parents should sign a waiver allowing the school to use epinephrine when school staff consider it necessary.
- Parents should be informed of the federal, state, and school district mandates that regulate the management of food allergies, including the use of epinephrine injections.
- Every child who has been prescribed an epinephrine auto-injector should have one labeled with his or her name and kept in a readily available location.
- Children who are old enough to use an epinephrine auto-injector should carry their own; assistance in administering a dose should be provided by a teacher or other caregiver.
- All teachers and other caregivers should be aware of children who have an allergy that may predispose them to anaphylaxis. These children should be properly identified and their allergy clearly stated (e.g., medical alert bracelet).
- Staff and students should be educated about anaphylaxis and how to treat it. Substitute teachers must also be informed of children with food allergies and the emergency plan.

14

Developmental Effects of Type 1 Diabetes*

Sarah A. Bassin, W. Mark Posey, and Elizabeth M. Schneider

Samantha is an 8-year-old female who was recently diagnosed with type 1 diabetes. Although she is a hardworking student, she missed more than 2 weeks of school at the beginning of third grade due to her initial diagnosis and hospital stay. At least three times during the school day, the teacher sends Samantha to the nurse's office to check her blood sugar.

Typically an active child, Samantha has felt sluggish due to recurrent hypoglycemic episodes since her diagnosis, which have limited her participation in physical activities. She has difficulties with concentration and reports feeling weak. Despite efforts to keep her condition managed, Samantha has already experienced one severe hypoglycemic episode during the school day. Emergency services were contacted immediately, as was her family. Since then, her teacher has worried about a recurrence and feels underprepared to handle such a situation. Moreover, the other children in the classroom were never briefed on the events of that day, leaving some children uneasy and others asking Samantha questions she is not prepared to answer.

In preparation for fourth grade, a meeting was arranged before the start of classes with Samantha's fourth-grade teacher and other relevant personnel. While an Individualized Health Plan was drawn up and reviewed, her parents decided that her teachers should be provided with something more practical. Consequently, the teachers were given a pocket-sized, laminated quick-reference guide that listed hypo- and hyperglycemic symptoms and the appropriate course of action to take in each case, along with Samantha's dietary and blood

*Adapted from Wilson, S., Posey, M., & Schneider, E. (in press). Type 1 diabetes in children. *Communiqué*, Copyright by the National Association of School Psychologists, Bethesda, MD. Use is by permission of the publisher. www.nasponline.org

glucose-monitoring schedule. In addition, arrangements were made so that Samantha could check her blood glucose in the classroom.

After speaking with Samantha and her parents, the teacher gave a short lesson to the class on diabetes, highlighting that it is not contagious and instructing the children on what they should do if they saw any symptoms. Not only did this address an important safety concern, it also opened the door for Samantha to discuss her condition openly with classmates. The steps taken by Samantha's parents and the school resulted in a much smoother fourth-grade year, with everyone involved feeling prepared to handle any incidents that might arise appropriately and promptly.

INTRODUCTION

Type 1 diabetes is a relatively common childhood chronic health condition in which the pancreas makes little or no insulin (Watson & Logan, 1998). Insulin is necessary to break down glucose or sugar in the blood, which the body can then use as energy. Type 1 diabetes can be described as an autoimmune disease because, in many children, the pancreas stops making sufficient insulin after the body's immune system destroys most of the beta cells in the pancreas. Yet for some children with type 1 diabetes, there is no known cause.

Prior to diagnosis, children with type 1 diabetes often experience a combination of the following symptoms: frequent urination, excessive thirst/appetite, weight loss, elevated blood sugar (hyperglycemia), glucose in the urine, and an abnormal increase in ketones in the blood and/or urine. Because the child's body does not produce sufficient insulin, the child must take insulin. Although new technologies are being developed for administering insulin, by far the most common forms of administration are an insulin pump or insulin injection. Most children maintain healthy blood sugar levels by using a combination of rapid-acting and long-acting insulin. The amount of insulin that the child needs throughout the day is determined, in part, by counting the number of carbohydrates the child will eat or has eaten during a meal or snack. Children must check their blood sugar multiple times per day using a blood glucose meter to determine how much insulin they need.

The treatment regimen for children diagnosed with type 1 diabetes requires frequent monitoring of the child's diet and blood sugar levels. Consequently, parents and children must be educated in the skills necessary for treatment adherence. A certified diabetes educator should provide this education to families, most commonly at a local hospital. Typically, an Individualized Health Plan (IHP) is developed with the school to ensure that child's health needs are recognized and addressed in the school setting.

Without acceptable treatment adherence and the availability of sufficient insulin, children with type 1 may experience a range of short-term and long-term effects (Watson & Logan, 1998). A child's treatment adherence determines how well the diabetes is controlled. Poor glycemic control has been associated with increased negative effects, which may be physical, cognitive, academic, psychosocial, or behavioral in nature.

BACKGROUND

Acute Effects

Diabetes often results in acute effects because of hypoglycemic or hyperglycemic episodes. These episodes occur when insulin, diet, and physical activity are not properly balanced. Consequently, short-term physical effects of poor control may include a return of prediagnosis symptoms. Individuals experiencing hyperglycemia or hypoglycemia may present with symptoms that include confusion, hunger, trembling, sweating, sleepiness, an inability to speak, blurred vision, fatigue, dry mouth, irritability, excessive thirst, and/or excessive urination. The similarity in symptoms highlights the importance of learning the unique behavioral symptoms of hypoglycemia and hyperglycemia for each child. Though these effects are transient when the condition is treated immediately, they do have important implications for school performance. Possible mood changes, as well as deficiencies in motor speed, attention, and mental efficiency, may result from an episode of hypoglycemia. These may lead to slowed performance on tasks requiring rapid reaction time (Ryan, Gurtunca, & Becker, 2006). Although hyperglycemia is also thought to affect mental efficiency, it has been reported to influence emotion and behavior more than intellectual performance (Martin, Davis, & Jones, 2006). Both hypoglycemia and hyperglycemia can lead to coma or death if not treated immediately.

Long-Term Effects

Physical Effects. The most commonly cited source of information on the physical long-term effects of diabetes is the Diabetes Control and Complications Trial (DCCT). The data for the DCCT were collected through the National Institute of Diabetes and Digestive and Kidney Diseases (NIDDK) and are based on information from 1,441 participants across North America (NIH, 2001). This study has provided strong evidence that when diabetes is not well controlled, individuals are at greater risk for heart disease, blindness, nerve damage, and kidney damage (NIH). In addition to these complications, there is some evidence that children with very poor control may also experience insufficient growth and are at risk for additional weight gain when they attempt to achieve better control (Ambler, Fairchild, Craig, & Cameron, 2006).

Cognitive Effects. Research focusing on cognitive development in children does imply differences between children with diabetes and healthy children in terms of cognitive and neuropsychological functioning, and most evidence relates differences to age at onset of diabetes and glycemic control. Earlier onset of diabetes is a risk factor for adverse developmental effects. Although deficits in functioning have been detected using measures of intelligence, attention, processing speed, long-term memory, and executive skills, intelligence for children with type 1 generally falls within the average range (Greer & Holmes, 1996; Holmes, O'Brien, & Greer, 1995; Northam et al., 2001). Hypoglycemia can be associated with verbal and nonverbal memory deficits, even more so for children who have experienced hypoglycemic seizures (Hershey, Lillie,

Sadler, & White, 2003). More specifically, memories that involve personal events and facts may be adversely affected (Desrocher & Rovet, 2004).

Early onset of diabetes negatively affects the same cognitive functions as hypoglycemia, such as verbal and nonverbal memory (Desrocher & Rovet, 2004). Ryan and colleagues' (1985) study shows slower motor speeds in children with early-onset diabetes, while Rovet's group has found and replicated decreased visual-spatial performance on construction and puzzle tasks (Rovet & Alvarez, 1997). These difficulties may be related to slower processing speed and diminished executive skills (Ferguson et al., 2005). In fact, attention abilities are reduced in children with early-onset diabetes (Desrocher & Rovet). Another difference that has been replicated across several research groups is decreased nonverbal intelligences scores, particularly on tasks that are timed (Rovet, Ehrlich, & Hoppe, 1988).

However, the effects of hypoglycemia and early-onset diabetes may be confounded with effects related to the duration of diabetes (Desrocher & Rovet, 2004). For example, Rovet's group has replicated a finding that difficulties with visual-spatial tasks increase the longer the child has type 1 diabetes. Similarly, visual-spatial and motor speed deficits are found in children with early-onset type 1 diabetes. Nonverbal intelligence scores are related to diabetes duration (Holmes, Cant, Fox, Lampert, & Greer, 1999). Other possible late effects include decreased performance on verbal intelligence and executive-functioning tasks (Northam et al., 2001).

Academic Achievement. A number of studies suggest that children with type 1 diabetes who report adverse effects on their academic achievement experience increased risk related to cognitive effects and school absenteeism. In one study, 24% of children with diabetes received special education, whereas only 13% of comparison children received these services (Holmes et al., 1995). Kovacs, Goldston, and Iyengar (1992) found that a sample of children over the first 6 years postdiagnosis experienced increasingly declining school grades (Kovacs et al.).

Although cognitive abilities are related to achievement, low academic achievement has been reported even when variation in intelligence was taken into account (Holmes et al., 1995). Low achievement scores may be related to aspects of intelligence that were not measured or other factors that contribute to decreased achievement. For example, children with diabetes miss more school than their peers (Holmes et al., 1999). In fact, Holmes and colleagues found a negative relationship between school absences and achievement, but absences only partially explained academic achievement scores. Kovacs and colleagues (1992) detected a similar relationship between school absences and grades. However, the effect of school absences may be mediated by factors besides absenteeism, such as glycemic control and/or cognitive effects. For example, Fowler, Johnson, and Atkinson (1985) reported decreased achievement in these children without an increase in school absences. In addition, two groups have found a relationship between poor control and lower math scores (Rovet et al., 1988). Academic achievement scores were not lower for children with diabetes in general, but decreased achievement was specifically related to poor control, as well as increased school absences (McCarthy, Lindgren, Mengeling, Tsalikian, & Engvall, 2002).

Social-Emotional Functioning. A study of over 2,600 children and adolescents with type 1 diabetes found mildly depressed mood in 14% of participants and moderately or severely depressed mood in approximately 9% (Lawrence et al., 2006). There are also increased psychiatric diagnoses among individuals with type 1 diabetes, with depression being most common and then anxiety (Eiber, Berlin, Grimaldi, & Bisserbe, 1997). Dantzer, Swendsen, Maurice-Tison, and Salamon (2003) reported that most studies indicate a positive correlation between internalizing psychological disorders and type 1 diabetes. More specifically, children with diabetes report more problems with depressive symptoms and anxiety immediately post-diagnosis, but after approximately 1 year, some studies have found that there are no longer differences in psychological adjustment (Northam, Anderson, Adler, Werther, & Warne, 1996).

Decreased participation in social activities has also been found in children with chronic health conditions (Sexson & Madan-Swain, 1995). This may be due, in part, to symptoms associated with acute complications of diabetes, such as fatigue or nausea due to hypoglycemia or hyperglycemia, which may affect the frequency or quality of participation. As many as 55% of children with newly diagnosed diabetes fail to discuss the condition with peers, with 35% of them reporting that their friends would like them better if they did not have the condition (Storch et al., 2004). Moreover, children with diabetes, in comparison to a control group, reported higher rates of relational victimization and less frequent supportive behavior from peers, with relational victimization associated with depression and social anxiety (Storch et al.). As such, teachers should be aware of this increased risk of bullying for children with diabetes.

Children with diabetes are especially at risk for poorer social-emotional outcomes and functioning if they have less developed social and coping skills (Wysocki, 2006) and if parental involvement, knowledge, and skills are low (Chisholm et al., 2007). Because type 1 is a lifelong illness, children diagnosed at a young age progress through the stages of development while attempting to regulate their condition. One of the most important skills that should be gradually fostered is that of self-care and independence (Bradford, 1997). In fact, decreased treatment adherence has been found in children of parents who lack developmentally appropriate expectations for diabetes management (Palmer et al., 2004).

IMPLICATIONS FOR EDUCATORS

Given that children with type 1 diabetes are at risk for negative physical, cognitive, academic, psychosocial, and behavioral effects, school psychologists and other school professionals should become educated about how students with diabetes may struggle and how best to help them. In one recent study, teachers were asked to determine the cause of students' behavior, with health factors as one possible cause (Wodrich, 2005). When teachers were blind to students' health conditions, only 2.6% correctly identified health factors as the cause of the students' behavior. In contrast, when the children's diagnosis was disclosed to the teachers and disease-specific behaviors were described, 50% of teachers correctly identified health factors as the cause of students' behavior.

Unfortunately, inaccurate assumptions may lead teachers to make incorrect choices about how best to address a student's classroom behavior. When teachers are provided with more information about type 1 diabetes, they may be better able to meet students' classroom learning needs (Cunningham & Wodrich, 2006). Another study found that when school personnel received diabetes education, students with type 1 diabetes demonstrated better control. When classmates received diabetes education, children with type 1 diabetes rated their quality of life higher than students whose classmates did not receive this training (Wagner, Heapy, James, & Abbott, 2006).

Therefore, education for school professionals, as well as children's classmates, may contribute to improved behavioral, academic, and quality-of-life outcomes for children with type 1 diabetes. Given the importance of the school for children's overall health and well-being, collaboration among school and medical professionals, as well as family members, is perhaps the most important contributor to successful management of childhood diabetes.

EDUCATIONAL STRATEGIES

- Develop an Individualized Health Plan for the student.
- Educate teachers, parents, and students about the symptoms and effects of diabetes.
- Know how to intervene to help the child with diabetes in school. This includes developing a close relationship with the school nurse and using appropriate behavioral strategies.
- Plan for potential intermittent absences due to health issues related to diabetes.
- Develop a monitoring strategy for the child while in school so that symptoms related to diabetes can be quickly identified. Intervention plans should be clear and easily implemented.

DISCUSSION QUESTIONS

1. When type 1 diabetes is not well controlled, for what types of problems are individuals at greater risk?

2. In children who have poor control, what behavioral-ecological issues should be considered?

3. What are some of the risk factors for lower cognitive functioning?

4. What are reasons, as educators, to stress control of his or her diabetes to a child?

5. Why might there be a risk of bullying with children who have type 1 diabetes?

6. What are the specific advantages of providing special training to school personnel who work with a child who has diabetes?

RESEARCH SUMMARY

- Poor control of diabetes is associated with short-term and long-term physical and psychological effects.
- Physical symptoms include (but are not limited to) confusion, hunger, trembling, sweating, sleepiness, blurred vision, fatigue, irritability, excessive thirst, and frequent urination.
- Younger age at onset and poor diabetic control lead to an increased risk for negative effects.
- Diabetes most commonly affects attention, processing speed, long-term memory, and executive skills.
- After an initial period of adjustment, psychological difficulties, such anxiety or depression, may reappear.

RESOURCES

National Diabetes Education Program (NDEP). (2003). *Helping the student with diabetes succeed: A guide for school personnel.* Retrieved October 1, 2009, from www.ndep.nih.gov/media/Youth_NDEPSSchoolGuide.pdf. The National Institutes of Health and Centers for Disease Control and Prevention jointly produced this guide, which includes action checklists for school personnel in various roles, sample emergency plans, and a resource list.

Children With Diabetes provides an online community for children, families, and adults with diabetes at its Web site: www.children withdiabetes.com.

H A N D O U T

GENERAL INFORMATION ABOUT TYPE 1 DIABETES

- Type 1 diabetes is a relatively common childhood condition in which the pancreas makes little or no insulin.
- Insulin is necessary to break down sugar in the blood for energy in the body.
- This condition is referred to as type 1 diabetes, insulin-dependent diabetes mellitus (IDDM), or juvenile-onset diabetes.
- Insulin is administered by injection or through a pump.
- Individuals with type 1 diabetes check their blood sugar multiple times per day, using a blood glucose meter, to determine how much insulin they need.
- The amount of insulin may also be determined by counting the number of carbohydrates the child will eat or has eaten during a meal or snack.

Short-Term Physical Effects and Behavior

- Prior to diagnosis, children often experience the following: frequent urination, excessive thirst/appetite, weight loss, and hyperglycemia (elevated blood sugar).
- Behavioral symptoms of hyperglycemia and hypoglycemia (low blood sugar) can include irritability, confusion, fatigue, attention problems, and headache.
- When blood sugar is extremely high or low, it can result in coma or death.
- A child with a rapid drop in blood sugar may seem shaky, pale, or sweaty.
- The effects of hypoglycemia may take 30 minutes or longer to subside.

Long-Term Effects

- A child's treatment adherence determines how well the diabetes is controlled; poor control has been associated with increased negative effects.
- Children in poor control of their diabetes are at greater risk for heart disease, blindness, nerve damage, kidney damage, and stroke.
- Although negative effects are somewhat related to the duration of the condition, increased negative long-term effects appear most closely related to early-onset age (less than 5 years old) and poor control of blood sugar levels.
- Areas of difficulty may include attention, cognitive and motor processing speed, long-term memory, verbal and visual-spatial reasoning, and executive skills.
- Broad intellectual abilities often remain within normal limits.
- Although most children's achievement is average, they are likely to miss more school, their grades may decline, and they are more likely to receive special education services.
- Initially, children are at an increased risk of depression and anxiety. Although children and families seem to adjust within about a year of diagnosis, the child's risk for mental health problems appears to increase again over the long term.
- Parent involvement, knowledge, and skills are critical for successful adjustment.

Glossary

Chapter 2

Bereavement—The process of managing and coping with grief

Catastrophe—A large-scale disaster that often leads to personal disruption and loss

Crisis—An unstable or abrupt change in present events with significant effects on personal adjustment

Grief—A multifaceted response to loss. Grief spans the emotions of numbness, disbelief, anxiety, despair, sadness, and loneliness.

Chapter 3

Angleman's Syndrome—A deletion on the 15th chromosome leading to lack of speech, intellectual disabilities, feeding problems, small head, and jerky motor movements

Autosome—Non-sex chromosome

Chromosome—An organized structure of DNA and protein found in cells. A chromosome is a single piece of DNA that contains many genes, regulatory elements, and other nucleotide sequences.

Cortex—The outermost layer of the brain that is critical in all higher-order thought

Cri-du-chat—A deletion on the 5th chromosome, leading to intellectual disabilities, speech problems, and a characteristic cry at birth that resembles a cat's cry.

Cytogenetics—A branch of genetics relating to the study of cells

DiGeorge Syndrome—A deletion on the 22nd chromosome, also known as velocardiofacial syndrome. Learning disabilities, behavior disorders, heart problems, and cleft palate are common features of the heterogeneous presentation of this disorder.

DNA—Deoxyribonucleic acid carries the genetic instructions used in the development and functioning of all known organisms.

Down Syndrome—An additional 21st chromosome is present, leading to heart malformations, distinct facial features, intellectual disabilities, and acid reflux disease.

FISH—Fluorescence in situ hybridization is a technique used to detect specific DNA sequences of chromosomes.

Fragile X—A mutation of the FMR1 gene leads to learning disabilities or intellectual disabilities, low muscle tone, and distinctive facial features.

Heterogeneous—Widely varying features

Hippocampus—A brain structure responsible for much of memory formation, storage, and retrieval

Homogeneous—Similar or unvarying features

IDEA—The Individuals with Disabilities Education Act is the U.S. law establishing and funding special education programming.

Intellectual Disabilities—Formerly known as mental retardation. Is defined in part as the lowest 2% of cognitive abilities.

Karyotype—The characteristic number and arrangement of chromosomes (i.e., 23 pairs for humans)

Klinefelter Syndrome—In males, an extra X chromosome results in reduced fertility and some behavior problems.

Mutagenic—Any substance known to increase the probability of a mutation

Phenotype—An observable trait

Polysaccharides—A family of complex carbohydrates essential for development

RNA—Ribonucleic acid is similar to DNA but has a single strand and, among other things, serves as part of a system to convert DNA information into proteins.

Synapse—A juncture between two neurons (i.e., nerve cells)

Turner Syndrome—In females, a missing X chromosome leads to a host of behavioral characteristics and physical abnormalities.

Williams Syndrome—A deletion in the 7th chromosome leads to intellectual disabilities, distinctive elfin facial appearance, and a distinct pattern of cognitive strengths and weaknesses.

Wolf-Hirschhorn—A deletion in the 4th chromosome leads to intellectual disabilities, seizures, low muscle tone, and small head.

Chapter 4

Amino Acid—Basic organic molecules that combine to form proteins

Dopamine—A neurotransmitter with many functions in the brain, including important roles in behavior and cognition, motor activity, motivation and reward, sleep, mood, attention, and learning

Enzyme—Complex proteins produced from living cells that are capable of producing chemical changes

Executive Function—An umbrella term used to classify different mental functions including problem solving, organizational skills, and learning techniques; attention and focus; planning and strategizing; the ability to follow rules; remembering details; and the ability to inhibit impulsive responses and initiate appropriate responses

Neurotransmitter—A chemical released by a neuron that stimulates an adjacent neuron, facilitating communication through the nervous system

Phenylalanine (Phe)—An essential amino acid that the body needs for development but does not produce. Sources are found in protein-containing foods such as meat and dairy, and it constitutes 50% of the artificial sweetener aspartame. In the body, it is metabolized into tyrosine.

Tyrosine—A nonessential amino acid produced by phenylalanine. It is used to synthesize proteins and is the precursor for the synthesis of adrenaline, noradrenalin, and dopamine.

Chapter 5

Candidate Gene—A gene that researchers think may be related to a particular condition

Chromosome—A strand of DNA that carries genetic material in a living organism. Humans possess 23 pairs of chromosomes.

DNA—Deoxyribonucleic acid is a nucleic acid that contains the genetic instructions required for the development and functioning of all living organisms.

Epidemiological Study—A statistical study on human populations that attempts to link human health effects to a specified cause

Gene—Genes are the basic units of heredity. They are made up of DNA and act as instructions to make proteins.

Genetic Counseling—A process during which trained counselors advise families about the consequences, heritability, and management of an inherited genetic disorder

Genotype—The genetic makeup of an individual

Heritability—The proportion of phenotypic variation (*see* Phenotype) in a population that is attributable to genetic variation (*see* Genotype) among individuals

Phenotype—An observable behavior arising from the expression of an organism's genes, the influence of environmental factors, and possible interactions between the two

Chapter 6

Amygdala—An almond-shaped brain structure, located in the limbic system at the inside base of each temporal lobe, controlling the experience and expression of emotion and involved in motivation, aggression, feeding, and long-term memory. Electrical stimulation of this area usually produces an intense emotion of fear.

Anxiety Disorder—Mental disorders marked by physiological arousal, feelings of tension, and intense apprehension, often without apparent reason

Autonomic—A branch of the nervous system involved in involuntary responses, especially with regard to organ or visceral changes, that occur without conscious intent or control

Corticosterone—A hormone secreted in response to serious injury or stress, sometimes suppressing immune responses

Cortisol—A hormone produced in response to stress or injury

Functional Magnetic Resonance Imaging (fMRI)—A brain-imaging technique that combines the benefits of both MRI and PET scans by using magnets to detect changes in the flow of blood to cells in the brain

Lesions—Any structural alteration of an organ or tissue to the body brought about by injury or disease

Limbic System—The region of the brain that regulates emotional behavior, basic motivational urges, and memory, as well as major physiological functions

Social Phobia—A persistent, irrational fear that arises in anticipation of a public situation in which an individual can be observed by others

Systematic Desensitization—A behavioral therapy technique in which a client is taught to prevent the arousal of anxiety by confronting the feared stimulus while simultaneously being relaxed. An adaptation of the technique involving exposure to the actual phobic stimulus or situation is called *in vivo desensitization*.

Temperament—A person's typical way of responding to his or her environment, often considered innate or genetically determined

Temporal Lobe—One of the four lobes of the cerebral cortex, the temporal lobe contains the auditory cortex and hippocampus and plays a role in receptive language, memory, and emotion.

Chapter 7

Developmental Disabilities—A blanket term for all forms of atypical development that lead to functional problems

Pervasive Developmental Disorder (PDD)—A developmental disability that includes a continuum of behaviors, including autism, Asperger disorder, Rett syndrome, and childhood disintegrative disorder

Resilience—The ability of individuals and families to overcome stressors, threats, and factors that place development, family dynamics, and general outcomes at risk for a negative outcome

Chapter 8

Alcohol-Related Birth Defects (ARBD)—One or more congenital abnormalities linked to confirmed heavy prenatal alcohol exposure

Alcohol-Related Neurodevelopmental Disorder (ARND)—Measurable but subtler neurobehavioral deficits than are seen with children with fetal alcohol syndrome. The individual presents with central nervous system or behavioral/cognitive abnormalities inconsistent with developmental level or environmental factors.

Cerebellum—Also known as the hindbrain, the cerebellum is the region of the brain that receives sensory information from muscles and helps coordinate movement.

Executive Function—*See* Chapter 4.

Fetal Alcohol Effects (FAE)—Refers to children exhibiting some, but not all, of the characteristics of fetal alcohol syndrome (FAS)

Fetal Alcohol Spectrum Disorders (FASD)—Collective term that includes fetal alcohol syndrome (FAS), partial fetal alcohol syndrome (partial FAS), alcohol-related birth defects (ARBD), and alcohol-related neurodevelopmental disorder (ARND)

Fetal Alcohol Syndrome (FAS)—Significant cognitive deficits and/or behavioral deficits, growth retardation, and physical deformities, including facial dysmorphology, associated with substantial prenatal alcohol exposure

Gray Matter—A major component of the central nervous system, gray matter is distributed throughout the cerebellum and brain hemispheres and serves to aid in sensory and motor communication to various centers of the brain.

Myelination—Process by which axons are insulated with myelin, improving and increasing the speed of brain signals

Partial Fetal Alcohol Syndrome—Refers to children with some facial dysmorphology and at least one of the following: growth retardation, neurodevelopmental abnormalities, or behavioral/cognitive abnormalities associated with confirmed heavy prenatal alcohol exposure

Teratogen—A harming agent, such as a drug or virus, that typically leads to a birth defect

Chapter 9

Apgar—An index used to evaluate the condition of a newborn infant based on a rating of 0, 1, or 2 for each of the following five characteristics: *A*ppearance (skin color), *P*ulse, *G*rimace (response to stimulation of the sole of the foot), *A*ctivity (muscle tone), and *R*espiration. A score of 10 is a perfect score.

Dopamine—A neurotransmitter in the brain that plays a role in behavior, cognition, motor activity, motivation, sleep, mood, attention, and learning

Monoamine Oxidase Inhibitors (MAOIs)—A class of medicines sometimes prescribed to treat severe depression. MAOIs increase the concentration of neurotransmitters responsible for relaying information between nerves in particular regions of the brain, thereby facilitating mental functioning.

Neonate—Newborn infant up to age 1 month

Norepinephrine—A neurotransmitter that plays a role in attention and alertness

Selective Serotonin Reuptake Inhibitors (SSRIs/SRIs)—A class of antidepressant drugs that help to increase serotonin. Representative drugs include fluoxetine (Prozac), paroxetine (Paxil), sertraline (Zoloft), citalopram (Celexa), and escitalopram (Lexapro).

Serotonin—A neurotransmitter that plays an important role in the modulation of anger, aggression, body temperature, mood, sleep, sexuality, appetite, and metabolism

Teratogen—An agent or substance that causes malformation or damage to an embryo

Tricyclic Antidepressants (TCAs)—Class of antidepressants used to treat depression by increasing the amount of available serotonin and norepinephrine in the brain. They can be helpful in restoring sleep and appetite. Examples include amitriptyline (Elavil) and imipramine (Tofranil).

Chapter 10

Autoimmune/Immune-Mediated Disease—*Auto* means "self." This class of diseases is so-called because a person's immune system attacks his or her own body tissues.

Endoscopy—A thin, flexible tube (endoscope) is inserted, typically through the mouth, into the upper gastrointestinal tract to examine the small intestine.

Gluten-Free Diet (GFD)—A special diet that involves the avoidance of all products derived from wheat, barley, and rye. In addition, oats may need to be avoided by those newly diagnosed with celiac disease (CD) until it can be clearly demonstrated that CD is well controlled. The proteins in oats (avenins) can trigger an immune response similar to that produced by gluten in some individuals with CD, and the growth and processing of oats in North American can lead to cross-contamination with wheat, barley, and rye. The only accepted treatment for CD is lifelong adherence to a gluten-free diet.

Intestinal T-Cell Lymphoma—A rare and aggressive malignancy usually arising in patients with a history of CD

Intestinal Villi/Villius—Tiny, fingerlike projections that come out from the wall of the small intestine and increase the absorptive surface area of the intestinal wall

Small Bowel Biopsy—Samples of a portion of the lining of the small intestine are removed for further examination via endoscopy.

T Cell—A kind of white blood cell that is of key importance to the immune system and is at the core of adaptive immunity. T cells serve like soldiers in the body by searching out and destroying targeted invaders.

Chapter 11

Externalizing Behavior—Behavior problems that are manifested outward and reflect the child negatively acting on the external environment. These externalizing disorders typically consist of disruptive, hyperactive, and aggressive behaviors.

Internalizing Behavior—A behavior that involves withdrawal, anxiety, inhibition, and/or depression. These problems affect the child's inner psyche more than the external world.

Chapter 12

Asthma—A chronic condition of the respiratory system in which airways sometimes constrict, become inflamed, and are lined with excessive amounts of mucus, often in response to one or more triggers such as illness or allergens

Asthma Action Plan—A written plan developed jointly by a health care provider and the patient or the patient's family that is used to recognize signs of asthma attacks, take specific steps based on symptoms and peak flow readings, manage medications, and organize contact information for the patient

Bronchodilators—Medications that relieve asthma symptoms by relaxing muscle bands that tighten around airways. This action rapidly opens the airways, resulting in improved breathing.

Controller Medications—Medicines that work over time to reduce airway inflammation and help prevent asthma symptoms from occurring. They may be inhaled or swallowed as a pill or liquid. Also called *preventive* or *maintenance medications.*

Corticosteroids—Anti-inflammatory medications that reduce swelling and mucus production in the airways, resulting in lower sensitivity and reactivity

Inhaler—A medical device used for delivering medication into the body via the lungs. Examples include metered-dose inhalers (MDIs), which deliver a specific amount of medication to the lungs in aerosolized form, and dry powder inhalers (DPIs), which deliver a specific amount of medication in dry powder form.

Leukotriene Modifiers—Medications that block the body's production or use of leukotrienes, which are chemicals that maintain inflammation, increase mucous production, and contribute to swelling of lungs

Peak Flow Meter—A portable handheld device that measures a person's ability to push air out of the lungs and helps determine the openness of airways

Rescue Medications—Medicines that work immediately to relieve asthma symptoms. They are often inhaled directly into the lungs, where they open up the airways and relieve symptoms such as wheezing, coughing, and shortness of breath. Also called *quick-relief* or *fast-acting medications.*

Chapter 13

Allergen—An environmental trigger leading to an allergic reaction

Allergies—Disorders of the immune system, often also referred to as *atopy*. Allergic reactions are hypersensitivities that occur to environmental substances known as *allergens*.

Anaphylactic Shock—Occurs when a severe allergic response (i.e., anaphylaxis) triggers a quick release of large quantities of immunological mediators (histamines, prostaglandins, leukotrienes) leading to systemic vasodilation (associated with a sudden drop in blood pressure) and edema of bronchial mucosa (resulting in bronchoconstriction and difficulty breathing)

Anaphylaxis—The most severe type of hypersensitivity to an allergen

Antibody IgE—Proteins used by the immune system to identify and neutralize foreign objects, such as bacteria and viruses. Also called *immunoglobulin antibodies*.

Injectable Epinephrine—Epinephrine is a neurochemical that narrows blood vessels and opens airways in the lungs. These effects can reverse severe low blood pressure, wheezing, severe skin itching, hives, and other symptoms of an allergic reaction.

Intolerances—Discomfort but not danger associated with specific foods. Whereas an allergy is caused by an immune reaction to a protein, intolerances are caused by the body having trouble absorbing a sugar.

Chapter 14

Autoimmune—An immune response in which the body attacks itself

Carbohydrate Counting—A technique used by many diabetics in meal planning that involves counting the amount of carbohydrates ingested to determine the necessary amount of insulin to take

Glucose—A simple sugar that the body uses as its main source of energy

Glycemic Control—The degree to which blood glucose is being maintained within the normal range of glucose values

HbA1c—Blood test that measures a type of hemoglobin, which reflects a person's average blood glucose over the past 2 to 3 months

Hyperglycemia—A condition in which blood glucose is abnormally high

Hypoglycemia—A condition in which blood glucose is abnormally low

Insulin—A hormone that acts to lower blood sugar

Insulin-Dependent Diabetes Mellitus (IDDM)—An autoimmune disease often diagnosed in childhood and adolescence in which the beta cells of the pancreas are destroyed, resulting in little, if any, insulin production to regulate blood glucose. IDDM is also referred to as *type 1 diabetes* or *juvenile-onset diabetes.*

Insulin Pump—A medical device that serves as an alternative to insulin injections. It continuously delivers insulin to the body through a small, flexible tube that is inserted under the skin. It attempts to mimic the actions of a functional pancreas.

Ketones—Chemicals produced when the body breaks down fat for energy, brought on by an insufficient amount or lack of insulin in the body

Pancreas—A glandular organ, located in the abdomen partially behind the stomach, responsible for the production of insulin

References

Chapter 1

Abdelmalek, M., & Elston, D. M. (2008). *Childhood HIV disease.* Retrieved October 1, 2009, from http://emedicine.medscape.com/article/1133546-overview

Akinbami, L. J. (2006). *The state of childhood asthma, United States, 1980–2005: Advance data from vital and health statistics* (No. 381). Hyattsville, MD: National Center for Health Statistics.

Bernstein, A. B., Hing, E., Moss, A. J., Allen, K. F., Siller, A. B., & Tiggle, R. B. (2003). *Health care in America: Trends in utilization.* Hyattsville, MD: National Center for Health Statistics.

Blank, R. H., & Burau, V. (2004). *Comparative health policy.* London: Palgrave Macmillan.

Bloom, B., & Cohen, R. A. (2009). *Summary health statistics for U.S. children: National Health Interview Survey, 2007 (Vital and Health Statistics, 10[239]).* Hyattsville, MD: National Center for Health Statistics, Centers for Disease Control and Prevention. Retrieved October 1, 2009, from http://www.cdc.gov/nchs/data/series/sr_10/sr10_239.pdf

Cooper, W. O., Arbogast, P. G., Ding, H., Hickson, G. B., Fuchs, D. C., & Ray, W. A. (2006). Trends in prescribing of antipsychotic medications for US children. *Ambulatory Pediatrics, 6*(2), 79–83.

Cox, E. R., Halloran, D. R., Homan, S. M., Welliver, S., & Mager, D. E. (2008). Trends in the prevalence of chronic medication use in children: 2002–2005. *Pediatrics, 122,* 1053–1061.

Iyasu, S., & Tomashek, K. (2002). Infant mortality and low birth weight among black and white infants—United States, 1980–2000. *MMWR Weekly, 51,* 589–592.

McCabe, P.C. (2008). Academic functioning and quality of life of children and adolescents with allergic rhinitis—Part I. *Communiqué, 37*(1), 1–10.

National Alliance on Mental Illness (NAMI). (2004). *Children and adolescents living with mental illnesses.* Retrieved January 31, 2009, from http://www.nami.org

National Institute of Diabetes and Digestive and Kidney Diseases (NIDDK). (2008). *National diabetes statistics: 2007 fact sheet.* Bethesda, MD: U.S. Department of Health and Human Services, National Institutes of Health.

Portuese, E., & Orchard, T. (1995). Mortality in insulin-dependent diabetes mellitus. In *Diabetes in America* (2nd ed.; NIH Publication No. 95–1468; pp. 221–232). Washington, DC: U.S. Department of Health and Human Services.

Ries, L. A. G., Melbert, D., Krapcho, M., Stinchcomb, D.G., Howlader, N., Horner, M. J., et al. (Eds). (2008). *SEER cancer statistics review, 1975–2005.* Bethesda, MD: National Cancer Institute. Retrieved October 1, 2009, from http://seer.cancer.gov/csr/1975_2005/

Shaw, S., & McCabe, P. C. (2008). Hospital to school transition for children with chronic illness: Meeting the new challenges of an evolving health care system. *Psychology in the Schools, 45,* 74–87.

Zito, J. M., Safer, S. J., dosReis, S., Gardner, J. F., Magder, L., Soeken, K., et al. (2003). Psychotropic practice patterns for youth: A 10-year perspective. *Archives of Pediatric & Adolescent Medicine, 157*(1), 17–25.

Chapter 2

American Association of Suicidology (AAS). (2009). *Youth suicide fact sheet* [based on 2006 national statistics]. Retrieved October 1, 2009, from http://www .suicidology.org/web/guest/stats-and-tools/fact-sheets

Ayyash-Abdo, H. (2001). Childhood bereavement: What school psychologists need to know. *School Psychology International, 22,* 417–433.

Boelen, P. A., van den Bout, J., & de Keijser, J. (2003). Traumatic grief as a distinct disorder from bereavement-related depression and anxiety: A replication study with bereavement mental health care patients. *American Journal of Psychiatry, 160,* 1339–1342.

Brown, E. J., & Goodman, R. F. (2005). Childhood traumatic grief: An exploration of the construct in children bereaved on September 11. *Journal of Clinical Child & Adolescent Psychology, 34,* 248–259.

Centers for Disease Control and Prevention (CDC). (2009). WISQARS injury mortality reports, 1999–2006. Retrieved October 1, 2009, from http://webappa.cdc .gov/sasweb/ncipc/mortrate10_sy.html

Dowdney, L. (2000). Annotation: Childhood bereavement following parental death. *Journal of Child Psychology and Psychiatry, 7,* 819–830.

Holland, J. (1993). Child bereavement in Humberside primary schools. *Educational Research, 35,* 289–297.

Jimerson, S., & Huff, L. (2002). Responding to a sudden, unexpected death at school: Chance favors the prepared professional. In S. E. Brock, P. J. Lazerus, & S. R. Jimerson (Eds.), *Best practice in school crisis prevention and intervention* (pp. 451–488). Bethesda, MD: National Association of School Psychologists.

Kato, P. M., & Mann, T. (1999). A synthesis of psychological interventions for the bereaved. *Clinical Psychology Review, 19,* 275–296.

Mauk, G. W., & Sharpnack, J. D. (1997). Grief. In G. G. Bear, K. M. Minke, & A. Thomas (Eds.), *Children's needs II: Development, problems and alternatives* (pp. 375–385). Bethesda, MD: National Association of School Psychologists.

Murphy, S., Chung, I., & Johnson, L. (2002). Patterns of mental distress following the violent death of a child and predictors of change over time. *Research in Nursing and Health, 25,* 425–437.

Nader, K. O. (1997). Childhood traumatic loss: The interaction of trauma and grief. In C. R. Figley, B. E. Bride, & N. Mazza (Eds.), *Death and trauma: The traumatology of grieving* (pp. 17–41). Washington, DC: Taylor & Francis.

Poland, S., & Poland, D. (2004, April). Dealing with death at school. *Principal Leadership,* 8–12.

Stroebe, W., Schut, H., & Stroebe, M. S. (2005). Grief work, disclosure and counseling: Do they help the bereaved? *Clinical Psychology Review, 25,* 395–414.

Tonkins, S. A. M., & Lambert, M. J. (1996). A treatment outcome study of bereavement groups for children. *Child and Adolescent Social Work Journal, 13,* 3–22.

Wass, H., Miller, M. D., & Thornton, G. (1990). Death education and grief/suicide intervention in the public schools. *Death Studies, 14,* 253–268.

Webb, N. B. (2002). Assessment of the bereaved child. In N. B. Webb (Ed.), *Helping bereaved children: A handbook for practitioners* (pp. 45–69). New York: Guilford.

Chapter 3

Anderlid, B. M., Schoumans, J., Anneren G., Tapia-Paez, I., Dumanski, J., Blennow, E., et al. (2002). Subtelomeric rearrangements detected in patients with idiopathic mental retardation. *American Journal of Medical Genetics, 107,* 275–284.

Baker, E., Hinton, L., Callen, D. F., Altree, M., Dobbie, A., Eyre, H. J., et al. (2002). Study of 250 children with idiopathic mental retardation reveals nine cryptic and diverse subtelomeric chromosome abnormalities. *American Journal of Medical Genetics, 107,* 285–293.

Burack, J. A., Hodapp, R. A., & Zigler, E. (Eds.). (1998). *Handbook of mental retardation and development.* Cambridge, England: Cambridge University.

Carey, G. (2003). *Human genetics for the social sciences.* London: Sage.

Dykens, E. M., Hodapp, R., & Evans, D. (2006). Profiles and development of adaptive behavior in children with Down syndrome. *Down Syndrome Research and Practice, 9,* 45–50.

Dykens, E. M., & Rosner, B. A. (1999). Refining behavioral phenotypes: Personality-motivation in Williams and Prader-Willi syndromes. *American Journal on Mental Retardation, 104,* 158–169.

Engels, H., Brockschmidt, A., Hoischen, A., Landwehr, C., Bosse, K., Walldorf, C., et al. (2007). DNA microarray analysis identifies candidate regions and genes in unexplained mental retardation. *Neurology, 68,* 743–750.

Fidler, D. J., Hodapp, R. M., & Dykens, E. M. (2002). Behavioral phenotypes and special education. *The Journal of Special Education, 36*(2), 80–88.

Hessl, D., Glaser, B., Dyer-Friedman, J., Blasey, C., Hastie, T., Gunnar, M., et al. (2005). Cortisol and behaviour in fragile X syndrome. *Psychoneuroendocrinology, 27,* 855–872.

Hodapp, R. M., DesJardin, J. L., & Ricci, L. A. (2003). Genetic syndromes of mental retardation: Should they matter for the early interventionist? *Infants and Young Children, 16,* 152–160.

Hodapp, R. M., & Dykens, E. M. (2005). Measuring behavior in genetic disorders of mental retardation. *Mental Retardation and Developmental Disabilities Research Reviews, 11,* 340–346.

Holland, A., Whittington, J., & Hinton, E. (2003). The paradox of Prader-Willi syndrome: A genetic model of starvation. *Lancet, 362,* 989–991.

Jones, K. L. (1997). *Smith's recognizable patterns of human malformation* (5th ed.). Philadelphia: W. B. Saunders.

Meyer-Lindenberg, A., Mervis, C. B., & Faith Berman, K. (2006). Neural mechanisms in Williams syndrome: A unique window to genetic influences on cognition and behaviour. *Nature Reviews Neuroscience, 7,* 380–393.

Singer, M., & Berg, P. (Eds.). (1997). *Exploring genetic mechanisms.* Sausalito, CA: University Science Books.

Udwin, O., & Yule, W. (1991). A cognitive and behavioural phenotype in Williams syndrome. *Journal of Clinical and Experimental Neuropsychology, 16,* 317–322.

Chapter 4

Antshel, K. M., & Waisbren, S. E. (2003). Timing is everything: Executive functions in children exposed to elevated levels of phenylalanine. *Neuropsychology, 17,* 458–468.

Arnold, G. L., Kramer, B. M., Kirby, R. S., Plumeau, P. B., Blakely, E. M., Sanger-Cregan, L. S., et al. (1998). Factors affecting cognitive, motor, behavioral and executive functioning in children with phenylketonuria. *Acta Paediatrica, 87,* 565–570.

Carey, K. T., & Lesen, B. M. (1998). Phenylketonuria. In L. Phelps (Ed.), *Health-related disorders in children and adolescents: A compilation of 96 rare and common disorders.* Washington, DC: American Psychological Association.

Cerone, R., Schiaffino, M. C., Di Stefano, S., & Veneselli, E. (1999). Phenylketonuria: Diet for life or not? *Acta Paediatirica, 88,* 664–666.

Griffiths, P. (2000). Neuropsychological approaches to treatment policy issues in phenylketonuria. *European Journal of Pediatrics, 159,* 82–86.

Hardelid, P., Cortina-Borja, M., Munro, A., Jones, H., Cleary, M., Champion, M. P., et al. (2006). The birth prevalence of PKU in populations of European, South Asian and Sub-Saharan African Ancestry Living in South East England. *Annals of Human Genetics, 72,* 65–71.

Huijbregts, S. C. J., De Sonneville, L. M. J., Van Spronsen, F. J., Berends, I. E., Licht, R., Verkerk, P. H., et al. (2003). Motor function under lower and higher controlled processing demands in early and continuously treated phenylketonuria. *Neuropsychology, 17,* 369–379.

Huttenlocher, P. R. (2000). The neuropsychology of phenylketonuria: Human and animal studies. *European Journal of Pediatrics, 159,* 102–106.

Koch, R. (1999). Issues in newborn screening for phenylketonuria. *American Family Physician, 60,* 1462–1466.

Koch, R., Moseley, K., Ning, J., Romstad, A., Guldberg, P., & Guttler, F. (1999). Long-term beneficial effects of the phenylalanine-restricted diet in late-diagnosed individuals with phenylketonuria. *Molecular Genetics and Metabolism, 67,* 148–155.

Levy, H., Burton, B., Cederbaum, S., & Scriver, C. (2007). Recommendations for evaluation of responsiveness to tetrahydrobiopterin (BH$_4$) in phenylketonuria and its use in treatment. *Molecular Genetics & Metabolism, 92,* 287–291.

Luciana, M., Sullivan, J., & Nelson, C. A. (2001). Associations between phenylalanine-to-tyrosine ratios and performances on tests of neuropsychological function in adolescents treated early and continuously for phenylketonuria. *Child Development, 72,* 1637–1652.

National Institutes of Health (NIH). (2000). *Phenylketonuria: Screening and management* (NIH Consensus Statement No. 113). Retrieved October 1, 2009, from http://consensus.nih.gov/2000/2000Phenylketonuria113html.htm

National Institutes of Health (NIH). (2002). *X-Plain™ phenylketonuria or PKU: Reference summary.* Retrieved October 1, 2009, from http://www.nlm.nih.gov/medlineplus/tutorials/pku/pd029102.pdf

Ogier de Baulny, H., Abadie, V., Feillet, F., & de Parscau, L. (2007). Management of phenylketonuria and hyperphenylalaninemia. *Journal of Nutrition, 13,* 1561–1563.

Rollins, J. A. (2008). Items of interest: First specific drug therapy approved for the treatment of PKU. *Pediatric Nursing, 4,* 181–182.

Seashore, M. R., Friedman, E., Novelly, R. A., & Bapat, V. (1985). Loss of intellectual function in children with phenylketonuria after relaxation of dietary phenylalanine restriction. *Pediatrics, 75,* 226–232.

Surtees, R., & Blau, N. (2000). The neurochemistry of phenlyketonuria. *European Journal of Pediatrics, 159,* 109–113.

van Calcar, S. C., MacLeod, E. L., Gleason, S. T., Etzel, M. R., Clayton, M. K., Wolff, J. A., et al. (2009). Improved nutritional management of phenylketonuria by using a diet containing glycomacropeptide compared with amino acids. *American Journal of Clinical Nutrition, 89,* 1068–1077.

Waisbren, S. E., & Azen, C. (2003). Cognitive and behavioral development in maternal phenylketonuria offspring. *Pediatrics, 112,* 1544–1547.

Welsh, M. C., Pennington, B. F., Ozonoff, S., Rouse, B., & McCabe, E. R. B. (1990). Neuropsychology of early-treated phenylketonuria: Specific executive function deficits. *Child Development, 61,* 1697–1713.

White, D. A., Nortz, M. J., Mandernach, T., Huntington, K., & Steiner, R. D. (2001). Deficits in memory strategy use related to prefrontal dysfunction during early development: Evidence from children with phenylketonuria. *Neuropsychology, 15,* 221–229.

Chapter 5

Autism Genome Project Consortium. (2007). Mapping autism risk loci using genetic linkage and chromosomal rearrangements. *Nature Genetics, 39*(3), 319–328.

Autism Speaks. (2009). *Treating autism.* Retrieved October 1, 2009, from http://www.autismspeaks.org/treatment/index.php

Bailey, A., Le Couteur, A., Gottesman, I., Bolton, P., Simonoff, E., Yuzda, E., et al. (1995). Autism as a strongly genetic disorder: Evidence from a British twin study. *Psychological Medicine, 25,* 63–78.

Bryson, S. E., Rogers, S. J., & Fombonne, E. (2003). Autism spectrum disorders: Early detection, intervention, education, and psychopharmacological management. *Canadian Journal of Psychiatry, 48,* 506–516.

Canadian Paediatric Society. (2004). Early intervention for children with autism. *Paediatric Child Health, 9,* 267–270.

Centers for Disease Control and Prevention (2009). *Autism spectrum disorders: Data & statistics.* Retrieved October 17, 2009, from http://www.cdc.gov/ncbddd/autism/data.html.

Cohen, D., Pichard, N., Tordjman, S., Bauman, C., Burglen, L., Excoffier, E., et al. (2005). Specific genetic disorders and autism: Clinical contribution towards their identification. *Journal of Autism and Developmental Disorders, 35,* 103–116.

Filipek, P. A., Accardo, P. J., Baranek, G. T., Cook, E. H., Dawson, G., Gordon, B., et al. (1999). The screening and diagnosis of autistic spectrum disorders. *Journal of Autism and Developmental Disorders, 29,* 439–484.

Fombonne, E. (2002). Epidemiological trends in the rates of autism. *Molecular Psychiatry, 7,* 4–6.

Fombonne, E. (2003). The prevalence of autism. *Journal of the American Medical Association, 289,* 87–89.

Fombonne, E., Zakarian, R., Bennett, A., Meng, L., & McLean-Heywood, D. (2006). Pervasive developmental disorders in Montreal, Quebec, Canada: Prevalence and links with immunizations. *Pediatrics, 118,* 139–150.

Freitag, C. M. (2007). The genetics of autistic disorders and its clinical relevance: A review of the literature. *Molecular Psychiatry, 12,* 2–22.

Gupta, A. R., & State, M. W. (2007). Recent advances in the genetics of autism. *Biological Psychiatry, 61,* 429–437.

Herbert, M. R., Russo, J. P., Yang, S., Roohi, J., Blaxill, M., Kahl, S. G., et al. (2006). Autism and environmental genomics. *Journal of NeuroVirology, 11,* 1–10.

Jones, G. (2002). *Educational provision for children with autism and Asperger syndrome.* London: David Fulton.

Muhle, R., Trencoste, S. V., & Rapin, I. (2004). Genetics of autism. *Pediatrics, 113,* 472–486.

Newschaffer, C. J., Croen, L. A., Daniels, J., Giarelli, E., Grether, J. K., Levy, S. E., et al. (2007). The epidemiology of autism spectrum disorders. *Annual Reviews of Public Health, 28,* 235–258.

Paris Autism Research International Sibpair Study. (1999). Genome-wide scan for autism susceptibility genes. *Human Molecular Genetics, 8,* 805–812.

Persico, A. M., & Bourgeron, T. (2006). Searching for ways out of the autism maze: Genetic, epigenetic and environmental clues. *Trends in Neuroscience, 29,* 349–356.

Rutter, M. (2005). Aetiology of autism: Findings and questions. *Journal of Intellectual Disability Research, 48,* 231–238.

Schanen, N. C. (2006). Epigenetics of autism spectrum disorders. *Human Molecular Genetics, 15,* R138–R150.

Simonoff, E. (1998). Genetic counseling in autism and pervasive developmental disorders. *Journal of Autism and Developmental Disorders, 28,* 447–456.

Skuse, D. H. (2000). Imprinting, the X-chromosome, and the male brain: Explaining sex differences in the liability to autism. *Pediatric Research, 47,* 9–16.

Smalley, S. L., Asarnow, R. F., & Spence, M. A. (1988). Autism and genetics: A decade of research. *Archives of General Psychiatry, 45,* 953–961.

Volker, M. A., & Lopata, C. (2008). Autism: A review of biological bases, assessment, and intervention. *School Psychology Quarterly, 23,* 258–270.

Wilson, H. L., Wong, A. C. C., Shaw, S. R., Tse, W-Y., Stapleton, G. A., Phelan, M. C., et al. (2003). Molecular characterization of the 22q13 deletion syndrome supports the role of haploinsufficiency of SHANK3/PROSAP2 in the major neurological symptoms. *Journal of Medical Genetics, 40,* 575–584.

Yang, M. S., & Gill, M. (2007). A review of gene linkage, association and expression studies in autism and an assessment of convergent evidence. *International Journal of Developmental Neuroscience, 25,* 69–85.

Chapter 6

Anderson, A., & Phelps, E. (2002). Is the human amygdala critical for the subjective experience of emotion? Evidence of intact dispositional affect in patients with amygdala lesions. *Journal of Cognitive Neuroscience, 14,* 709–720.

Beyond shyness and stage fright: Social anxiety disorder. (2003). *Harvard Mental Health Letter, 20,* 1–4.

Chung, J., & Evans, M. (2000). Shyness and symptoms of illness in young children. *Canadian Journal of Behavioural Science, 32,* 49–57.

Crozier, W. R., & Hostettler, K. (2003). The influence of shyness on children's test performance. *British Journal of Educational Psychology, 73,* 317–328.

De Bellis, M., Casey, B., Dahl, R., Birmaher, B., Williamson, D., Thomas, K., et al. (2000). A pilot study of amygdala volumes in pediatric generalized anxiety disorder. *Biological Psychiatry, 48,* 51–57.

Greco, L., & Morris, T. (2001). Treating childhood shyness and related behavior: Empirically evaluated approaches to promote positive social interactions. *Clinical Child and Family Psychology Review, 4,* 299–318.

Henderson, H. A., & Fox, N. A. (1998). Inhibited and uninhibited children: Challenges in school settings. *School Psychology Review, 27,* 492–506.

Kagan, J., & Snidman, N. (1999). Early childhood predictors of adult anxiety disorders. *Biological Psychiatry, 46,* 1536–1541.

Kemple, K. (1995). Shyness and self-esteem in early childhood. *Journal of Humanistic Education & Development, 33*(4), 173–183.

Phillips, M., Drevets, W., Rauch, S., & Lane, R. (2003). Neurobiology of emotion perception I: The neural basis of normal emotion perception. *Biological Psychiatry, 54,* 504–514.

Poulou, M., & Norwich, B. (2000). Teachers' perceptions of students with emotional and behavioural difficulties: Severity and prevalence. *European Journal of Special Needs Education, 15,* 171–187.

Robinson, J., Kagan, J., Reznick, J., & Corley, R. (1992). The heritability of inhibited and uninhibited behavior: A twin study. *Developmental Psychology, 28,* 1030–1037.

Schmidt, L. A., Fox, N. A., Rubin, K. H., & Sternberg, E. M. (1997). Behavioral and neuroendocrine responses in shy children. *Developmental Psychobiology, 30,* 127–140.

Schulkin, J., Gold, P., & McEwen, B. (1998). Induction of corticotrophin-releasing hormone gene expression by glucocorticoids: Implication for understanding the states of fear and anxiety and allostatic load. *Psychoneuroendocrinology, 23,* 219–243.

Schwartz, C., Wright, C., Shin, L., Kagan, J., Whalen, P., McMullin, K., et al. (2003). Differential amygdalar response to novel versus newly familiar neutral faces: A functional MRI probe developed for studying inhibited temperament. *Biological Psychiatry, 53,* 854–862.

Smoller, J. W., Paulus, M. P., Fagerness, J. A., Purcell, S., Yamaki, L. H., Hirshfeld-Becker, D., et al. (2008). Influence of RGS2 on anxiety-related temperament, personality, and brain function. *Archives of General Psychiatry, 65,* 298–308.

Stein, M. (1998). Neurobiological perspectives on social phobia: From affiliation to zoology. *Biological Psychiatry, 44,* 1277–1285.

Zimmermann, L., & Stansbury, K. (2004). The influence of emotion regulation, level of shyness, and habituation on the neuroendocrine response of three-year-old children. *Psychoneuroendocrinology, 29,* 973–982.

Chapter 7

Baker, B. L., & Blacher, J. (2002). For better or worse? Impact of residential placement on families. *Mental Retardation, 40,* 1–13.

Baker, B. L., Blacher, J., & Olsson, M. B. (2005). Preschool children with and without developmental delay: Behaviour problems, parents' optimism and well-being. *Journal of Intellectual Disability Research, 49,* 575–590.

Baker-Ericzen, M. J., Brookman-Frazee, L., & Stahmer, A. (2005). Stress levels and adaptability in parents of toddlers with and without autism spectrum disorders. *Research & Practice for Persons With Severe Disabilities, 30,* 194–204.

Bayat, M. (2007). Evidence of resilience in families of children with autism. *Journal of Intellectual Disability Research, 51,* 702–714.

Boss, P. (2006). *Loss, trauma, and resilience: Therapeutic work with ambiguous loss.* New York: Norton.

Byrnes, A. L., Berk, N. W., Cooper, M. F., & Marazita, M. L. (2003). Parental evaluation of informing interviews for cleft lip and/or palate. *Pediatrics, 112,* 308–314.

Cohen, M. S. (1999). Families coping with childhood chronic illness: A research review. *Family Systems & Health, 17,* 149–164.

Dellve, L., Samuelsson, L., Tallborn, A., Fasth, A., & Hallberg, L. R.-M. (2006). Stress and well-being among parents of children with rare diseases: A prospective intervention study. *Journal of Advanced Nursing, 53,* 392–402.

Giallo, R., & Gavidia-Payne, S. (2006). Child, parent and family factors as predictors of adjustment for siblings of children with a disability. *Journal of Intellectual Disability Research, 50,* 937–948.

Grant, G., Ramcharan, P., McGrath, M., Nolan, M., & Keady, J. (1998). Rewards and gratifications among family caregivers: Towards a refined model of caring and coping. *Journal of Intellectual Disability Research, 42,* 58–71.

Gray, D. (2003). Gender and coping: The parents of children with high functioning autism. *Social Science & Medicine, 56,* 631–642.

Guralnick, M. J. (2000). An agenda for change in early childhood inclusion. *Journal of Early Intervention, 23,* 213–222.

Hastings, R. P., Allen, R., McDermott, K., & Still, D. (2002). Factors related to positive perceptions in mothers of children with intellectual disabilities. *Journal of Applied Research in Intellectual Disabilities, 15,* 269–275.

Kaminsky, L., & Dewey, D. (2002). Psychosocial adjustment in siblings of children with autism. *Journal of Child Psychology and Psychiatry, 43,* 225–235.

Lietz, C. A. (2006). Uncovering stories of family resilience: A mixed methods study of resilient families, part 1. *Families in Society: The Journal of Contemporary Social Services, 87,* 575–582.

Longo, D. C., & Bond, L. (1984). Families of the handicapped child: Research and practice. *Family Relations, 33,* 57–65.

Mansell, W., & Morris, K. (2004). A survey of parents' reactions to the diagnosis of an autistic spectrum disorder by a local service: Access to information and use of services. *Autism, 8,* 387–407.

Mauldon, J. (1992). Children's risks of experiencing divorce and remarriage: Do disabled children destabilize marriages? *Population Studies, 46,* 349–362.

Minnes, P., & Nachshen, J. S. (1997). The Family Stress and Support Questionnaire: Focusing on the needs of parents. *Journal on Developmental Disabilities, 5,* 67–76.

O'Brien, M. (2007). Ambiguous loss in families of children with autism spectrum disorders. *Family Relations, 56,* 135–146.

Olsson, M. B., & Hwang, P. C. (2001). Depression in the mothers and fathers of children with intellectual disabilities. *Journal of Intellectual Disability Research, 45,* 1–9.

Patterson, J. (2002). Integrating family resilience and family stress theory. *Journal of Marriage and Family, 64,* 349–360.

Seligman, M., & Darling, R. B. (2007). *Ordinary families, special children: A systems approach to childhood disability* (3rd ed.). New York: Guilford Press.

Seltzer, M. M., Greenberg, J. S., Floyd, F. J., Pettee, Y., & Hong, J. (2001). Life course impacts of parenting a child with a disability. *American Journal on Mental Retardation, 106,* 265–286.

Sharpe, D., & Rossiter, L. (2002). Siblings of children with a chronic illness: A meta-analysis. *Journal of Pediatric Psychology, 27,* 699–710.

Siegel, B., & Silverstein, S. (1994). *What about me? Growing up with a developmentally disabled sibling.* New York: Plenum Press.

Stainton, T., & Besser, H. (1998). The positive impact of children with an intellectual disability on the family. *Journal of Intellectual & Developmental Disability, 23,* 57–70.

Stoneman, Z., & Gavidia-Payne, S. (2006). Marital adjustment in families of young children with disabilities: Associations with daily hassles and problem-focused coping. *American Journal on Mental Retardation, 111,* 1–14.

Tarleton, B., & Ward, L. (2007). "Parenting with support": The views and experiences of parents with intellectual disabilities. *Journal of Policy and Practice in Intellectual Disabilities, 4,* 194–202.

Werner, E., & Smith, R. (1992). *Overcoming the odds: High risk children from birth to adulthood.* New York: Cornell University Press.

Witt, W. P., Riley, A. W., & Cairo, M. J. (2003). Childhood functional status, family stressors, and psychological adjustment among school-aged children with disabilities in the United States. *Archives of Pediatric Adolescent Medicine, 157,* 687–695.

Chapter 8

Coles, C. D. (2001). Fetal alcohol exposure and attention: Moving beyond ADHD. *Alcohol Research and Health, 25,* 199–204.

Floyd, R. L., O'Connor, M. J., Bertrand, J., & Sokol, R. (2006). Reducing adverse outcomes from prenatal alcohol exposure: A clinical plan of action. *Alcoholism: Clinical and Experimental Research, 30,* 1271–1275.

Green, J. (2007). Fetal alcohol spectrum disorders: Understanding the effects of prenatal alcohol exposure and supporting students. *Journal of School Health, 77,* 103–108.

Guerri, C. (1998). Neuroanatomical and neurophysiological mechanisms involved in central nervous system dysfunctions induced by prenatal alcohol exposure. *Alcoholism: Clinical and Experimental Research, 22,* 304–312.

Jacobson, J. L., & Jacobson, S. W. (2002). Effects of prenatal alcohol exposure on child development. *Alcohol Research and Health, 26,* 282–286.

Jones, K. L. (1986). Fetal alcohol syndrome. *Pediatrics in Review, 8,* 122–126.

Kelly, S. J., Day, N., & Streissguth, A. P. (2000). Effects of prenatal alcohol exposure on social behavior in humans and other species. *Neurotoxicology and Teratology, 22,* 143–149.

Kodituwakku, P. W., Handmaker, N. S., Cutler, S. K., Weathersby, E. K., & Handmaker, S. D. (1995). Specific impairments in self-regulation in children exposed to alcohol prenatally. *Alcoholism: Clinical and Experimental Research, 19,* 1558–1564.

Krahl, S. E., Berman, R. F., & Hannigan, J. H. (1999). Electrophysiology of hippocampal CA1 neurons after prenatal ethanol exposure. *Alcohol, 17,* 125–131.

Mattson, S. N., Riley, E. P., Gramling, L., Delis, D. C., & Jones, K. L. (1998). Neuropsychological comparison of alcohol-exposed children with or without physical features of fetal alcohol syndrome. *Neuropsychology, 12,* 146–153.

O'Connor, M. J., Shah, B., Whaley, S., Cronin, P., Gunderson, B., & Graham, J. (2002). Psychiatric illness in a clinical sample of children with prenatal alcohol exposure. *The American Journal of Drug and Alcohol Abuse, 28,* 743–754.

Olney, J. W., Farber, N. B., Wozniak, D. F., Jevtovic-Todorovic, V., & Ikonomidou, C. (2000). Environmental agents that have the potential to trigger massive apoptotic neurodegeneration in the developing brain. *Environmental Health Perspectives, 108,* 383–388.

O'Malley, K. D., & Nanson, J. (2002). Clinical implications of a link between fetal alcohol spectrum disorder and attention-deficit hyperactivity disorder. *Canadian Journal of Psychiatry, 47,* 349–354.

Paley, B., O'Connor, M. J., Kogan, N., & Findlay, R. (2005). Prenatal alcohol exposure, child externalizing behavior, and maternal stress. *Parenting: Science and Practice, 5,* 29–56.

Schonfeld, A. M., Paley, B., Frankel, F., & O'Connor, M. J. (2006). Executive functioning predicts social skills following prenatal alcohol exposure. *Child Neuropsychology, 12,* 439–452.

Sowell, E. R., Thompson, P. M., Peterson, B. S., Mattson, S. N., Welcome, S. E., Henkenius, A.L., et al. (2002). Mapping cortical gray matter asymmetry patterns in adolescents with heavy prenatal alcohol exposure. *NeuroImage, 17,* 1807–1819.

Streissguth, A. P., Aase, J. M., Clarren, S. K., Randels, S. P., LaDue, R, A., & Smith, D. F. (1991). Fetal alcohol syndrome in adolescence and adults. *Journal of the American Medical Association, 265,* 1961–1967.

Teeter, P. A., & Semrud-Clikeman, M. (1997). *Child neuropsychology: Assessment and interventions for neurodevelopmental disorders.* Boston: Allyn & Bacon.

Chapter 9

Altshuler, L. L., Cohen, L., Szuba, M. P., Burt, V. K., Gitlin, M., & Mintz, J. (1996). Pharmacologic management of psychiatric illness during pregnancy: Dilemmas and guidelines. *American Journal of Psychiatry, 153*(5), 592–606.

Altshuler, L. L., & Szuba, M. P. (1994). Course of psychiatric disorders in pregnancy. *Neurologic Clinics, 12,* 613–635.

Arnon, J., Shechtman, S., & Ornoy, A. (2000). The use of psychiatric drugs in pregnancy and lactation. *Israeli Journal of Psychiatry and Related Sciences, 37,* 205–222.

Barki, Z. H. K., Kravitz, H. M., & Berki, T. M. (1998). Psychotropic medications in pregnancy. *Psychiatric Annals, 28,* 486–500.

Barnet, B., Duggan, A. K., & Devoe, M. (2003). Reduced low birth weight for teenagers receiving prenatal care at a school-based health center: Effect of access and comprehensive care. *Journal of Adolescent Health, 33,* 349–358.

Baum, A. L., & Misri, S. (1996). Selective serotonin-reuptake inhibitors in pregnancy and lactation. *Harvard Review of Psychiatry, 4,* 117–125.

Blier, P. (2006). Pregnancy, depression, antidepressants and breast-feeding. *Journal of Psychiatry and Neuroscience, 31,* 226–228.

Brent, N., & Wisner, K. (1998). Fluoxetine and carbamazepine concentrations in a nursing mother/infant pair. *Clinical Pediatrics, 37,* 41–44.

Cohen, L. S., Altshuler, L. L., Harlow, B. L., Nonacs, R., Newport, D. J., Viguera, A. C., et al. (2006). Relapse of major depression during pregnancy in women who maintain or discontinue antidepressant treatment. *JAMA, 295,* 499–507.

Einarson, A., Selby, P., & Koren, G. (2001). Abrupt discontinuation of psychotropic drugs during pregnancy: Fear of teratogenic risk and impact of counseling. *Journal of Psychiatry and Neuroscience, 26,* 44–49.

Evans, J., Heron, J., Francomb, H., Oke, S., & Golding, J. (2001). Cohort study of depressed mood during pregnancy and after childbirth. *British Medical Journal, 323*, 257–260.

Food and Drug Administration (FDA). (2006). Treatment challenges of depression in pregnancy and the possibility of persistent pulmonary hypertension in newborns. Retrieved October 1, 2009, from http://www.fda.gov/Drugs/DrugSafety/PublicHealthAdvisories/ucm124348.htm

Gentile, S. (2006). Escitalopram late in pregnancy and while breastfeeding. *Annals of Pharmacotherapy, 26*, 256–258.

Hendrick, V., Stowe, Z. N., Altshuler, L. L., & Hwang, S. (2003). Placental passage of antidepressant medications. *The American Journal of Psychiatry, 160*, 993–997.

Iqbal, M. M. (1999). Effects of antidepressants during pregnancy and lactation. *Annals of Clinical Psychiatry, 11*, 237–256.

Kristensen, J., Ilett, K., Hackett, L., Yapp, P., Paech, M., & Begg, E. J. (1999). Distribution and excretion of fluoxetine and norfluoxetine in human milk. *British Journal of Clinical Pharmacology, 48*, 521–527.

Misri, S., Kostaras, D., & Kostaras, X. (2000). The use of selective serotonin reuptake inhibitors during pregnancy and lactation: Current knowledge. *Canadian Journal of Psychaitry, 45*, 285–288.

National Institute of Mental Health (NIMH). (2008). *The numbers count: Mental disorders in America.* Retrieved October 1, 2009, from http://www.nimh.nih.gov/publicat/numbers.cfm

Simon, G. E., Cunningham, M. L., & Davis, R. L. (2002). Outcomes of prenatal antidepressant exposure. *American Journal of Psychiatry, 159*, 2055–2061.

Stowe, Z. N., Strader, J. R., & Nemeroff, C. B. (2001). Psychopharmocology during pregnancy and lactation. In A. F. Schatzberg & C. B. Nemeroff (Eds.), *Essentials of clinical psychopharmacology* (pp. 659–680). Washington, DC: American Psychiatric Association.

Zayas, L. H., Cunningham, C., McKee, M. D., & Jankowski, K. R. B. (2002). Depression and negative life events among pregnant African-American and Hispanic women. *Women's Health Issues, 12*(1), 16–22.

Chapter 10

Addolorato, G., Capristo, E., Ghittoni, G., Valeri, C., Mascianà, R., Ancona, C., et al. (2001). Anxiety but not depression decreases in celiac patients after one-year gluten-free diet: A longitudinal study. *Scandinavian Journal of Gastroenterology, 5*, 502–506.

Cárdenas, A., & Kelly, C. (2002). Celiac sprue. *Seminars in Gastrointestinal Disease, 13*, 232–244.

Catassi, C., & Fasano, A. (2002). New developments in childhood celiac disease. *Current Gastroenterology Reports, 4*, 238–243.

Ciacci, C., D'Agate, C., DeRosa, A., Franzese, C., Errichiello, S., Gasperi, V., et al. (2003). Self-rated quality of life in celiac disease. *Digestive Diseases and Sciences, 48*, 2216–2220.

Ciacci, C., Iavarone, A., Mazzacca, G., & DeRosa, A. (1998). Depressive symptoms in adult coeliac disease. *Scandinavian Journal of Gastroenterology, 33*, 247–250.

Collin, P., Reunala, T., Pukkala, E., Laippala, P., Keyriläinen, O., & Pasternack, A. (1994). Coeliac disease: Associated disorders and survival. *Gut, 35*, 1215–1218.

Corrao, G., Corazza, G., Bagnardi, V., Brusco, G., Ciacci, C., Cottone, M., et al. (2001). Mortality in patients with celiac disease and their relatives: A cohort study. *Lancet, 358*, 356–361.

Crannery, A., Zarkadas, M., Graham, I., & Switer, C. (2003). The Canadian celiac health survey: The Ottawa chapter pilot. *BMC Gastroenterology, 3*, 8–13.

Dennis, M., & Case, S. (2004). Going gluten-free: A primer for clinicians. *Practical Gastroenterology, 28,* 86–104.

Devlin, S., Andrews, C., & Beck, P. (2004). Celiac disease: CME update for family physicians. *Canadian Family Physician, 50,* 719–725.

DiMatteo, R., Lepper, H., & Croghan, T. (2000). Depression is a risk factor for non-compliance with medical treatment: Meta-analysis of the effects of anxiety and depression on patient adherence. *Archives of Internal Medicine, 160,* 2101–2107.

Edwards George, J. B., Leffler, D. A., Dennis, M. D., Franko, D. L., Blom-Hoffman, J., & Kelly, C. P. (2008). Psychological correlates of gluten-free diet adherence in adults with celiac disease [Electronic version]. *Journal of Clinical Gastroenterology, 43*(4), 301–306. Retrieved January 2009 from http://journals.lww.com/jcge

Fasano, A. (2003). Celiac disease: How to handle a clinical chameleon. *New England Journal of Medicine, 348,* 2568–2570.

Fasano, A., Berti, I., Gerarduzzi, T., Not, T., Colletti, R., Dargo, S., et al. (2003). Prevalence of celiac disease in at-risk groups in the United States. *Archives of Internal Medicine, 163,* 286–292.

Green, P. H., & Jabri, B. (2003). Coeliac disease, *Lancet, 362,* 383–391.

Kumar, P., Walker-Smith, J., Milla, P., Harris, G., Colyer, J., Halliday, R., et al. (1988). The teenage celiac: Follow-up study of 102 patients. *Archives of Disease in Childhood, 63,* 916–920.

Mayer, M., Greco, L., & Troncone, R. (1991). Compliance of adolescents with celiac disease with a gluten-free diet. *Gut, 32,* 881–885.

Pietzak, M. (2005). Follow-up of patients with celiac disease: Achieving compliance with treatment. *Gastroenterology, 128,* S135–S141.

Pietzak, M., Catassi, C., Drago, S., Fornaroli, F., & Fasano, A. (2001). Celiac disease: Going against the grains. *Nutrition in Clinical Practice, 16,* 335–344.

Rashid, M., Crannery, A., Graham, I., Zarkardas, M., Switer, C., Case, S., et al. (2003). Canadian celiac health survey: Pediatric data. *Journal of Pediatric Gastroenterology and Nutrition, 37,* A127.

Schuppan, D. (2000). Current concepts of celiac disease pathogenesis. *Gastroenterology, 119,* 234–242.

Talley, N., Valdovinos, M., Petterson, T., Carpenter, H., & Melton L. (1994). Epidemiology of celiac sprue: A community-based study. *American Journal of Gastroenterology, 89,* 843–846.

Treem, W. (2004). Emerging concepts in celiac disease. *Current Opinion in Pediatrics, 16,* 552–559.

Chapter 11

Ashman, S. B., Dawson, G., & Panagiotides, H. (2008). Trajectories of maternal depression over 7 years: Relations with child psychophysiology and behavior and role of contextual risks. *Development and Psychopathology, 20,* 55–77.

Chronis, A. M., Lahey, B. B., Pelham, W E., Jr., Williams, S. H., Baumann, B. L., Kipp, H., et al. (2007). Maternal depression and early positive parenting predict future conduct problems in young children with attention-deficit/hyperactivity disorder. *Developmental Psychology, 43,* 70–82.

Cicchetti, D., Rogosch, F. A., & Toth, S. L. (1998). Maternal depressive and contextual risk: Contributions to the development of attachment insecurity and behavior problems in toddlerhood. *Development and Psychopathology, 10,* 283–300.

Dawson, G., Ashman, S. B., Panagiotides, H., Hessl, D., Self, J., Yamada, E., et al. (2003). Preschool outcomes of children of depressed mothers: Role of maternal behavior, contextual risk, and children's brain activity. *Child Development, 74,* 1158–1175.

Elgar, F. J., Curtis, L. J., McGrath, P. J., Waschbusch, D. A., & Stewart, S. H. (2003). Antecedent-consequence conditions in maternal mood and child adjustment: A four-year cross-lagged study. *Journal of Clinical Child and Adolescent Psychology, 32,* 362–374.

Franck, K. L., & Buehler, C. (2007). A family process model of marital hostility, parental depressive affect, and early adolescent problem behavior: The roles of triangulation and parental warmth. *Journal of Family Psychology, 21,* 614–625.

Garstein, M. A., & Sheeber, L. (2004). Child behavior problems and maternal symptoms of depression: A mediational model. *Journal of Child and Adolescent Psychiatric Nursing, 17,* 141–150.

Grace, S. L., Evindar, A., & Stewart, D. E. (2003). The effect of postpartum depression on child cognitive development and behavior: A review and critical analysis of the literature. *Archives of Women's Mental Health, 6,* 263–274.

Gross, H. E., Shaw, D. S., & Moilanen, K. L. (2008). Reciprocal associations between boys' externalizing problems and mothers' depressive symptoms. *Journal of Abnormal Child Psychology, 36,* 693–709.

Knitzer, J., Theberge, S., & Johnson, K. (2008). *Reducing maternal depression and its impact on young children: Toward a responsive early childhood policy framework.* Retrieved October 1, 2009, from http://www.nccp.org/publications/pub_791.html

McFarland, M. L., & Sanders, M. R. (2003). The effects of mothers' depression on the behavioral assessment of disruptive child behavior. *Child & Family Behavior Therapy, 25,* 39–63.

Murray, L., Sinclair, D., Cooper, P., Ducournay, P., Turner, P., & Stein, A. (1999). The socioemotional development of 5-year-old children of postnatally depressed mothers. *Journal of Child Psychology and Psychiatry, 40,* 1259–1271.

Phillips, L. H. C., & O'Hara, M. W. (1991). Prospective study of postpartum depression: 4½-year follow-up of women and children. *Journal of Abnormal Psychology, 100*(2), 151–155.

Shin, D. W., & Stein, M. A. (2008). Maternal depression predicts maternal use of corporal punishment in children with attention-deficit/hyperactivity disorder. *Yonsei Medical Journal, 49,* 573–580.

West, A. E., & Newman, D. L. (2003). Worried and blue: Mild parental anxiety and depression in relation to the development of young children's temperament and behavior problems. *Parenting: Science and Practice, 3,* 133–154.

Chapter 12

Alati, R., O'Callaghan, M., Najman, J. M., Williams, G. M., Bor, W., & Lawlor, D. A. (2005). Asthma and internalizing behavior problems in adolescence: A longitudinal study. *Psychosomatic Medicine, 67,* 462–470.

American Lung Association (ALA). (2009, January). *Asthma medicines chart.* Retrieved October 1, 2009, from http://www.lungusa.org/site/c.dvLUK 9O0E/b.22581/

Annett, R. D., Aylward, E. H., Bender, B. G., Lapidus, J., & DuHamel, T. (2000). Neurocognitive functioning in children with mild and moderate asthma in the Childhood Asthma Management Program. *Journal of Asthma and Clinical Immunology, 105,* 717–724.

Calam, R. M., Gregg, L., & Goodman, R. (2005). Psychological adjustment and asthma in children and adolescents: The UK nationwide mental health survey. *Psychosomatic Medicine, 67,* 105–110.

Centers for Disease Control and Prevention (CDC). (2009). *Summary health statistics for U.S. children: National health interview survey, 2007.* Retrieved October 1, 2009, from http://www.cdc.gov/nchs/data/series/sr_10/sr10_239.pdf

Figueroa-Muñoz, J. I., Chinn, S., & Rona, R. J. (2001). Association between obesity and asthma in 4–11 year old children in the UK. *Thorax, 56,* 133–137.

Grant, E. N., Lyttle, C. S., & Weiss, K. B. (2000). The relation of socioeconomic factors and racial/ethnic differences in US asthma mortality. *American Journal of Public Health, 90,* 1923–1925.

Halterman, J. S., Conn, K. M., Forbes-Jones, E., Fagnano, M., Hightower, A. D., & Zilagyi, P. G. (2006). Behavior problems among inner-city children with asthma: Findings from a community-based sample [Electronic version]. *Pediatrics 117*(2), 192–199.

Johansen, S. E. (2004). *School functioning of children with asthma: A study of the elementary and middle school years.* Unpublished master's thesis, University of South Florida, Tampa.

Kimes, D., Ullah, A., Levine, E., Nelson, R., Timmins, S., Weiss, S., et al. (2004). Relationships between pediatric asthma and socioeconomic/urban variables in Baltimore, Maryland. *Health and Place, 10,* 141–152.

Klinnert, M. D., McQuaid, E. L., & Gavin, L. A. (1997). Assessing the Family Asthma Management System. *Journal of Asthma, 34,* 77–88.

Klinnert, M. D., McQuaid, E. L., McCormick, D., Adinoff, A. D., & Bryant, N. E. (2000). A multimethod assessment of behavioral and emotional adjustment in children with asthma. *Journal of Pediatric Psychology, 25,* 35–46.

Lara, M., Akinbami, L., Flores, G., & Morgenstern, H. (2006). Heterogeneity of childhood asthma among Hispanic children: Puerto Rican children bear a disproportionate burden. *Pediatrics, 117,* 43–53.

Lenney, W. (1997). The burden of pediatric asthma. *Pediatric Pulmonology, 15,* 13–16.

McQuaid, E., Kopel, S. J., & Nassau, J. H. (2001). Behavioral adjustment in children with asthma: A meta-analysis. *Journal of Developmental and Behavioral Pediatrics, 22,* 430–439.

National Heart, Lung, and Blood Institute (NHLBI). (2007). *Expert panel report 3 (EPR3); Guidelines for the diagnosis and management of asthma.* Bethesda, MD: U.S. Department of Health and Human Services; National Institutes of Health; National Heart, Lung, and Blood Institute; National Asthma Education and Prevention Program. Available October 1, 2009, at http://www.nhlbi.nih.gov/guidelines/asthma/

Peck, H. L, Bray, M. A., & Kehle, T. J. (2003). Relaxation and guided imagery: A school-based intervention for children with asthma. *Psychology in the Schools, 40,* 657–675.

Schipper, H., Clinch, J., & Powell, V. (1990). Definitions and conceptual issues. In B. Spilker (Ed.), *Quality of life assessment in clinical trials* (pp. 11–24). New York: Raven Press.

Shohat, T., Graif, Y., Garty, B., Livne, I., & Green, M. S. (2005). The child with asthma at school: Results from a national asthma survey among schoolchildren in Israel. *Journal of Adolescent Health, 37,* 275–280.

Starfield, B., Riley, A. W., Green, B. F., Ensminger, M. E., Ryan, S. A., Kelleher, K., et al. (1995). The Adolescent and Child Health and Illness Profile: A population-based measure of health. *Medical Care, 33,* 553–566.

Wright, R. J., Rodriguez, M., & Cohen, S. (1998). Review of psychosocial stress and asthma: An integrated biopsychosocial approach. *Thorax, 53,* 1066–1074.

Yawn, B. P., Brenneman, S. K., Allen-Ramey, F. C., Cabana, M. D., & Markson, L. E. (2006). Assessment of asthma severity and asthma control in children. *Pediatrics, 118,* 322–329.

Chapter 13

American Academy of Pediatrics (AAP). (2009). *Policy statement—Guidance for the administration of medication in school* [Electronic version]. *Pediatrics, 124,* 1244–1251. Retrieved October 1, 2009, from http://aappolicy.aappublications.org/cgi/content/abstract/pediatrics;124/4/1244

Ben-Shoshan, M., Kagan, R., Primeau, M.-N., Alizadehfar, R., Verreault, N., Yu, J. W., et al. (2008). Availability of the epinephrine autoinjector at school in children with peanut allergy. *Annals of Allergy, Asthma and Immunology, 100,* 570–575.

Bollinger, M. E., Dahlquist, L. M., Mudd, K., Sonntag, C., Dillinger, L., & McKenna, K. (2006). The impact of food allergy on the daily activities of children and their families. *Annals of Allergy, Asthma and Immunology, 96,* 415–421.

Food Allergy and Anaphylaxis Network (FAAN). (2008a). *Five steps forward for food allergy.* Retrieved October 1, 2009, from http://www.foodallergy.org/FAAW/FAAW%202008/magnacarta3c_small.pdf

Food Allergy and Anaphylaxis Network (FAAN). (2008b, December 12). *Incidence of anaphylaxis higher than previously reported* [press release]. Retrieved October 1, 2009, from http://foodallergy.org/media/press_releases/anaphylaxisstudy.html

Freund, L. H., & Ryaunier, J. (2003). *The complete idiot's guide to food allergies.* Indianapolis, IN: Alpha Books.

Hannaway, P. J. (2007). *On the nature of food allergy: A complete handbook on food allergy for patients, parents, restaurant personnel, child-care providers, educators, school nurses, dieticians and health-care providers.* Marblehead, MA: Lighthouse Press.

Isolauri, E., Huure, A., Salminen, S., & Impivaara, O. (2004). The allergy epidemic extends beyond the past few decades. *Clinical and & Experimental Allergy, 34,* 1007–1010.

LeBovidge, J. S., Stone, K. D., Twarog, F. J., Raiselis, S., Kalish, L. A., Bailey, E. P., et al. (2006). Development of preliminary questionnaire to assess parental response to children's food allergies. *Annals of Allergy, Asthma, and Immunology, 96,* 473–477.

Lyons, A. C., & Forde, E. M. E. (2004). Food allergy in young adults: Perceptions and psychological effects. *Journal of Health Psychology, 9,* 497–504.

McIntyre, C. L., Sheetz, A. H., Carroll, C. R., & Young, M. C. (2005). Administration of epinephrine for life-threatening allergic reactions in school settings. *Pediatrics, 116,* 1134–1140.

Powers, J., Bergren, M. D., & Finnegan, L. (2007). Comparison of school food allergy emergency plans to the food allergy and anaphylaxis network's standard plan. *The Journal of School Nursing, 23,* 252–258.

Rakel, D. (2007). *Integrative medicine.* New York: Saunders.

Sicherer, S. H. (2006*). Understanding and managing your child's food allergies.* Baltimore, MD: John Hopkins University Press.

Sicherer, S. H., Munoz-Furlong, A., Murphy, R., Wood, R., & Sampson, H. A. (2003). Food allergies in children. *Pediatrics, 111,* 1591–1596.

Stern, L., Francouer, M. J., Primeau, M. N., Sommerville, W., Fombonne, E., & Mazer, B. D. (2005). Immune function in autistic children. *Annals of Allergy, Asthma & Immunology, 95,* 558–565.

Szpir, M. (2006). Tracing the origins of autism: A spectrum of new studies. *Environmental Health Perspectives, 114,* 412–418.

Vickerstaff, J. J. (2007). *Dealing with food allergies in babies and children.* Boulder, CO: David Bull.

Williams, G. P., Dalrymple, N., & Neal, J. (2000). Eating habits of children with autism. *Pediatric Nursing, 26*(3), 259–264.

Chapter 14

Ambler, G. R., Fairchild, J., Craig, M. E., & Cameron, F. J. (2006). Contemporary Australian outcomes in childhood and adolescent type 1 diabetes: 10 years post the Diabetes Control and Complications Trial. *Journal of Pediatrics and Child Health, 42,* 403–410.

Bradford, R. (1997). *Children, families, and chronic disease: Psychological models and methods of care.* London: Routledge.

Chisholm, V., Atkinson, L., Donaldson, C., Noyes, K., Payne, A., & Kelnar, C. (2007). Predictors of treatment adherence in young children with type 1 diabetes. *Journal of Advanced Nursing, 57*(5), 482–493.

Cunningham, M., & Wodrich, D. L. (2006). The effect of sharing health information on teachers' production of classroom accommodations. *Psychology in the Schools, 43,* 553–564.

Dantzer, C., Swendsen, J., Maurice-Tison, S., & Salamon, R. (2003). Anxiety and depression in juvenile diabetes: A critical review. *Clinical Psychology Review, 6,* 787–800.

Desrocher, M., & Rovet, J. (2004). Neurocognitive correlates of type 1 diabetes mellitus in childhood. *Child Neuropsychology, 10,* 36–52.

Eiber, R., Berlin, I., Grimaldi, A., & Bisserbe, J. C. (1997). Insulin-dependent diabetes and psychiatric pathology: General clinical and epidemiologic review. *Encephale, 23,* 351–357.

Ferguson, S. C., Blane, A. B., Wardlaw, J. A., Frier, B. M., Perros, P., McCrimmon, R. J., et al. (2005). Influence of an early-onset age of type 1 diabetes on cerebral structure and cognitive function. *Diabetes Care, 28,* 1431–1437.

Fowler, M. G., Johnson, M. P., & Atkinson, S. S. (1985). School achievement and absence in children with chronic health conditions. *Journal of Pediatrics, 106,* 683–687.

Greer, T. F., & Holmes, C. S. (1996). Effects of IDDM on cognitive functioning: A meta-analysis. *Diabetes, 45,* S1.

Hershey, T., Lillie, R., Sadler, M., & White, N. H. (2003). Severe hypoglycemia and long-term spatial memory in children with type 1 diabetes mellitus: A retrospective study. *Journal of the International Neuropsychological Society, 9,* 740–750.

Holmes, C. S., Cant, M. C., Fox, M. A., Lampert, N. L., & Greer, T. (1999). Disease and demographic risk factors for disrupted cognitive functioning in children with insulin-dependent diabetes mellitus (IDDM). *School Psychology Review, 28,* 215–227.

Holmes, C. S., O'Brien, B., & Greer, T. (1995). Cognitive functioning and academic achievement in children with insulin-dependent diabetes mellitus (IDDM). *School Psychology Quarterly, 10,* 329–344.

Kovacs, M., Goldston, D., & Iyengar, S. (1992). Intellectual development and academic performance of children with insulin-dependent diabetes mellitus: A longitudinal study. *Developmental Psychology, 28,* 676–684.

Lawrence, J. M., Standiford, D. A., Loots, B., Klingensmith, G. J., Williams, D. E., Ruggiero, A., et al. (2006). Prevalence and correlates of depressed mood among youth with diabetes: The SEARCH for diabetes in youth study. *Pediatrics, 117,* 1348–1358.

Martin, D. D., Davis, E. A., & Jones, T. W. (2006). Acute effects of hyperglycaemia in children with type 1 diabetes mellitus: The patient's perspective. *Journal of Pediatric Endocrinology and Metabolism, 19,* 927–936.

McCarthy, A. M., Lindgren, S., Mengeling, M. A., Tsalikian, E., & Engvall, J. (2002). Effects of diabetes on learning in children. *Pediatrics, 109,* e9.

National Institutes of Health (NIH). (2001). *Diabetes Control and Complications Trial (DCCT)* (NIH Publication No. 02–3874). Bethesda, MD: National Diabetes Information Clearinghouse.

Northam, E., Anderson, P. J., Adler, R., Werther, G., & Warne, G. (1996). Psychosocial and family functioning in children with insulin-dependent diabetes at diagnosis and one year later. *Journal of Pediatric Psychology, 21,* 699–717.

Northam, E., Anderson, P. J., Jacobs, R., Hughes, M., Warne, G. L., & Werther, G. A. (2001). Neuropsychological profiles of children with type 1 diabetes 6 years after disease onset. *Diabetes Care, 24,* 1541–1546.

Palmer, D. L., Berg, C. A., Wiebe, D. J., Beveridge, R. M., Korbel, C. D., Upchurch, R., et al. (2004). The role of autonomy and pubertal status in understanding age differences in maternal involvement in diabetes responsibility across adolescence. *Journal of Pediatric Psychology, 29*, 35–46.

Rovet, J., & Alvarez, M. (1997). Attentional functioning in children and adolescents with IDDM. *Diabetes Care, 20*, 803–810.

Rovet, J. F., Ehrlich, R. M., & Hoppe, M. (1988). Specific intellectual deficits in children with early onset diabetes mellitus. *Child Development, 59*, 226–234.

Ryan, C., Gurtunca, N., & Becker, D. (2006). Hypoglycemia: A complication of diabetes therapy in children. *Seminars in Pediatric Neurology, 12*, 163–177.

Ryan, C., Vega, A., & Drash, A. (1985). Cognitive deficits in adolescents who developed diabetes early in life. *Pediatrics, 75*, 921–927.

Sexson, S., & Madan-Swain, A. (1995). The chronically ill child in the school. *School Psychology Quarterly, 10*, 359–368.

Storch, E. A., Lewin, A., Silverstein, J. H., Heidgerken, A. D., Strawser, M. S., Baumeister, A., et al. (2004). Peer victimization and psychosocial adjustment in children with type 1 diabetes. *Clinical Pediatrics, 43*, 467–471.

Wagner, J., Heapy, A., James, A., & Abbott, G. (2006). Brief report: Glycemic control, quality of life, and school experiences among students with diabetes. *Journal of Pediatric Psychology, 31*, 764–769.

Watson, T. S., & Logan, P. (1998). Diabetes mellitus (insulin dependent). In A. Phelps (Ed.), *Health-related disorders in children and adolescents: A guidebook for understanding and educating* (pp. 238–247). Washington, DC: American Psychological Association.

Wodrich, D. L. (2005). Disclosing information about epilepsy and type 1 diabetes mellitus: The effect on teachers' understanding of classroom behavior. *School Psychology Quarterly, 20*, 288–303.

Wysocki, T. (2006). Behavioral assessment and intervention in pediatric diabetes. *Behavior Modification, 30*, 72–92.

Index

CORWIN

A SAGE Company

The Corwin logo—a raven striding across an open book—represents the union of courage and learning. Corwin is committed to improving education for all learners by publishing books and other professional development resources for those serving the field of PreK–12 education. By providing practical, hands-on materials, Corwin continues to carry out the promise of its motto: **"Helping Educators Do Their Work Better."**

**NATIONAL
ASSOCIATION OF
SCHOOL
PSYCHOLOGISTS**

The National Association of School Psychologists represents school psychology and supports school psychologists to enhance the learning and mental health of all children and youth.